# IT'S A CONSPIRACY!

## The National Insecurity Council

EarthWorks Press
Berkeley, California

> "Sunshine is the best disinfectant."
> —*Justice Louis Brandeis*

Pages 213-217 are adapted from *Unreliable Sources: A Guide
to Detecting Bias in News Media,* by Martin A. Lee and
Norman Solomon. Copyright © 1990 by Martin A. Lee
and Norman Solomon. Published by arrangement with
Carol Publishing Group. A Lyle Stuart Book.

*Supressing Sarkhan* © 1992 by William Lederer. Used with permission.
*Deadly Secrets* © 1992 by Warren Hinkle and Bill Turner, 1992. Published by Thunder's Mouth Press.
Used with permission.

*Produced and packaged by Javnarama*
*Design by Javnarama*

*Cover design by Michael Brunsfeld, Andrea Sohn,
John Javna, and Lenna Lebovich
Artwork by Kirk Henderson*

10 9 8 7 6 5 4 3 2 1
First Printing, 1992

**For ordering information, write:**
EarthWorks Press
1400 Shattuck Avenue, # 25
Berkeley, CA 94709

*Bulk rates are available.*

# ACKNOWLEDGMENTS

*We would like to thank the people whose advice and
assistance made this book possible, including:*

John Javna
Kristina Filipovich
John Dollison
Jack Mingo
Sven Newman
Catherine Dee
mr minimal
Dayna Macy
Kim Koch
Emma Lauriston
Lenna Lebovich
Joanne Miller
Melanie Foster
Denise Silver
Fritz Springmeyer
Phil Catalfo
Dennis Bernstein
Paul Krassner
Mark Friedman
Leder Norahs
Gordon Javna
Neil Shapiro
KPFA
The Data Center
Peter Dale Scott
Jonathan Marshall

William J. Lederer
Phillip Melanson
Alison Kennedy
*Mondo 2000*
Curt Gentry
Christopher Simpson
Anthony Summers
Jim Marrs
Robert Sherrill
Peter Matthiessen
Martin Lee
Norman Solomon
Noam Chomsky
Alexander Cockburn
Russell Mokhiber
*The Nation*
Larry Bensky
Scott Armstrong
Jonathan Vankin
Arts & Entertainment
Network
Bob & Doc
Sharilyn Hovind
Penelope Houston
Carl Wells
The EarthWorks Group

# CONTENTS

# INTRODUCTION

T his book began in France in 1990, when three vacationing American couples met at a dinner party. Knowing nothing about each other, they groped for something to talk about. At first the conversation was self-conscious. Then somebody mentioned JFK's assassination. Suddenly they had a lot in common, and plenty to talk about.

As it happened, the publisher of this book was a member of that group—but you've probably had a similar experience. It seems as though everyone you talk to has their own "pet" conspiracy theories.

That's not surprising. The official versions of pivotal events like the Kennedy assassinations, the Iran-Contra scandal and the S&L mess seem so much like fiction that any number of conspiracy theories look more plausible in comparison.

Unfortunately, most of us don't have the time or inclination to wade through the hundreds of books and articles that chronicle each of these events. As a result, most of us can't tell the difference between really farfetched conspiracy theories and realistic ones.

That's the reason the National Insecurity Council has put together *It's a Conspiracy!*—a digest of four or five dozen of America's most intriguing conspiracy theories. We pored through thousands of newspapers, government documents, and books, gathering facts—so you wouldn't have to—and then arranged them in an easy-to-read format.

## WHAT'S IN THE BOOK?

Naturally, we've included the Big Conspiracies—JFK, Robert Kennedy, Martin Luther King, Jr., Marilyn Monroe, Pearl Harbor, Watergate, etc. But we've also uncovered—and included—

dozens of fascinating, lesser-known conspiracy theories, like:

√ Hitler's bribe to William Randolph Hearst

√ The U.S. plan to import Nazis after WWII

√ The plot to destroy mass transit in America

√ How the CIA introduced LSD to the USA

√ Why George Bush may have wanted a war with Iraq

Conspiracy buffs will notice that we haven't included every conspiracy theory ever concocted. That's intentional; this book is a "reader," after all—not an encyclopedia. Besides, some popular theories are too unbelievable to deserve attention; others are overtly bigoted; and still others just aren't that interesting. And, there are an important handful—like Pope John Paul I's death, the imprisonment of Leonard Peltier, and the FBI's COINTEL operations—that we're saving for volume two.

In any case, we think you'll find an interesting mix of political, business, military, and social conspiracies here.

## ARE CONSPIRACIES REAL?

The word "conspire" comes from the Latin *conspirare*, "to breathe together." Certainly, it's a vivid image—conspirators huddled so closely together that they seem to share the same breath. And, according to the *Oxford English Dictionary*, a conspiracy is:

> a combination of persons for an evil or unlawful purpose; an agreement between two or more persons to do something criminal, illegal, or reprehensible...

The 1990 *Encyclopedia Brittanica* adds:

> Conspiracy is perhaps the [vaguest] area in Anglo-American criminal law....Although many statutes now require an overt act as proof of an agreement to commit a felony, conspiracy is still largely inferred from circumstantial evidence.

Note that last point. Because most conspiracies are hatched in secret and are almost impossible to detect—even decades later—we have to rely on circumstantial evidence to determine whether they've occurred.

Some people, looking for this evidence, get carried away and begin to see conspiracies everywhere.

We don't encourage that.

However, conspiracies *do* exist. In their quest for power and riches, people conspire to cheat business competitors, rig elections, steal from and lie to the public, falsely imprison enemies, and murder heads of state—as they have throughout recorded history. When you consider that conspirators deposed six Caesars in a row (starting with Julius), one American president murdered by a conspiracy in Dallas is not so hard to believe.

We hope you'll find this book entertaining. But we also hope you'll take it seriously. The theories included here may be incredible...but they're all the more amazing because they might just be true.

# PEARL HARBOR

*Japan's attack on Pearl Harbor is one of the most dramatic incidents in U.S. history—and the source of one of the most persistent conspiracy theories. Did President Roosevelt know the attack was coming? If so, why didn't he defend against it?*

Shortly after dawn on Sunday, December 7, 1941, Japanese planes launched an all-out attack on Pearl Harbor, the major U.S. military base in Hawaii. Within two hours, they had damaged or destroyed eighteen warships and more than 200 aircraft, killing 2,403 American soldiers, sailors, and marines, and wounding 1,178. Americans were stunned and outraged.

The next day, FDR delivered a stirring speech to Congress in which he referred to the day of the attack as "a date which will live on in infamy." In response, Congress declared war, and the U.S. closed ranks behind the president.

Despite America's commitment to the war, however, questions arose about Pearl Harbor that were not easily dismissed: How were we caught so completely by surprise? Why were losses so high? Who was to blame? Did the president know an attack was coming? Did he purposely do nothing so America would be drawn into the war? Although there were seven full inquiries before the war ended, the questions persist to this day.

## WAS IT A CONSPIRACY? #1
*Did the U.S. intercept Japanese messages long before the attack, but fail to warn the Hawaiian base?*

### Suspicious Facts
• By the summer of 1940, the U.S. had cracked Japan's top-secret diplomatic code, nicknamed "Purple." This enabled U.S. intelligence agencies to monitor messages to and from Tokyo.

• Although several U.S. command posts received machines for decoding "Purple," Pearl Harbor was never given one.

• Messages intercepted in the autumn of 1941 suggested what the Japanese were planning:

√ On October 9, 1941, Tokyo told its consul in Honolulu to "divide the water around Pearl Harbor into five sub-areas and report on the types and numbers of American war craft." (*Revisionism and the Origins of Pearl Harbor*)

√ The Japanese foreign minister urged negotiators to resolve issues with the U.S. by November 29, after which "things are automatically going to happen." (ibid.)

√ On December 1, after negotiations had failed, the Navy intercepted a request that the Japanese ambassador in Berlin inform Hitler of an extreme danger of war...coming "quicker than anyone dreams." (ibid.)

### On the Other Hand

• Although the United States had cracked top-secret Japanese codes several years earlier, "the fact is that code-breaking intelligence did not prevent and could not have prevented Pearl Harbor, because Japan never sent any message to anybody saying anything like 'We shall attack Pearl Harbor,'" writes military historian David Kahn in the autumn 1991 issue of *Military History Quarterly*.

• "The [Japanese] Ambassador in Washington was never told of the plan," Kahn says, "Nor were other Japanese diplomats or consular officials. The ships of the strike force were never radioed any message mentioning Pearl Harbor. It was therefore impossible for cryptoanalysts to have discovered the plan. Despite the American code breakers, Japan kept her secret."

• Actually, Washington *had* issued a warning to commanders at Pearl Harbor a few weeks earlier. On November 27, 1941, General George Marshall sent the following message: "Hostile action possible at any moment. If hostilities cannot, repeat CANNOT, be avoided, the United States desires that Japan commit the first overt act. This policy should not, repeat NOT, be construed as restricting you to a course of action that might jeopardize your defense."

• But the commanders at Pearl Harbor were apparently negligent. The base should have at least been on alert, but the antiaircraft guns were unmanned and most people on the base were asleep when the attack came.

## WAS IT A CONSPIRACY? #2

*Did a sailor pick up signals from the approaching Japanese fleet and pass the information on to the White House—which ignored it?*

### Suspicious Facts

• This theory is promoted in John Toland's bestselling book, *Infamy*. He asserts that in early December, an electronics expert in the Twelfth Naval District in San Francisco (whom Toland refers to as "Seaman Z") identified "queer signals" in the Pacific. Using cross-bearings, he identified them as originating from a "missing" Japanese carrier fleet which had not been heard from in months. He determined that the fleet was heading directly for Hawaii.

• Toland says that although Seaman Z and his superior officer allegedly reported their findings to the Office of Naval Intelligence, whose chief was a close friend of the president, Pearl Harbor never got the warning.

### On the Other Hand

• Gordon Prange, author of *Pearl Harbor: The Verdict of History*, refutes many of Toland's assertions. Although he concedes that there may have been unusual Japanese signals that night, Prange says that they were almost certainly signals *to* the carriers from Tokyo—and thus would have been useless in locating the carriers.

• To prove his point, Prange quotes reports written by Mitsuo Fuchida, who led the air attack on Pearl Harbor: "The Force maintained the strictest silence throughout the cruise....[Admiral] Genda stressed that radio silence was so important that the pilots agreed not to go on the air even if their lives depended upon it." The chief of staff for Fleet Admiral Nagumo adds, "All transmitters were sealed, and all hands were ordered to be kept away from any key of the machine."

• Prange notes, "It would be interesting to know how the Twelfth Naval District in San Francisco could pick up information that the Fourteenth Naval District, much nearer the action [in Honolulu], missed."

• Finally, Prange reports that years after the war, "Seaman Z" was identified as Robert D. Ogg, a retired California businessman. Ogg flatly denied that he had said the unusual signals were "the missing carrier force," nor was he even sure that the transmissions were in Japanese—"I never questioned them at the time."

## WAS IT A CONSPIRACY? #3

*Even if FDR didn't specifically know about an impending attack on Pearl Harbor, he may have done his best to provoke the Japanese into attacking the U.S. to gain the support of the American public for his war plans.*

### Suspicious Facts

• FDR told close aides that if the Allies were to be victorious, the U.S. had to enter the war before Japan overran the Pacific and Germany destroyed England.

• FDR told a British emissary that the United States "would declare war on Japan if the latter attacked American possessions... [but] public opinion would be unlikely to approve of a declaration of war if the Japanese attack were directed only against British or Dutch territories."

• Earlier that year, on July 25, 1941, Roosevelt froze Japanese assets in the United States.

• In 1937, Japan sank a U.S. warship in China's Yangtze River, and relations between America and Japan began deteriorating. Both countries made a public effort to negotiate, but FDR presented a series of impossible ultimatums to the Japanese negotiators and openly loaned money to the Nationalist Chinese, whom the Japanese were fighting at the time.

• According to columnist Pat Buchanan, Roosevelt also committed an act of war against Japan in August 1941, when he secretly approved sending a crack U.S. Air Force squadron, the "Flying Tigers," to fight alongside the Chinese Nationalists. Although these fliers were officially "volunteers," Buchanan claims that they were "recruited at U.S. bases, offered five times normal pay [and] sent off to fight Japan months before Pearl Harbor, in a covert operation run out of FDR's White House....Though their planes carried the insignia of the Chinese army, [they] were on active duty for the United States."

## On the Other Hand

No evidence *proving* a conspiracy to goad the Japanese into attacking has come to light in the fifty-plus years since Pearl Harbor.

## RECOMMENDED READING

*You could easily spend a lifetime reading all the books about Pearl Harbor. Here are two good ones to start with:*

• *Pearl Harbor: The Verdict of History*, by Gordon Prange (McGraw Hill, 1986)

• *Revisionism and the Origins of Pearl Harbor*, by Frank Mintz (University Press of America, 1985)

## MEDIA CONSPIRACIES

In June 1990, an NBC staffer contacted Todd Putnam, editor of *National Boycott News*, about appearing on the "Today Show."

"Today" was planning a program about boycotting products to change corporate behavior, and the NBC staffer asked for "the biggest boycott going on right now." Putnam asked for a little time. He recalls: "When I looked at major boycotts in terms of visibility, effectiveness, scope and public support, one stood out: the boycott of GE products led by the group INFACT, prompted by GE's leading role in the production and promotion of nuclear weapons."

The only trouble was, GE has owned NBC since 1986, when the company bought RCA. Would NBC be willing to discuss a boycott against its own corporate parent?

"When I talked next to [the NBC staffer]," Putnam says, " I broke the news to her: 'The biggest boycott in the country is against General Electric,' I said."

" 'We can't do that one,' she responded immediately.…'Well, we could do that one, but we won't.' "

—From *Extra!*, published by FAIR
(Fairness and Accuracy in Reporting)

# BLOWING SMOKE

*When a convicted drug dealer claimed to be Dan Quayle's college marijuana connection, the Feds tossed him into solitary. If it was all just a pipe dream, why did they need to shut him up?*

With the 1988 election a month away, the Republicans should have been happy. Their presidential candidate, George Bush, held a comfortable lead. But the GOP had a problem: Bush's running mate, Senator J. Danforth Quayle.

Quayle, a staunch conservative, mouthed the usual hawkish rhetoric about fighting communism. Yet when the press reported that his father had pulled strings to get him into the National Guard and keep him out of Vietnam, the tough talk sounded hypocritical. His hard line on defense became a joke: "What do you get when you cross a hawk and a chicken?—A Quayle."

Quayle also had the reputation of being a lightweight who was more interested in his golf than his legislative duties. Polls showed that public uneasiness about Quayle was eroding Bush's lead. One more embarrassing disclosure about the vice presidential nominee could have endangered the ticket.

## WHAT HAPPENED

• In mid-October, a federal prisoner named Brett Kimberlin, serving time in the El Reno Correctional Institution in Oklahoma, told reporters that he had sold marijuana to Dan Quayle "fifteen to twenty times" between 1971 and 1973 when Quayle was a law student in Indianapolis.

• Kimberlin offered to take a polygraph test and promised to detail his allegations in a press conference later that month. Since the Republicans had made fighting drugs a centerpiece of their political agenda, the charges could have had a devastating effect.

• But the press conference never happened. Four days before the election, Bureau of Prisons Director Michael Quinlan, a political appointee in Washington, D.C., contacted the warden and told him to cancel Kimberlin's conference. Kimberlin, who was serving a 51-year sentence for drug-smuggling and bombing offenses, was thrown into solitary confinement less than an hour before he was supposed to detail his story. According to *American Lawyer* magazine, he "remained in solitary...until eight days after the election." The story died, and Quayle's accuser was generally ignored or dismissed by the media.

• Meanwhile, Kimberlin stuck to his story. In a lawsuit against the government, he claimed that "Quinlan was pressured into silencing him by politically connected higher-ups." (*San Francisco Examiner*)

## THE OFFICIAL STORY

When Gary Trudeau ran a series of "Doonesbury" comic strips about the case a few years later, the vice president's spokesperson, David Beckwith, dismissed the accusation, saying: "This belongs in the comics pages. The allegations are going to run exactly where they belong." (*The New York Times*)

## SUSPICIOUS FACTS

• The vice president denies that he ever smoked or bought pot. Still, if Quayle was like most college students in the sixties, he was probably exposed to it. In fact, his fraternity at DePauw University, Delta Kappa Epsilon, had a reputation as a great place for parties.

• One memorable party was "The Trip" in 1968. In DePauw's yearbook, the party is described as "a colorful psychedelic journey into the wild sights and sounds produced by LSD." The description appears in the caption above Quayle's yearbook photograph.

• Kimberlin wasn't the first to accuse Quayle of taking drugs. In 1982, the Drug Enforcement Agency investigated charges that the young senator had used cocaine and Quaaludes.

• There was no credible reason given for placing Kimberlin in solitary confinement; furthermore, the warden of his prison had already approved the press conference. As *The New York Times* noted, "It appears to be unprecedented for a solitary confinement order to come from the Bureau of Prisons director in Washington."

• Some people accuse Kimberlin of trying to reduce his sentence with wild charges. Kimberlin replies that he expected "nothing but grief" from prison authorities for going public—and he's gotten it. According to the *San Francisco Examiner*, "Last year the presidentially appointed U.S. Parole Commission decided to keep him imprisoned until February 1994, despite an exemplary prison record. The 180 months of incarceration would be twice the maximum time recommended in federal guidelines (64-92 months) for a prisoner in his category."

## WAS IT A CONSPIRACY?

The White House and the presidential campaign team, of course, denied that there was any attempt to silence Kimberlin. *The New York Times* quoted a Justice Department aide as saying that he "knew of no evidence to suggest that Mr. Kimberlin was confined to avoid any damage his statements might cause the Bush-Quayle campaign." But the facts suggest otherwise.

## BEHIND THE SCENES

A Washington-based weekly, *The Legal Times*, found "intense interest" in Kimberlin's activities among top GOP campaign aides:

• "Mark Goodin, deputy press secretary to the campaign, says he briefed campaign chairman James Baker on Kimberlin's status five times during the final days of the campaign. Goodin, who says he was in regular contact with the Justice Department about Kimberlin, also says that he briefed Lee Atwater, Bush's campaign manager, and Stuart Spencer, Quayle's campaign manager."

• Moreover, said *The Legal Times*, Director Quinlan's order that Kimberlin be isolated was "highly unusual." Disciplining prisoners is routinely handled by local wardens. *The Legal Times* also noted that, "several factors, in addition to Quinlan's personal involvement, led to the conclusion that the decisions to silence Kimberlin were not simply the product of routine prison administration."

• Loye Miller, the Justice Department's director of public affairs, seems to have been a key player in the affair. Miller at first denied discussing Kimberlin's case with his superiors at the Justice Department. But, according to Martin Lee and Norman Solomon, authors of *Unreliable Sources*, "while increasingly drawn into fielding pre-election media calls on the matter, Loye Miller apparently served as a savvy switchboard between Bush-Quayle strategists and the ostensibly non-political Bureau of Prisons operating under the wing of the Justice Department."

• In the end, Miller all but admitted to the conspiracy to silence Kimberlin: "The Bureau of Prisons caught on that he [Kimberlin] was going to hold another press conference," he said. "So they put him back in." (*The Legal Times*)

# SEEING RED

*The Communist conspiracy—and how to fight it—was on the minds of millions of Americans in the late '40s and early '50s. Here's what the "experts" had to say about it.*

"If we are to win over the Communists, we must not only out-think them, out-live them, but out-sing them."
—F. Olin Stockwell,
The Power of Song

"Fishing promotes a clean mind, healthy body and leaves no time for succumbing to Communistic or Socialistic propaganda."
—Ivar Hemmings, chairman,
South Bend Bait Company

"We must recognize Communism for what it is—a vast international conspiracy with tentacles in every country in the world, our own included."
—Senator Styles Bridges
(New Hampshire), 1948

"Schools and colleges should be on the alert against Communist infiltration.... Parents should take a greater interest in school affairs and know what organizations attract their children."
—J. Edgar Hoover

"You hear about 'constitutional rights,' 'free speech,' and the 'free press.' Every time I hear these words I say to myself, 'That man is a Red!!...' You never hear a *real* American talk like that!"
—Mayor Frank Hague,
Jersey City

"In every country the Communists have taken over, the first thing they do is outlaw cockfighting."
Rep. John Monks
(Oklahoma)

"This country today is in the hands of a secret inner coterie...which is directed by agents of the Soviet Union....Our only choice is to impeach President Truman to find out who is the secret invisible government."
—Senator William Jenner
(Indiana), 1948

"A red cancer is gnawing at the vitals of this nation and the world. The Communists are working at being Communists 24 hours a day. Let us work at being Americans 24 hours a day."
—Cecil B. deMille,
movie director, 1948

# SUSPICIOUS DEATH #1: WILLIAM SULLIVAN

*Like a secret society, the American intelligence community keeps its secrets and protects its own—until they break the code of silence.*

The deceased: William C. Sullivan, former third-in-command under J. Edgar Hoover. For a decade, he ran the FBI's domestic intelligence division (which oversaw the Bureau's investigations of the Kennedy and King assassinations). After Hoover summarily fired him in 1971, Sullivan became an active and effective critic of the Bureau.

How he died: On November 9, 1977, shortly after daybreak, Sullivan went to meet two hunting companions near his Sugar Hill, New Hampshire, home. He never made it. On the way, he was shot to death by the 18-year-old son of a state policeman. The young man claimed that even though his rifle was equipped with a telescopic sight, he had mistaken Sullivan for a deer. Two months later, the killer received his sentence: a $500 fine and a ten-year suspension of his hunting license.

## SUSPICIOUS FACTS

• Sullivan could have been seen as a threat to the FBI:

√ As the FBI's illegal activities came to light after Watergate, a number of agents were brought to trial. Sullivan was testifying against them. At the time of his death, for example, he was scheduled to be the chief witness against John Kearny, an ex-agent indicted for illegal wiretapping.

√ Sullivan was writing a tell-all book about his years in the FBI. The book, called *The Bureau*, was eventually completed by his co-author and was published by W.W. Norton.

• Sullivan was shot just a week before he was scheduled to appear before the House Select Committee on Assassinations.

• In his book *Conspiracy*, Anthony Summers wrote: "Sullivan had been head of the FBI's Division Five, which handled much of the

King and Kennedy investigations....In 1975, Sullivan responded in opaque fashion to a question from a Congressional committee about [Lee Harvey] Oswald. Asked whether he had seen anything in the files to indicate a relationship between Oswald and the CIA, he replied...'I don't recall ever having seen anything like that, but I think there is something on that point....It rings a bell in my head.' Sullivan's fatal accident occurred before the Assassinations Committee could ask him to be more specific about...that bell in his mind."

## PLAUSIBLE EXPLANATIONS

• **It really was a hunting accident.** Sullivan's coauthor on *The Bureau*, Bill Brown, says that he flew to New Hampshire and checked it out—and was satisfied that it was an accident.

• **It was an assassination.** The day after Sullivan was shot, attorney William Kunstler called a press conference and postulated that the former FBI official had been murdered before he could "blow the whistle" on FBI operations connected to the deaths of not only Kennedy and King, but Malcolm X as well.

Some experienced hunters are also skeptical that a seasoned hunter with a telescopic sight could confuse a deer with a person. Among other reasons, the hunter would have had to look carefully to verify that the deer was old enough—and the right gender—to shoot legally.

## RECOMMENDED READING

*Conspiracy*, by Anthony Summers (McGraw Hill, 1980)

## TALES OF THE CIA

As the Cold War ended, the CIA decided it needed to project "a greater openness and sense of public responsibility." So it commissioned a task force. On December 20, 1991, the committee submitted a 15-page "Task Force Report on Greater Openness." It is stamped SECRET, and agency officials refuse to disclose any of the contents.

# NEIL BUSH AND THE S&L BAILOUT

*When he joined the board of directors of a Colorado S&L, Neil Bush neglected to mention that a pair of the thrift's borrowers were his business partners. Then he voted to approve more than $100 million in loans to them. Was it really just bad judgment?*

I n 1983, Neil Bush, the son of then-Vice President George Bush, started an oil company called JNB Exploration, with partners Kenneth Good and Bill Walters. He put in $100 of his own money; his partners put in $160,000. For his $100 investment, Bush received a 32 percent share of the company and a $75,000-a-year salary. (*Savings & Loan Scandal Cards*)

## BANKING ON IT

• Two years later, in 1985, Bush was offered membership on the board of directors of Silverado Savings and Loan, a Denver, Colorado, thrift. He accepted.

• Without disclosing his connections to Good and Walters, Bush asked the Silverado board of directors to give a $900,000 line of credit to a joint venture in which he and Good were partners. Then he voted with the board to lend Walters $100 million. (ibid.)

• "By late 1986, Good had borrowed nearly $32 million from Silverado and was having trouble making payments on the loans. He requested that they be restructured" to give him more time to pay. At the same time, however, he invested another $5 million in JNB Exploration. (*Inside Job*)

• By 1987, JNB was losing money: it had drilled 30 oil wells, and all of them turned up dry. Even so, Good raised Bush's salary to $120,000, gave him a $22,500 bonus, and lent him an additional $100,000 to invest in high-risk commodities—with the stipulation that Bush didn't have to pay the money back if the commodities flopped. They did, and Bush didn't. (ibid.)

• Good and Walters ultimately "borrowed and defaulted on over $130 million in loans from Silverado" and on November 9, 1988—

the day *after* George Bush was elected president—Silverado was declared insolvent and was seized by federal regulators. (ibid.)

• The cost to taxpayers for all of Silverado's bad loans is estimated to be $1 billion.

## WAS IT A CONSPIRACY? #1

*Was Neil Bush an innocent blunderer? Or did he and his partners intentionally milk Silverado?*

• Neil Bush claimed he made "an innocent mistake." But Edward Conry, a University of Colorado law professor hired by regulators to evaluate Bush's performance as a Silverado director, dismissed that claim: "It is nearly inconceivable that a well-educated, experienced person receiving ongoing legal advice would not have been jarred out of innocence by $100 million in transactions." (ibid.)

• Even worse, Conry noted, "Bush was entirely dependent upon Good for his income." If Good had decided not to fund JNB, he would have "perhaps greatly embarrassed the son of a candidate for the presidency. This appears to be a relationship of very substantial power. Mr. [Neil] Bush appears to have been captured." (ibid.)

• Critics of Bush's actions urged that he be barred from future S&L dealings. However, the Office of Thrift Supervision gave him the lightest penalty it could have imposed, merely ordering him "to avoid future conflicts of interest in the banking industry."

## WAS IT A CONSPIRACY? #2

*U.S. regulators waited until the day after the 1988 presidential elections tv close Silverado. Was the timing part of a conspiracy to protect George Bush's candidacy? Were they helping Republicans avoid major embarrassment? Or was it just a lucky coincidence?*

### Suspicious Facts

• In March 1987, federal examiners studying Silverado Savings and Loan recommended that a cease-and-desist order be placed against it—a move that would have effectively shut down operations. But Kermit Mowbray, the top S&L regulator in the district, felt the order was too severe a penalty; he put off issuing a "c&d" for almost 18 months. (ibid.)

• Finally, in the late summer of 1988, Mowbray told "the Silverado board of directors that he could no longer hold off the obvious—Silverado was insolvent. Neil Bush resigned two days later, just days before his father won the Republican nomination for president." (*Inside Job*)

• But Mowbray didn't seize Silverado immediately. After he notified the board of directors that the seizure was imminent, he received instructions from his superiors in Washington to delay it for 60 days—until after the presidential elections. The alleged reason for the holdup was that "there wasn't enough money in the budget to pay off depositors." (ibid.)

• Thus voters went to the polls, as *Inside Job* put it, "without having their minds cluttered with the unsettling news that candidate George Bush's son had been a director at one of the failed savings and loans." The news came the day *after* the election.

## THE FURTHER ADVENTURES OF NEIL BUSH

• In May 1989, six months after Silverado crashed, Neil Bush formed a new oil company, Apex Energy Corp. It was capitalized with $2.3 million that Neil borrowed from Wood River Capital, a company owned by a Bush family friend. In 1990, the Small Business Administration (SBA) declared Wood River to be in "technical default" on $25 million in loans from the SBA. (*Inside Job*)

### Walters and Good

• In June 1990, Walters and Good testified before a congressional committee investigating their connection with Silverado and Bush. They said they were broke.

• But a few weeks later, a California news team trailing Walters discovered that he and his wife were living in a $1.9 million home, owned two Mercedes-Benzes, and had a $1 million Palm Springs condominium. Everything was in Walters's wife's name.

• Good owned a $450,000 home, a Maserati, "a $4 million IOU from his sale of [a business] and at least 175 trusts." (*Inside Job*)

## RECOMMENDED READING

• *Inside Job: The Looting of America's Savings and Loans*, by Stephen Pizzo, Mary Fricker, and Paul Muolo (HarperCollins, 1991)

- "The Looting Decade: S&Ls, Big Banks and Other Triumphs of Capitalism," by Robert Sherrill (*The Nation*, Nov. 19, 1990)
- *Savings & Loan Scandal Trading Cards*, by Dennis Bernstein and Laura Sydell (Eclipse Enterprises, Forestville, CA)

### TALES OF THE CIA

"It was, even by Georgetown standards, one helluva dinner party. It was the spring of 1960. The hosts were Senator and Mrs. John F. Kennedy. The guest of honor was John Kennedy's favorite author, Ian Fleming.

"Kennedy asked Fleming what his man James Bond might do if M. assigned him to get rid of Castro. Fleming had been in British intelligence....He was quick to answer. According to his biographer, John Pearson, Fleming thought he would have himself some fun....

"[He] said there were three things which really mattered to the Cubans—money, religion, and sex. Therefore, he suggested a triple whammy. First the United States should send planes to scatter [counterfeit] Cuban money over Havana. Second, using the Guantanamo base, the United States should conjure up some religious manifestation, say, a cross of sorts in the sky which would induce the Cubans to look constantly skyward. And third, the United States should send planes over Cuba dropping pamphlets to the effect that owing to American atom bomb tests the atmosphere over the island had become radioactive; that radioactivity is held longest in beards, and that radioactivity makes men impotent. As a consequence the Cubans would shave off their beards, and without bearded Cubans there would be no revolution.

"Fleming was staying at the house of British newsman Henry Brandon. The next day CIA Director Allen Dulles called Brandon to speak to Fleming. Brandon said his guest had already left Washington. Dulles expressed great regret. He had heard about Fleming's terrific ideas for doing in Castro and was sorry he wouldn't be able to discuss them with him in person.

"It is testimony to the resounding good sense exercised by the CIA during the Secret War that all three of Fleming's spoof ideas were in one form or another attempted—or at least seriously considered."

—Warren Hinkle and William Turner, *Deadly Secrets*

# THE BEAST OF BAGHDAD

*Despite the Bush administration's public outrage over Iraq's invasion of Kuwait, there's good reason to believe that Washington knew Saddam wanted war—and suckered him into it.*

On August 2, 1990, Saddam Hussein's troops and tanks rolled into neighboring Kuwait, taking total control of the country within three days.

Although Bush had reportedly been informed by CIA Director William Webster that an attack was imminent five days before it happened, administration officials said they were surprised by it. "Nobody was sure he was going to pull the trigger," commented a White House source.

Within a few weeks, President Bush began talking tough, and five months later the U.S. started bombing Iraq. It was a brief and very popular war. But when the patriotic fervor died down and Hussein was still in power, people began asking: Why didn't Bush act to prevent the Iraqi invasion in the first place?

## BACKGROUND

• In 1980, ten years before the Gulf War, Iraq and Iran went to war over a border dispute. The war dragged on for eight bloody years, causing more than a million casualties.

• Iraq, whose soldiers were outnumbered three to one, was able to stay in the war only because it could buy high-tech weapons on credit from countries like the U.S. But after spending $40 billion and losing "rivers of blood," Iraq was bankrupt. In 1990, its president, Saddam Hussein, appealed to other Arab states. Since Iran's Islamic fundamentalism had threatened their governments as well, he said, it was only fair that they should help pay for the war.

• Hussein's cash problems were exacerbated by low oil prices. He blamed this situation on the other OPEC countries—and he had a point. OPEC members had agreed to keep the price of oil at $18 a barrel. But Saudi Arabia, Kuwait, and the United Arab Emirates were overproducing by so much—500,000 barrels per day—that prices fell to $13.54 a barrel. And for every dollar the price slipped, Iraq lost nearly $1 billion in revenue. Its economy was hemorrhaging.

• Iraq wasn't the only oil producer hurt by low prices. Back in the U.S., oil-rich states like Louisiana, Alaska, Arizona, and Texas were experiencing a near depression. Oil prices (after adjusting for inflation) had sunk below 1973 levels; U.S. oil producers watched the Arab struggle closely.

## THE THREAT

• Throughout 1990, Hussein verbally attacked OPEC members who were violating the agreed-upon production quotas. At an Arab Cooperation Council in February he also "threatened reprisals if Kuwait and Saudi Arabia did not forgive Iraq's $30 billion in war debt and provide Iraq with an additional $30 billion in new grants." (*Village Voice*)

• Hussein was particularly angry with Kuwait. He charged that in addition to violating the quota, Kuwait had stolen 2.4 billion barrels of oil—worth more than $40 billion—from the vast Rumailah oil field located beneath their border (95% is on Iraq's side). At an Arab summit in May 1990, he warned that if Kuwait did not stop its "economic warfare" against his country, Iraq might attack Kuwait.

• Hussein also repeatedly told the United States how he felt. In January, he reportedly met with U.S. diplomats in New York to discuss the price of oil. On April 12, 1990, he met with a delegation of U.S. senators led by Robert Dole; on July 25, he met for two hours with U.S. Ambassador April Glaspie.

• As Hussein publicly escalated his demands, his ministers worked quietly behind the scenes to negotiate a settlement with the other Arab states. For a while it looked as though they would succeed. On July 31, representatives of Iraq, Kuwait, and Saudi Arabia met and agreed to a partial payment of $10 billion to Iraq for costs incurred during the war with Iran. But, according to several sources, Kuwait abruptly reneged, killing the accord, and told Hussein to "sit on it."

• That was the last straw. Two days later, on August 2, Iraqi troops invaded Kuwait, quickly taking control of the whole country.

## WAS IT A CONSPIRACY?

*Although the U.S. said it was surprised by Iraq's invasion of Kuwait, there is compelling evidence to suggest that the Bush administration knew Hussein's plans—and encouraged him to attack.*

### SUSPICIOUS FACTS

• George Bush told Congress: "In the early morning hours of August 2, following negotiations and promises by Iraq's dictator Saddam Hussein not to use force, a powerful Iraqi army invaded its trusting and much weaker neighbor, Kuwait."

• Hussein made no such promises. On the contrary, he had been warning Kuwait for months that he *would* use force. And in his July 25 meeting with U.S. Ambassador April Glaspie—eight days before the invasion—he told her that Kuwait's economic war was slowly killing his people. Referring to impending talks with the Kuwaitis, he said, "If we are unable to find a solution, then it will be natural that Iraq will not accept death" (*The New York Times*).

• Hussein made it clear that even U.S. retaliation wouldn't deter him: "You can come to Iraq with aircraft and missiles...but do not push us to the point that we cease to care....When we feel that you want to injure our pride and take away the Iraqi's chance of a high standard of living, then we will cease to care and death will be the choice for us."

• Glaspie's response to Hussein was curiously noncommittal, considering that he was clearly threatening war against Kuwait. She replied: "We have no opinion on the Arab-Arab conflicts, like your border dispute with Kuwait," and added, "James Baker has directed our official spokesman to emphasize this instruction." (*The New York Times*)

### A Green Light?

When details of the Glaspie meeting leaked out, reporters asked White House spokesperson Marlin Fitzwater if the administration hadn't always supported Hussein and in fact sent Iraq a "green light to invade." He answered that such assertions were "stupid" and "ludicrous."

• However, although Glaspie was later criticized for mishandling the situation, she was clearly echoing White House policy. On July 24, the day before the meeting, State Department spokesperson

Margaret Tutwiler stated, "We do not have any defense treaties with Kuwait, and there are no special defenses or security commitments to Kuwait." On July 31, six days after Glaspie's meeting, Assistant Secretary of State John Kelly reiterated that position before a House subcommittee. "Historically," he said, "the U.S. has taken no position on the border disputes in the area."

• When Secretary of Defense Dick Cheney asserted that the U.S. *would* defend Kuwait if it were attacked, his remarks were quickly repudiated by the Defense Department. A spokesperson claimed that Cheney had spoken "with some degree of liberty." One Pentagon insider noted, "The White House cut the secretary down to size rather quickly. They said: 'You're committing us to a war we might not want to fight.' He was told quite pointedly that, from then on, statements on Iraq would be made by the White House and the State Department."

• Until the morning of the invasion, the Bush administration stuck to its position of remaining officially and publicly "neutral in any Iraq-Kuwait conflict"—despite the fact that on July 28 (according to the *Village Voice*), CIA Director William Webster informed President Bush that an Iraqi invasion was imminent.

### POSSIBLE MOTIVES
*Why would the Bush administration want to lure Saddam Hussein into war?*

### THEORY #1: Oil
• Low oil prices had sent American oil-producing states into a tailspin, so former Texas oilmen George Bush and Jim Baker may have tailored U.S. foreign policy to help them out. Washington's staunch ally, Saudi Arabia, also smiled on Hussein's attempts to raise oil prices. Saudi Arabia even encouraged negotiations with the Kuwaitis, hoping that there would be modest price increases without an invasion.

• According to Helga Graham of the *London Observer*, the Bush administration had been encouraging Hussein to pursue an "aggressive policy of higher oil prices" seven months before he invaded Kuwait. Graham wrote, "It was discreetly suggested at a New York meeting in January…between an American former ambassador and one of Saddam's top Ministers...that Iraq should engineer a big oil price rise at OPEC."

• In his July 25 meeting with Glaspie, Saddam announced that Kuwait's actions had hurt Iraq and that he hoped to drive the price of oil up to $25. State Department cables show that Glaspie responded: "We have many Americans who would like to see the price go above $25 because they come from oil-producing states."

• At best, Washington was sending mixed signals. It's possible that the administration was willing to let Iraq take a few oil fields. (Even while Hussein threatened OPEC members, Washington continued to talk about "improved relations" with Iraq.) But, apparently, the U.S. was surprised when Hussein took the whole country. Glaspie, for example, was quoted in *The New York Times* as commenting: "Obviously I didn't think, and nobody else did, that the Iraqis were going to take *all* of Kuwait."

## THEORY #2: The U.S. needed an excuse to staff a top-secret base in the Middle East.

• Investigative reporter Scott Armstrong may have uncovered a key to the Gulf War. In a *Mother Jones* article, he revealed something that most Americans and even most members of Congress had not been aware of—the White House, the Pentagon, and the Saudi royal family have worked together secretly for the last decade to build a network of high-tech military superbases in the Saudi Arabian desert.

• Built at a cost of more than $200 billion, the network includes five regional outposts and offers the Saudis "the most advanced warfare command system in the world, with conventional military capabilities beyond those available to defend Europe or even the continental United States." (*Mother Jones*)

• The "sophisticated network of superbases and advanced weapons systems" was designed to protect the region's oil fields from Soviet or Islamic revolutionary attacks. The bases were fully armed and equipped—in the event of war, all they needed were several thousand U.S. troops to run them.

• But stationing those troops permanently in Saudi Arabia was unacceptable to the royal family. In fact, some Saudi princes bittterly objected to the plan, for religious reasons. Since the Saudi royal family claims to be the "protector of Islam," it must keep "infidels" from ever entering the holiest mosques in Medina and Mecca. Even the *appearance* of working too closely with the U.S. could undermine the royal family's legitimacy.

• However, the Bush administration had compelling reasons to staff the bases as soon as possible. The secret defense agreement with Saudi Arabia was legally shaky—"under the Constitution, the president may enter into treaties with other governments only with the advice and consent of the Senate." If the secret agreement with the Saudis became known, pro-Israel senators in Congress might have tried to kill it. But more important, the secret bases are so advanced that they essentially determine who controls the Middle East. What if they were seized by Islamic fundamentalists?

• Thus Bush may have decided to startle the Saudis into action. The Bush administration had been arming and sharing intelligence with Saddam Hussein for years (until, in fact, only a few months before the invasion). Then, suddenly, after encouraging Hussein to invade Kuwait, the U.S. turned against him and rushed to Saudi Arabia's rescue.

• Scott Armstrong makes it clear that the superbases were the focus of the U.S. war effort: without them, the U.S. could not have won the Gulf War so quickly—and perhaps not at all. According to Armstrong, even after the war King Fahd still resisted staffing the bases, but a compromise was reached. "While the Saudis have apparently agreed to station as many as seven thousand military personnel at Saudi bases, including at least some Special Forces advisers, the deployment will be treated publicly...merely as rotating units of technicians on temporary exercises and training assignments." Thus, when hundreds of thousands of Desert Storm troops left Saudi Arabia, seven thousand Americans quietly stayed behind. (*Mother Jones*)

• In that light, leaving Hussein in power makes a lot of sense. With the Beast of Baghdad still around, that's one more reason why we've got to stay over there. Ironically, Secretary of State Baker may have spelled it all out on September 4, months *before* the Gulf War—if you knew how to read between the lines. When some people hoped aloud that an Iraqi withdrawal might avert war, Baker replied, "the Administration intends to maintain a long-term military presence in the Persian Gulf even if Iraq agrees to withdraw from Kuwait." (*The New York Times*)

**THEORY #3: The defense industry pushed for a war to keep itself in business.**

• As the Soviet threat began to dissipate in 1990, the American public began talking about a "peace dividend." The U.S. military budget was in danger.

• By sending so many troops to the Middle East while negotiations were still under way and by refusing to consider any of Hussein's overtures before the war, Bush made it clear he wasn't interested in negotiations. Even the Saudis—whose defense was our official reason for being there—thought some of Hussein's proposals looked promising. But Bush dismissed them all and went ahead with the war.

• After the war, America was so supportive of the military—a feeling created, in part, by the government's manipulation of news coverage in Kuwait—that budget cuts that had seemed inevitable only months earlier never happened.

• Defense contractors even wound up with *more* business as a result of the Gulf War: "The war itself," said *The New York Times*, "has done the most to stir interest in the acquisition of high-tech weapons. Even the most backward and isolated national leader can hardly be unaware today that Iraq's vaunted army—said to be the world's fourth-largest—was quickly blown to pieces by the advanced armaments the U.S. and its allies used so effectively."

**RECOMMENDED READING**

• Two excellent compilations of newspaper articles are available from the DATACENTER, 464 19th Street, Oakland, CA 94612:
   √ *The Persian Gulf War, Background and Analysis*
   √ *The Persian Gulf War, The Media and Our Right to Know*

• "Eye of the Storm," by Scott Armstrong (*Mother Jones* magazine, Nov./Dec. 1991)

• "Who Lost Kuwait?" by Murray Waas (*Village Voice*, Jan. 22, 1991)

# THE PLOTS AGAINST CASTRO QUIZ

*After the Bay of Pigs invasion of Cuba failed in 1961, the CIA became obsessed with eliminating Fidel Castro. Guess which of these plots were really conceived by the CIA—and which are the National Insecurity Council's own disinformation.*

**1.** Use agents in Cuba to spread rumors that the Second Coming of Christ is imminent and that Castro is the Anti-Christ.
❏ Real   ❏ Disinformation

**2.** Give Castro pills containing botulism.
❏ Real   ❏ Disinformation

**3.** Recruit infected prostitutes to give him syphilis.
❏ Real   ❏ Disinformation

**4.** Recruit Mafia hit men.
❏ Real   ❏ Disinformation

**5.** Stage a phony Cuban invasion of the Guantanamo naval base as a pretext to invade with full military force.
❏ Real   ❏ Disinformation

**6.** Surprise him at the beach with an exploding conch shell.
❏ Real   ❏ Disinformation

**7.** Put thalium salts in his shoes or cigars during an appearance on the David Susskind Show, to make his beard and hair fall out.
❏ Real   ❏ Disinformation

**8.** Put itching powder in his scuba suit and LSD on his mouthpiece so that he would be driven crazy and drown.
❏ Real   ❏ Disinformation

**9.** Offer him exploding cigars designed to blow his head off.
❏ Real   ❏ Disinformation

**10.** Shoot him with a TV camera that has machine gun inside.
❏ Real   ❏ Disinformation

**11.** Spray his broadcasting studio with hallucinogens.
❏ Real   ❏ Disinformation

**12.** Kill him with a poison pen— a ballpoint with a hypodermic needle built in.
❏ Real   ❏ Disinformation

**Answer: Only #3 is false.**

# J. EDGAR HOOVER AND THE RED MENACE

*When America wanted to know about the Communist conspiracy in the early 1950s, FBI Director J. Edgar Hoover was ready to explain it.*

J Edgar Hoover was an expert on Communist infiltration in America and how Americans could guard against the Red Menace. Here are excerpts from different interviews he gave from 1947 to 1950, at the height of the Red Scare.

**INTERVIEWER:** "How can you tell a Communist?"

**HOOVER:** "A Communist is not always easy to identify. It is possible that a concealed Communist may hide in the most unsuspected and unlikely place. He is trained in deceit and uses cleverly camouflaged movements to conceal his real purposes. But he may frequently be detected by certain characteristics. He will always espouse the cause of Soviet Russia over that of the United States. His viewpoint and position will shift with each change in the Communist Party 'line.' He will utilize a language of 'double talk'—referring to the Soviet-dominated countries as 'democracies' and complain that the United States is 'imperialistic.' He will attempt to infiltrate and gain control of organizations and subvert them to the use of the party.

"My advice to the public is this: Be alert to the dangers of Communism. Report your information immediately and fully to the FBI."

**INTERVIEWER:** "Where do you find Communists?"

**HOOVER:** "Communists may be found in most sections of the United States. Of course, in some areas, the Communists are more thickly located than others. As a general rule, the Communists are less strong in agricultural areas. The Communists are strongest today in the industrial areas. The Communists, as a basic principle of infiltration, are interested in possessing strength in heavy industry, that is coal, steel, rubber, automobile, etc. It is here that, in event of an emergency, they can do their greatest harm to the country. That is one of the potential sabotage dangers facing America today."

INTERVIEWER: "Is the FBI interested in any Communist, or only those connected with espionage rings or possible sabotage?"

HOOVER: "The FBI is interested in knowing the identity of all Communists in the United States, as any Communist, properly qualified, might be recruited into espionage. He may today be circulating peace petitions or selling Communist literature. Tomorrow he may be sabotaging American industry or serving as an espionage courier. Every member of this international conspiracy is a potential saboteur and espionage agent."

INTERVIEWER: "Don't you draw a distinction between philosophical Communists and those who are tools of spy rings?"

HOOVER: "Any person who subscribes to these teachings, regardless of his reason, is working against American democracy and for the benefit of Soviet Russia. Stalin is his omnipotent oracle from whom all wisdom flows. The Communist party is today a Trojan horse of disloyalty, coiled like a serpent in the very heart of America.

"It may mouth sweet words of 'peace,' 'democracy,' 'equality,' and flourish gay slogans of 'international solidarity' and 'brotherhood of men,' but its body and feet are from the Russian bear."

INTERVIEWER: "Are Communists trained to lie?"

HOOVER: "The concept of morality and fair play, as practiced in our democracy, is alien and repugnant to him. Moreover, the Communists employ a purposeful double-talk, roundabout style, known as 'Aesopian language,' in their literature and speeches, designed to deceive and evade, to clothe their true thoughts. This technique, utilized by Lenin, is the very epitome of deceit."

INTERVIEWER: "Would you say it was a favorite Communist technique to belittle the amount of Communist activity here?"

HOOVER: "Very definitely. As an illustration, a few years ago there was a Communist Action group which was hard pressed in a given area, prima ily through the energetic efforts of a few individuals. So, to counteract these few anti-Communists, the Communists developed a technique: Whenever anybody would denounce Communists, they would say, 'What's wrong with being a Communist?' And the average person had given little thought to the subject. They knew they didn't like Communism, but were at a disadvantage with a trained Communist agitator."

**INTERVIEWER:** "Do you have many Communists whom you are actually watching from day to day?"

**HOOVER:** "We have a relatively small force when you take into consideration that there is approximately one special agent to every 29,000 inhabitants in this country. With some 43,217 members of the Communist Party and only 5,200 agents—it's a physical impossibility to keep all of them under surveillance."

**INTERVIEWER:** "What would you say to the charge often made that we are engaging in 'thought control' with our constant watching of Communists?"

**HOOVER:** "The FBI is concerned not with what Communists think, but with what they do—their actions, just as in any other field of its investigative activity. There is no scintilla of evidence to substantiate the charge that the FBI is engaged in 'thought control' activities."

**INTERVIEWER:** "Isn't it possible that by asking citizens to report subversive activities, some may be encouraged to circulate gossip and rumor and engage in 'witch hunts'?"

**HOOVER:** "I think that citizens cooperating with the FBI provide the greatest barrier you could possibly have against 'witch hunts' and hysteria; because, if the citizen has a suspicion, it is his duty to turn it over to the FBI and from that time on do nothing unless he receives a request. A 'Gestapo' under the American system would be an impossibility. In addition to the protection of our courts and Congress, we have a free press, which would quickly spot injustices or any excesses on the part of any government agency."

# EMBALMED BEEF

*One of the better-known conspiracy theories at the turn of the century in America was this one about Armour & Company.*

Of the 5,462 Americans who died in the Spanish-American War, only 379 were battle casualties. The rest of the deaths were attributed to "disease and other causes." One of the "other causes," soldiers said, was the tinned beef supplied to troops by Armour & Company, a Chicago meat packer. Although a death toll was never tallied, thousands of troops became ill after eating it. One Army inspector called it "embalmed beef."

Under a deal struck with War Secretary Russell Alger in May, 1898, Armour sold the U.S. Army 500,000 pounds of beef. But rumors quickly spread that Armour had sold soldiers tainted food—and that crooked members of the government were in on the scheme. President William McKinley was forced to appoint a special commission to look into the matter.

## WAS IT A CONSPIRACY?
*Did Armour intentionally sell rotten meat to the U.S. Army?*

## SUSPICIOUS FACTS
• The cases of beef sold to the Army had already been rejected once—by inspectors in Liverpool, England—because that meat was unsatisfactory.

• The shipment had been "stamped and approved by an inspector of the Bureau of Animal Industry." Yet two months later, an army inspector found "751 cases containing rotten meat. In the first sixty cases he opened, he found fourteen tins already burst, 'the effervescent putrid contents of which were distributed all over the cases.' " (*The Twentieth Century*)

• Among witnesses called by the special commission were Major General Nelson Miles, commander of the troops that invaded and occupied Puerto Rico in 1898. "Miles claimed that Alger and other War Department officials had deliberately connived with American meat packers to buy and send impure meat....to the country's fighting men overseas. Miles' charges could not be substantiated, but they helped bring on the resignation of Alger." (*Encyclopedia of American Scandal*)

• After reading about the tragic deaths during the war, Thomas Dolan, a former Armour plant superintendent, swore in an affidavit published in the *New York Journal*, "I have seen as much as forty pounds of flesh afflicted with gangrene cut from the carcass of a beef, in order that the rest of the animal might be utilized in trade....Of all the evils of the stockyards, the canning department is perhaps the worst." The company, said Dolan, "was selling carrion."

• Armour & Company called Dolan's charges "absolutely false." But the company never sued him or the newspaper that printed the story for libel. In fact, not long after the flap, Armour allegedly offered Dolan $5,000 to contradict his earlier charges and say that the *Journal* had paid him to fabricate his account. Dolan refused.

**FOOTNOTE**
Charges that Armour had bribed War Department officials were never proved, and in time the scandal blew over. Within twenty years, Armour & Co. was the biggest meat packer in the world.

**RECOMMENDED READING**
• *Encyclopedia of American Scandal*, by George Kohn (Facts on File, 1989)
• *The Twentieth Century: A People's History*, by Howard Zinn (Harper & Row, 1984)

## TAKING LIBERTIES: The Huston Plan

In 1970, President Nixon set up a committee of senior intelligence officials, headed by J. Edgar Hoover of the FBI, to consider ways the intelligence community could better silence Communists, hippies, anti-Vietnam protesters, and other administration opponents. Three weeks later the committee submitted a 43-page report, the Huston Plan (named after 29-year-old Charles Huston, the White House liaison to the committee).

The plan proposed a variety of illegal activities (infiltrating campus political groups, increased wiretapping, using military undercover agents, etc.) and was approved by Nixon in July 1970. But it was never put into practice. Hoover stopped it—not because it was unconstitutional, but because it infringed on the FBI's turf.

# PROJECT PAPERCLIP

*Did the Pentagon sneak Nazi scientists into the U.S. after World War II—and put them to work in American labs?*

After World War II ended in 1945, victorious Russian and American intelligence teams began a treasure hunt through occupied Germany for military and scientific booty. They were looking for things like new rocket and aircraft designs, medicine, and electronics. But they were also hunting down the most precious "spoils" of all: the scientists whose work had nearly won the war for Germany.

The U.S. military rounded up Nazi scientists and brought them to America. It had originally intended merely to debrief them and send them back to Germany. But when it realized the extent of the scientists' knowledge and expertise, the War Department decided it would be a waste to send the scientists home. It decided to keep the Nazi scientists in America and make them U.S. citizens.

There was only one problem: it was illegal. U.S. law explicitly prohibited Nazi officials from immigrating to America—and as many as three-quarters of the scientists in question had been committed Nazis.

## WHAT HAPPENED

• Convinced that German scientists could help America's postwar efforts, President Harry Truman agreed in September 1946 to authorize "Project Paperclip," a program to bring selected German scientists to work on America's behalf during the Cold War.

• However, Truman expressly excluded anyone found "to have been a member of the Nazi party and more than a nominal participant in its activities, or an active supporter of Naziism or militarism."

• The War Department's Joint Intelligence Objectives Agency (JIOA) conducted background investigations on the scientists. In February 1947, JIOA Director Bosquet Wev submitted the first set of scientists' dossiers to the State and Justice Departments for review.

• The dossiers were damning. Samuel Klaus, the State Department's representative on the JIOA board, claimed that all the scientists in this first batch were "ardent Nazis." Their visa requests were denied.

## A DIFFERENT APPROACH

• Wev was furious. He wrote a memo warning that "the best interests of the United States have been subjugated to the efforts expended in 'beating a dead Nazi horse.' " He also declared that the return of these scientists to Germany, where they could be exploited by America's enemies, presented "a far greater security threat to this country than any former Nazi affiliations which they may have had or even any Nazi sympathies that they may still have."

• Apparently, Wev decided to sidestep the problem. Since he couldn't persuade the State Department to allow hard-core Nazi scientists into the country, he asked U.S. military intelligence to rewrite the scientists' dossiers to eliminate incriminating evidence.

• Military intelligence cooperated, "cleansing" the files of Nazi references. By 1955, more than 760 German scientists had been granted citizenship in the U.S. and given prominent positions in the American scientific community. Many had been longtime members of the Nazi party and the Gestapo, had conducted experiments on humans at concentration camps, had used slave labor, and had committed other war crimes.

## WAS IT A CONSPIRACY?

• In a 1985 exposé in the *Bulletin of the Atomic Scientists*, Linda Hunt wrote that she had examined more than 130 reports on Project Paperclip subjects—and every one "had been changed to eliminate the security threat classification."

• President Truman, who had explicitly ordered that no committed Nazis be admitted under Project Paperclip, was evidently never aware that his directive had been violated. State Department archives and the memoirs of officials from that era confirm this. In fact, according to Clare Lasby's book *Operation Paperclip*, project officials "covered their designs with such secrecy that it bedeviled their own President; at Potsdam he denied their activities and undoubtedly enhanced Russian suspicion and distrust," quite possibly fueling the Cold War even further.

• A good example of how these dossiers were changed is the case of Wernher von Braun. A September 18, 1947, report on the German rocket scientist stated, "Subject is regarded as a potential security threat by the Military Governor."

• The following February, a new security evaluation of von Braun said, "No derogatory information is available on the subject....It is the opinion of the Military Governor that he may not constitute a security threat to the United States."

## ROGUES' GALLERY

*Here are a few of the suspicious characters who were allowed to immigrate through Project Paperclip:*

**Arthur Rudolph.** During the war, Rudolph was operations director of the Mittelwerk factory at the Dora-Nordhausen concentration camp, where 20,000 workers died from beatings, hangings, and starvation. Rudolph had been a member of the Nazi party since 1931; a 1945 military file on him said simply: "100% Nazi, dangerous type, security threat...!! Suggest internment."

But the JIOA's final dossier on him said there was "nothing in his records indicating that he was a war criminal, an ardent Nazi or otherwise objectionable." Rudolph became a U.S. citizen and later designed the Saturn 5 rocket used in the Apollo moon landings. In 1984, when his war record was finally investigated, he fled to West Germany.

**Wernher von Braun.** From 1937 to 1945, von Braun was the technical director of the Peenemunde rocket research center, where the V-2 rocket—which devastated England—was developed. As noted previously, his dossier was rewritten so he didn't appear to have been an enthusiastic Nazi.

Von Braun worked on guided missiles for the U.S. Army and was later director of NASA's Marshall Space Flight Center. He became a celebrity in the 1950s and early 1960s, as one of Walt Disney's experts on the "World of Tomorrow." In 1970, he became NASA's associate administrator.

**Kurt Blome.** A high-ranking Nazi scientist, Blome told U.S. military interrogators in 1945 that he had been ordered in 1943 to experiment with plague vaccines on concentration camp prisoners. He was tried at Nuremberg in 1947 on charges of practicing euthanasia (extermination of sick prisoners), and conducting experiments on humans. Although acquitted, his earlier admissions were well known, and it was generally accepted that he had indeed participated in the gruesome experiments.

Two months after his Nuremberg acquittal, Blome was interviewed at Camp David, Maryland, about biological warfare. In 1951, he was hired by the U.S. Army Chemical Corps to work on chemical warfare. His file neglected to mention Nuremberg.

**Major General Walter Schreiber.** According to Linda Hunt's article, the U.S. military tribunal at Nuremberg heard evidence that "Schreiber had assigned doctors to experiment on concentration camp prisoners and had made funds available for such experimentation." The assistant prosecutor said the evidence would have convicted Schreiber if the Soviets, who held him from 1945 to 1948, had made him available for the trial.

Again, Schreiber's Paperclip file made no mention of this evidence; the project found work for him at the Air Force School of Medicine at Randolph Field in Texas. When columnist Drew Pearson publicized the Nuremberg evidence in 1952, the negative publicity led the JIOA, says Hunt, to arrange "a visa and a job for Schreiber in Argentina, where his daughter was living. On May 22, 1952, he was flown to Buenos Aires."

**Hermann Becker-Freysing and Siegfried Ruff.** These two, along with Blome, were among the 23 defendants in the Nuremberg War Trials "Medical Case." Becker-Freysing was convicted and sentenced to 20 years in prison for conducting experiments on Dachau inmates, such as starving them, then force-feeding them seawater that had been chemically altered to make it drinkable. Ruff was acquitted (in a close decision) on charges that he had killed as many as 80 Dachau inmates in a low-pressure chamber designed to simulate altitudes in excess of 60,000 feet. Before their trial, Becker-Freysing and Ruff were paid by the Army Air Force to write reports about their grotesque experiments.

NOTE: Project Paperclip was stopped in 1957, when West Germany protested to the U.S. that these efforts had stripped it of "scientific skills." There was no comment about supporting Nazis.

### RECOMMENDED READING
- *Operation Paperclip*, by Clare Lasby (Athenaeum, 1975)
- "U.S. Coverup of Nazi Scientists," by Linda Hunt (*Bulletin of Atomic Scientists*, April 1985)

# NOTABLE QUOTES

*Here are some of The National Insecurity Council's favorite quotes:*

"Every government is run by liars and nothing they say should be believed."
—*I.F. Stone*

"Your theory is crazy, but it's not crazy enough to be true."
—*Niels Bohr (to a young physicist)*

"Though a good deal is too strange to be believed, nothing is too strange to have happened."
—*Thomas Hardy*

"What the American people don't know can kill them."
—*Fred Friendly*

"National Security is the cause of National Insecurity."
—*Hagbard Celine*

"Once we decide that anything goes, anything can come home to haunt us."
—*Bill Moyers*

"A democracy cannot be both ignorant and free."
—*Thomas Jefferson*

"We have met the enemy, and he is us."
—*Pogo (Walt Kelly)*

"Anyone in the United States today who isn't paranoid must be crazy."
—*Robert Anton Wilson*

"I keep reading between the lies."
—*Goodman Ace*

"The dream of every leader, whether a tyrannical despot or a benign prophet, is to regulate the behavior of his people."
—*Colin Blakemore*

"Secrecy, being an instrument of conspiracy, ought never to be the system of a regular government."
—*Jeremy Bentham*

"Secrecy...has become a god in this country, and those people who have secrets travel in a kind of fraternity....
They will not speak to anyone else."
—*Sen. William J. Fulbright*

# WHO WAS OSWALD?

*For all the millions of words written about him, Lee Harvey Oswald remains a mystery. And the part he played in JFK's killing is anyone's guess.*

Lee Harvey Oswald was first arrested as a suspect in the slaying of Dallas policeman J. D. Tippit on November 22, 1963, less than two hours after President John Kennedy's assassination. The following day, 24-year-old Oswald was charged with killing the president. On Sunday, November 24, as he was being transferred from the Dallas city jail to the county jail, Oswald was shot dead by Jack Ruby.

The portrait we have of Oswald as a lonely and deranged gunman comes, for the most part, from the Warren Commission Report. Some excerpts:

√ Oswald "was born in New Orleans on October 18, 1939, two months after the death of his father." His mother remarried briefly, but Oswald's childhood was an unsettled one of intermittent moves and spotty schooling. A New York City social worker described young Lee as "rather pleasant, appealing" but "emotionally scarred, affectionless...with fantasies of being all-powerful and hurting people."

√ At 16, "he started to read Communist literature...he wrote to the Socialist Party of America, professing his belief in Marxism." When he turned 17, Oswald dropped out of high school and joined the U.S. Marines.

## A RESTLESS LIFE

• "Most people who knew Oswald in the Marines described him as a 'loner' who...resented authority. He spent much of his free time reading....During this period he expressed strong admiration for Fidel Castro and an interest in joining the Cuban army." His three-year stint in the Marines, which included 15 months in Japan and a final year in California, ended in September 1959.

• A month later, Oswald emigrated to Russia and announced his intention to become a citizen. During the thirty months he lived there, he married a Russian woman, Marina Pruskova, and had a daughter. But Oswald was restless, and on June 1, 1962, after a determination that he had retained his American citizenship, the Oswalds left Moscow for the U.S., "assisted by a loan of $435.71 from the U.S. Department of State." They settled in Fort Worth, Texas.

• "During this period...Oswald was interviewed twice by agents of the FBI...Oswald denied that he was involved in Soviet intelligence activities and promised to advise the FBI if Soviet representatives attempted to enlist him in intelligence activities."

• The Oswalds were befriended by a group of Russian-speaking people in the Dallas-Fort Worth area, but Lee reportedly had trouble holding a job, and his marriage soon became strained. Leaving Marina with a friend in a Dallas suburb, Lee moved to New Orleans in April, 1963. While in that city he "formed a fictitious New Orleans Chapter of the Fair Play for Cuba Committee," and was arrested in August after his pro-Castro pamphleteering sparked a scuffle with anti-Castro Cuban exiles.

• By October, he was back in Dallas, where he got an apartment apart from Marina. With the help of Marina's friend Ruth Paine, Oswald got a job at the Texas School Book Depository on October 16. Little more than a month later, he was arrested for shooting President Kennedy from that building.

### Second Thoughts

Except for its conclusion that Oswald killed JFK, the Warren Report's biography of Lee Harvey Oswald is known to be factual. But had the Commission dug deeper and fleshed out the facts further, a more complicated Oswald might have emerged.

## WHO WAS OSWALD?

### THEORY #1: He was a CIA agent.

*Oswald's Marine Corps assignment, his ease returning to the U.S. after defecting to the Soviet Union, his fluency in Russian, and his subsequent involvement with CIA operatives in Texas and New Orleans suggest that he may have been a CIA agent.*

## SUSPICIOUS FACTS

### Atsugi, Japan

• Despite Oswald's alleged Marxist beliefs while in the Marines, he was posted to—and had security clearance for—one of the most sensitive U.S. bases in the world: Atsugi, Japan. According to Jim Marrs in his book *Crossfire: The Plot That Killed Kennedy*, Atsugi was the point of origin for U-2 spy plane flights over the Soviet Union and "the main CIA operational base in the Far East." Oswald served as "a radar operator monitoring the supersecret U-2 flights over the Soviet Union."

• Former CIA finance officer James Wilcott testified to the House Select Committee on Assassinations in 1977 that "he learned that Oswald was paid by the CIA while still stationed at Atsugi."

• It was revealed in 1977 that the CIA had a "201 file"—a personnel file—on Oswald. In the military, a 201 file means that the person is part of the organization, drawing a salary. The CIA handed over a "virtually empty folder" on Oswald to the House Select Committee on Assassinations, but an internal CIA document described Oswald's 201 file as filling "two four-drawer safes."

• While investigating JFK's death, New Orleans District Attorney Jim Garrison tried to get Lee Harvey Oswald's tax records. According to Garrison, those tax records were "classified," as were the "1200 CIA files on Oswald that were part of the Warren Report."

### Curious Travels

• Although Oswald was a high school dropout, his Russian was so good that when he first met his bride-to-be, Marina, she thought he was a native-born Russian "with a Baltic area accent." That kind of fluency suggests that Oswald got extensive language training while in the Marines.

• Oswald renounced his American citizenship when he entered Russia, and his Marine Corps discharge was changed to "dishonorable" after the Corps got word that he had offered to tell military secrets to the Russians. Yet Oswald had no trouble returning to the States with his Russian bride.

• Surprisingly, branches of the U.S. government even gave the Oswalds money for their trip to America and helped them get settled in the States. Notes Marrs in *Crossfire*, "The Department of

Health, Education and Welfare (HEW) had approved the financial aid to Oswald upon urging from the State Department. In Dallas HEW records, it states that Oswald went to Russia 'with State Department approval.' "

## Dallas CIA Connections

• The Oswalds settled in the Dallas area in 1962 with the help of a Russian-speaking couple, George and Jeanne DeMohrenschildt, who, the Warren Commission found, were "the people closest to Lee Harvey Oswald and his wife Marina just before the assassination." Socially, it was a curious match: the DeMohrenschildts traveled in the best social circles and were close friends of Jackie Kennedy's parents, the Bouviers.

• George DeMohrenschildt's pedigree in U.S. intelligence was equally impressive. A young Russian emigré during World War II, he had joined the Vlasov Army, a corps of anti-Communist Russians who fought alongside the Nazis against the Soviet Army. The Vlasov Army later became part of the CIA intelligence network set up by former Nazi spy chief Reinhard Gehlen (see p. 192). CIA memos released under the Freedom of Information Act showed that DeMohrenschildt continued to work for the Agency well into the 1960s.

• On March 29, 1977, shortly after an investigator for the House Select Committee on Assassinations tried to contact him, George DeMohrenschildt was found dead from a shotgun blast to the head. His death was ruled a suicide.

## New Orleans CIA Connections

• The Warren Report notes that Oswald set up the avowedly pro-Castro "Fair Play for Cuba Committee" (FPCC) in New Orleans during 1963. However, considerable evidence suggests that Oswald actually worked that summer with a fervently *anti*-Castro group, which included a number of CIA operatives.

• The location of Oswald's FPCC office—544 Camp Street—was very suspicious. The building also housed the CIA-backed Cuban Revolutionary Council, a militantly anti-Castro group, as well as the offices of Guy Banister, who was running an anti-Castro guerrilla training camp for the CIA in the woods outside New Orleans.

• According to Anthony Summer's book *Conspiracy*, Banister had been a renowned FBI agent in the 1930s, helping to capture public enemy number one, John Dillinger. During the war, Banister worked for the Office of Naval Intelligence, a connection he reportedly maintained all his life. And, according to Banister's secretary Delphine Roberts, "he received funds from the CIA—he had access to large funds at various times in 1963." Lee Harvey Oswald was on Banister's payroll that summer, says Summer, and was in and out of the office continually.

• New Orleans businessman Clay Shaw and pilot David Ferrie also worked with Banister that summer, and, according to former CIA officer Victor Marchetti and director of the CIA Richard Helms, they were also CIA operatives. On at least one occasion, said secretary Roberts, Ferrie took Oswald to an "anti-Castro guerrilla training camp outside New Orleans....to train with rifles." In fact, it's possible that Ferrie and Oswald knew each other before this time: in 1955, sixteen-year-old Oswald had been a cadet in a Civil Air Patrol unit which Ferrie was part of.

• A CIA-Mafia link? Ferrie had worked for the CIA at various times, yet, according to Summers, a "contemporary Border Patrol report" stated that Ferrie was the pilot of a private plane that surreptitiously flew Mob boss Carlos Marcello back into the United States two years after he had been deported by Attorney General Robert Kennedy.

### One for the Books

• According to one of Ferrie's friends, not long after the assassination a mob lawyer named C. Wray Gill visited Ferrie and told him that Oswald had been carrying Ferrie's library card when he was arrested in Dallas. Gill (who sometimes represented Carlos Marcello) promised to represent Ferrie, and went with him to the authorities the following day. Ferrie denied knowing anything about Oswald or the assassination and was later released. (*Crossfire*)

• According to *Crossfire*, there is no *official* public record that Ferrie's card was found on Oswald; nonetheless, the Secret Service reportedly asked Ferrie about it when they questioned him.

## THEORY #2: He was working for the FBI.

*Oswald played both sides of the Cuba issue, involving himself with both pro- and anti-Castro activities. Was he an agent provocateur or an undercover infiltrator in the pay of the FBI?*

### SUSPICIOUS FACTS

• On January 22, 1964, Warren Commission general counsel J. Lee Rankin received a call from Waggoner Carr, the Texas attorney general. Carr reported that Dallas district attorney Henry Wade, a former FBI agent, had told him that Oswald was recruited as an FBI informant in September 1962. Carr added that the FBI had paid Oswald $200 a month and had given him "Informant Number S-179." (*Crossfire*)

• Rankin had received the same information from the Secret Service, who "named a Dallas deputy sheriff, Allan Sweatt, as its source."

• The allegations threw the commissioners into a tizzy. Meeting with them that day, Rankin said that he and Justice Warren agreed that "if that [information about Oswald as FBI informant] was true and it ever came out, could be established, then you would have people think that there was a conspiracy to accomplish this assassination that nothing the Commission did or anybody could dissipate." (*Crossfire*)

• Some commissioners suggested destroying the transcript of their discussion on the subject. Meanwhile, the FBI was denying the allegation. The Warren Commission "decided just to drop the entire matter."

### THE OFFICIAL CONCLUSION

"All of the evidence before the Commission established that there was nothing to support the speculation that Oswald was an agent, employee, or informant of the FBI, the CIA, or any other governmental agency. It has thoroughly investigated Oswald's relationships prior to the assassination with all agencies of the U.S. government. All contacts with Oswald by any of these agencies were made in the regular exercise of their responsibilities."

—The Warren Commission Report

# WHERE WAS GEORGE?

*George Bush has been in public life for more than thirty years, but where was he when some of America's greatest conspiracies took place?*

## BAY OF PIGS

• Although this ill-fated invasion of Cuba occurred shortly after JFK took office, it was originally a CIA operation overseen by then-Vice President Richard Nixon. Bush has repeatedly denied any Agency involvement before he became its director in 1976, but Mark Lane and other conspiracy theorists claim that Bush actually helped recruit Cuban exiles in Miami for the 1961 invasion.

• According to Lane, two Navy vessels commandeered for the invasion and repainted to disguise their origin were also given new names: *Houston* and *Barbara*. The CIA's top-secret name for the invasion was Operation Zapata. At the time, George Bush was CEO of the Zapata Off-Shore Company, was living in Houston, and was then, as now, married to Barbara.

## JFK'S ASSASSINATION

• Although practically everyone else in America at the time remembers where they were when President John Kennedy was shot, George Bush isn't sure. He thinks he was in Texas.

• A look at an FBI file might refresh his memory. An August 13, 1988, article in *The Nation* reported a memo from FBI Director J. Edgar Hoover on November 23, 1963, which stated that "Mr. George Bush of the CIA" had been briefed about the reaction of anti-Castro Cuban exiles to the killing of President Kennedy.

• The CIA rarely confirms or denies such information, but in this instance the Agency said the memo in question referred to another George Bush—George *William* Bush. But when George William Bush was tracked down, he said he had worked for the CIA for six months as "a lowly researcher and analyst" and had certainly never been briefed by the head of the FBI about anything. Yet the CIA still denies that George Herbert Walker Bush was working for it in 1963.

## HEADING THE CIA

• George Bush was appointed director of the CIA by President Gerald Ford in 1976, one of the most critical times in the Agency's history. Congress was talking about limiting its powers and former Director Richard Helms was being investigated for perjury.

• Although Bush claims that he never worked for the CIA before then, he did a remarkable job of damage control for someone unfamiliar with the Agency. Among other things, he resisted disclosing the Agency's MK-ULTRA program, in which the CIA tested drugs on unwitting American citizens (see p. 165), and he hushed up the Agency's role in the murder of a Chilean diplomat, Orlando Letelier.

## IRAN-CONTRA

• Then-Vice President Bush claimed that he was "left out of the loop" on the Iran-Contra connection and knew nothing about it. However, *Covert Action* magazine reported in 1990 that Bush had "attended all but one of the important White House meetings about arms sales to Iran." (The one meeting he missed conflicted with the Army-Navy football game.)

• Bush may have also forgotten that, as head of Reagan's Drug Interdiction Task Force, head of the Counterterrorism Task Force, and chair of the Special Situation Group, which oversaw "covert operations related to terrorism policy," he got regular briefings on the progress of counterinsurgency efforts in Central America.

• Nor is it Bush's fault that his longtime aide and NSA advisor, Donald Gregg, talked so often with Oliver North's contra-supply manager, Felix Rodriguez, that conservatives warned that Rodriguez's "daily contact" with Bush's office could "damage President Reagan and the Republican party."

• However, in the 1988 primaries, Bush *was* willing to take credit for opposing the Iran-Contra operation he supposedly knew nothing about. As he candidly admitted, "I think the key players around there know I expressed certain reservations about certain aspects."

# THE MAN SHORTAGE

*Were men really scarce during the Reagan years, or did the government just want women to think they were?*

I n February 1986, Lisa Marie Petersen, a reporter for the *Stamford* (Connecticut) *Advocate*, called a Yale sociologist named Neil Bennett looking for statistics she could include in a Valentine's Day article about romance.

Bennett and two colleagues (one at Harvard) had almost completed a study on women's marriage patterns, so he had plenty of information. But he cautioned Petersen that the study wasn't really finished. Nonetheless, as Susan Faludi wrote in her book *Backlash*, Bennett indicated that there was a shortage of eligible men in the U.S., and "college-educated women who put schooling and careers before their wedding date were going to have a harder time getting married." His figures showed that at age 30, never-married, college-educated women had a 20% chance of getting married. By age 35, their odds went down to 5%, and by age 40, to 1.3%.

Petersen was shocked but didn't question the numbers because they came from Yale. Her article was picked up by the Associated Press, and the statistics were eventually publicized worldwide.

According to *Backlash*, however, Petersen didn't realize that the research methods used by the Yale-Harvard team were questionable. Bennett and colleagues David Bloom and Patricia Craig had used a controversial "parametric model" originally designed to analyze marriage patterns of older women who had already been through their marriage cycles. The team had also used a 1982 *Current Population Survey*, "an off year in census-data collection that taps a much smaller number of households than the decennial census study." The researchers had broken the sample down by age, race, and education—"making generalizations based on small unrepresentative samples of women."

## EXPLORING DOUBTS

Jeanne Moorman, a demographer at the U.S. Census Bureau's Marriage and Family Statistics branch, decided to calculate her own marriage study, using a more conventional statistical method and figures from the 1980 census, which included more households.

Her findings were dramatically different: "At 30, never-married college-educated women have a 58-66% chance at marriage—three times the Harvard-Yale study's predictions." At age 35, her model showed, the odds were 32-41%, and at age 40, they were 17-23%—up to 23 times greater than the Yale study.

Moorman and U.S. Census Bureau colleague Robert Fay realized that the Yale-Harvard team had "forgotten to factor in the different patterns in college- and high school-educated women's marital histories. (High school-educated women tend to marry in a tight cluster right after graduation, making for a steep and narrow bell curve skewed to the left. College-educated women tend to spread out the age of marriage over a longer and lower curve skewed to the right.)"

At the census industry's Population Association of America (PAA) conference, Bennett reported that his findings had been "preliminary" and didn't say much else. Moorman also attended the conference and had intended to refute Bennett's findings. But she didn't. The director of the Census Bureau, "looking to avoid further controversy, had ordered her to remove all references to the Harvard-Yale marriage study from her conference speech." (*Backlash*)

Was suppressing these statistics a part of the Reagan administration's political agenda? Were they trying to keep women out of the workforce...and in the home?

## SUSPICIOUS FACTS

• A study by the University of Illinois in October 1985—a few months before Bennett's statistics were released—found no evidence of a "man shortage."

• After Moorman publicized her findings, she was invited to appear on several TV news shows. But Reagan administration officials ordered her to stop talking to the press about the study. According to Faludi, "She was told to concentrate instead on a study that the White House wanted—about how poor unwed mothers abuse the welfare system."

• In an article published in *The New York Times*, *Boston Globe*, and *Advertising Age*, Bennett and Bloom complained that

Moorman shouldn't have done her study because it only "further muddied the discussion." But when Moorman and two Census Bureau colleagues responded, the Census Bureau wouldn't release their piece for months.

## WAS IT A CONSPIRACY?

• Faludi stops just short of saying that the government actually planned a campaign to encourage women to stay home. She quotes the chief of the Census Bureau, Martin O'Connell, as saying, "People I've dealt with in the [Reagan] government seem to want to re-create the fantasy of their own childhood." She also points out that the Republicans were concerned because a "gender gap" in voting had appeared in the 1980 election, with more women than men favoring the Democrats.

• "The split...[was] striking enough to inspire Reagan to commission pollster Richard Wirthlin to investigate how to combat it in the next election," she says. The Republican party chairman also alluded to the problem: "We are particularly vulnerable, if I can use that word, among young women between the ages of 18 and 35 who work outside the home and particularly within that subgroup, those young women who are single parents."

• The Republicans seemed to be trying to convince women to embrace "family values" over women's values. "U.S. Census Bureau demographers found themselves under increasing pressure to generate data for the government's war against women's independence," says Faludi, "to produce statistics 'proving' the rising threat of infertility, the physical and psychic risks lurking in abortion, the dark side of single parenthood, the ill effects of day care."

• If government employees didn't comply, there were consequences: "The Public Health Service demoted and fired federal scientists whose findings conflicted with the administration's so-called pro-family policy." Unfavorable data was discarded.

## RECOMMENDED READING

*Backlash: The Undeclared War Against American Women,* by Susan Faludi (Crown Publishers, 1991)

# SUSPICIOUS DEATH #2: WARREN G. HARDING

*Did Warren Harding die of a heart attack or a poisoned relationship?*

T he deceased: Warren G. Harding, 29th president of the United States (1921-1923)

How he died: In the summer of 1923, President Harding was visiting Vancouver when he became gravely ill. He was rushed to San Francisco and seemed to recover. But then, on August 2, 1923, he suddenly died of a heart attack. *The New York Times* reported: "Mrs. Harding was reading to the President, when utterly without warning, a slight shudder passed through his frame; he collapsed....A stroke of apoplexy was the cause of his death."

Although initial newspaper accounts didn't mention it, the White House physician, General Sawyer, was probably in the room as well when the president died.

## SUSPICIOUS FACTS
### Warren and the Duchess

• Harding owed his political success to his ambitious wife, Florence (nicknamed "the Duchess"). But his marriage wasn't a happy one; he strayed often. During the 1920 campaign, for example, the Republican National Committee paid a former lover of Harding's $20,000 for incriminating letters, paid her $2,000 a month for her silence, and sent her to Europe to keep her away from reporters.

• Harding had a child by Nan Britten, daughter of an Ohio friend. In fact, they had regular trysts in a large White House closet.

• According to former Treasury agent Gaston Means, who worked for Mrs. Harding, the president's wife despised her husband for his affairs and his ingratitude. In his bestselling book about Harding's death, Means reported that when the president's wife found out Harding had fathered Britten's baby, she got hysterical and vowed revenge. "I made him, I made him president!" she raved. When she confronted her husband, there was a nasty scene. He roared that he had never loved her, was sick of the whole presidential charade, and wanted to live with Britten and his child.

## After Harding's Death

• To everyone's surprise, Mrs. Harding refused to allow either an autopsy or a death mask.

• The *New York World* reported: "There will be no death mask made of President Harding....Although it is the usual custom, when a Chief Executive dies, to have a mask made that his features may be preserved for posterity, Mrs. Harding demurred."

• About a year later, while the president's widow was visiting General Sawyer, the former White House physician unexpectedly died in his sleep.

• According to the account in *The New York Times*: "General Sawyer's death was almost identical with the manner of death of the late Warren G. Harding when General Sawyer was with the President in San Francisco. Mrs. Harding was at White Oaks Farm (Sawyer's home) when General Sawyer was found dead. Members of his family had no intimation of the seriousness of the General's condition up to the moment he expired."

## POSSIBLE CONCLUSIONS

• **Harding really did have a heart attack.** His administration was riddled with scandals, and people were calling for his impeachment. The president, who'd previously had five nervous breakdowns, was said to be despondent. He apparently succumbed to the stress.

• **Harding was poisoned by his wife.** If Harding was really ready to give up his political career and marriage, then the Duchess may have poisoned him either to avoid disgrace or to exact revenge. She may have tried first in Vancouver; when Harding didn't die, the attempt was dismissed as food poisoning. Five days later, in San Francisco, she succeeded.

√ Refusing a death mask and an autopsy is consistent with this scenario. (Poison victims sometimes die with horrible grimaces.)

√ Sawyer's death is either a remarkable coincidence or proof of Mrs. Harding's guilt. Even if he wasn't involved in killing the president, as a physician Sawyer may have guessed what had happened and helped to cover it up. Mrs. Harding could have poisoned him to keep her secret safe.

# THE S&L SCANDAL: TRUE OR FALSE?

*"I think we've hit the jackpot."*
—Ronald Reagan to assembled S & L executives, as he signed the Garn-St. Germaine Act deregulating the Savings and Loan industry

You, your children and your grandchildren are going to be paying for the Savings & Loan Scandal for years, but how much do you know about it? See if you can tell which of the following statements are true:

**1.** The S&L scandal is the second-largest theft in the history of the world.

**2.** Deregulation eased restrictions so much that S&L owners could lend money to themselves.

**3.** The Garn Institute of Finance, named after Senator Jake Garn—who co-authored the S&L deregulation bill—received $2.2 million from S&L industry executives.

**4.** For his part in running an S&L into the ground, Neil Bush, George's son, served time in jail and was banned from future S&L involvement.

**5.** Rep. Fernand St. Germain, House Banking chairman and co-author of the S&L deregulation bill , was voted out of office after some questionable financial dealings were reported. The S&L industry immediately sent him back to Washington...as its lobbyist.

**6.** When asked whether his massive lobbying of government officials had influenced their conduct, Lincoln Savings president Charles Keating said, "Of course not. These are honorable men."

**7.** The S&L rip-off began in 1980, when Congress raised federal insurance on S&L deposits from $40,000 to $100,000, even though the average depositor's savings account was only $20,000.

**8.** Assets seized from failed S&Ls included a buffalo sperm bank, a racehorse with syphilis and a kitty-litter mine.

**9.** Working with the government in a bailout deal, James Fail invested $1 million of his own money to purchase 15 failing S&Ls. In return, the government gave him $1.85 billion in federal subsidies.

**10.** Federal regulators sometimes stalled as long as seven years before closing hopelessly insolvent thrifts.

**11.** When S&L owners who stole millions went to jail, their jail sentences averaged about five times the average sentence for bank robbers.

**12.** The government S&L bailout will cost taxpayers as much as $500 billion.

**13.** If the White House had admitted the problem and bailed out failing thrifts in 1986, instead of waiting until after the 1988 election, the bailout might have cost only $20 billion.

**14.** With the money lost in the S&L rip-off, the federal government could provide prenatal care for every American child born in the next 2,300 years.

**15.** With the money lost in the S&L rip-off, the federal government could have bought 5 million average houses.

**16.** The authors of *Inside Job*, a bestselling exposé of the S&L scandal, found evidence of criminal activity in 50% of the thrifts they investigated.

**ANSWERS**
(1) F; it's the *largest*. (2) T (3) T  (4) F  (5) T  (6) F; actually he said: "I certainly hope so." (7) F; all true, except the average savings account was only $6,000. (8) T  (9) F; it was only $1,000 of his own money.  (10) T; partly because of politics, partly because Reagan's people had fired 2/3 of the bank examiners needed to investigate S&L management. (11) F; they served only a fifth of the time. (12) F; it may hit $1.4 *trillion*. (13) T  (14) T (15) T  (16) F; they found criminal activity in *all* of the S&Ls they researched.

**SCORING**
13-16 right: Sadder, but wiser.
6-12 right: Just sadder.
0-5 right: Charlie Keating would like to talk to you about buying some bonds.

Thanks to *The Nation* and *Inside Job* for the facts cited.

# SILKWOOD

*Karen Silkwood has been the subject of numerous articles, books, and a major movie, but few people know what really happened to her. Here are the details of her controversial life and mysterious death.*

On November 13, 1974, Karen Silkwood left a group of co-workers at the Hub Cafe in Crescent, Oklahoma, headed to a crucial meeting with a *New York Times* reporter. On her way out, she told them that she was planning to show the reporter proof that the plutonium plant where they all worked—Kerr-McGee's Cimarron River plant—had repeatedly covered up safety violations and falsified records.

But she never made it to her meeting. A little more than 7 miles outside of Crescent, Silkwood's car went flying off the straight highway and crashed into a concrete culvert, silencing her forever. Official statements claim that Silkwood fell asleep at the wheel, but evidence suggests another conclusion.

## KAREN SILKWOOD VS. KERR-McGEE

• Soon after she started working for Kerr-McGee in 1972, Karen Silkwood joined the local branch of the Oil, Chemical, and Atomic Workers Union (OCAW). In the spring of 1974, she was elected to the governing committee and began to voice her concerns about the company's safety record. She believed Kerr-McGee was sloppy in its handling of radioactive materials and indifferent to the health of its workers.

• She became even more concerned when several coworkers were directly exposed to plutonium—perhaps the most toxic substance on earth. And a production speedup that required employees to work 12-hour shifts increased the danger.

• On August 1, 1974, Silkwood herself was contaminated when airborne plutonium entered the room in which she was working. She began worrying about the effects of the company's safety lapses on her own health and that of her coworkers, so she began carrying a notebook around with her to record the infractions she observed.

• On September 26, she and two other local union officials flew to Washington, D.C., to meet with national OCAW leaders. They alleged serious health and safety violations and charged that plant documents had been falsified to conceal defective fuel rods. National union leaders were so alarmed that they immediately took Silkwood to testify before the Atomic Energy Commission.

• This charge had "very deep and very grave [consequences]," according to OCAW official Steve Wodka—"not only for the people in the plant, but for the entire atomic industry and the welfare of the country. If badly made pins were placed into the reactor without deficiencies being caught, there could be an incident exposing thousands of people to radiation."

• After presenting her charges in Washington, Silkwood returned to Kerr-McGee and continued to document the safety violations she observed on the job.

## CONTAMINATION

• On Tuesday, November 5, Silkwood was in the metallography lab, where she was handling plutonium in a safety case called a "glovebox." When she finished her work, monitoring devices revealed that she had been contaminated again—this time from her hands all the way up to her scalp.

• The contamination on her coveralls was up to forty times the company limit. Any exposure above the company limit required emergency decontamination—scrubbing repeatedly with a mixture of Tide and Clorox, which left Silkwood's skin raw and stinging. Within a few days, she noted, "It hurt to cry because the salt in my tears burned my skin."

• Health officials required Silkwood to supply urine and fecal samples so they could monitor the radioactivity level in her system. Samples taken over the next few days showed new, extremely high levels of radiation. Baffled by the source of the contamination, officials eventually checked her apartment. They found that it was so contaminated that most of its contents had to be removed and buried. While officials gutted her apartment, Kerr-McGee lawyers interrogated Silkwood, insinuating that she had smuggled plutonium out of the plant.

• Her health began to deteriorate. She began to lose weight and had trouble sleeping. A series of doctors prescribed sedatives to relieve her anxiety. Now, terrified by the trauma of decontamination scrubbings, the burial of her belongings, and the high levels of contamination in her body, Karen Silkwood believed she was dying.

• She spent November 10 to 12 in Los Alamos, New Mexico, undergoing tests to assess how much radiation she had absorbed. Doctors determined that she was in no imminent danger—the amount of plutonium that her body had absorbed was below the maximum absorption that "cannot be exceeded without risk." But no one could assure her that the radioactivity would not lead to cancer or other health problems in the future.

• Then, on November 13, six days after the contamination was discovered in her house, Silkwood drove to meet a reporter from *The New York Times*, with documents she believed would prove Kerr-McGee's criminal neglect. En route, her car veered across the road and down the left-hand shoulder, and slammed head on into a concrete culvert, killing her.

## WAS IT A CONSPIRACY? #1

*Was her car wreck an accident—or murder?*

• The official explanation of Karen Silkwood's death is that she brought it on herself: she took too many tranquilizers and dozed off while driving. "An autopsy revealed that her blood, stomach, and liver contained methaqualone, a sleep-inducing drug, and it was surmised that she fell asleep at the wheel," according to the *Encyclopedia of American Scandal*. "Justice Department and FBI investigations found no wrongdoing."

• This was possible. To cope with insomnia, changes in her work shift, and growing tension at the plant, Silkwood had gotten a prescription for sleeping pills. Her boyfriend, Drew Stephens, says that she had taken them for tranquilization, not for sleep—especially during the last week of her life. (*Ms.*)

• But colleagues who had been with Silkwood shortly before the accident said she appeared alert, spoke clearly, and acted normally. "It would never have crossed my mind that she might not be capable of driving a car safely," one coworker said. What's more, the road her car went off was perfectly straight, and Karen was an excellent driver—she'd won several road rallies in previous years.

• When Silkwood left her colleagues to meet with the reporter from *The New York Times,* she was carrying a brown manila folder and a large notebook. One coworker who had been at the Hub Cafe recounted some of Silkwood's last words: "She then said there was one thing she was glad about, that she had all the proof concerning the health and safety conditions in the plant, and concerning falsification. As she said this, she clenched her hand more firmly on the folder and the notebook she was holding." (*Ms.*)

## Suspicious Facts

• Silkwood's manila folder and notebook disappeared after the accident. "A trooper at the scene reported stuffing the papers back into the car," said one reporter, "but they were gone when it was checked a day later."

• The road was straight. If, as the police suggested, she fell asleep, her car would probably have drifted to the right because of the road's centerline, or crown, and the pull of gravity. But instead it crossed the road and went off the left shoulder.

• Experts disagreed about the meaning of the tire marks at the accident. Police said her car left two sets of rolling tracks with no evidence of having attempted to brake or control the car. An investigator hired by the OCAW, however, thought the car had been out of control, as if it had been hit or pushed by another car.

• Experts also disagreed about a scratch along the side of the car. Police said it was made when the car was towed away from the culvert. But the OCAW analyst said microscopic exams showed metal and rubber fragments in the scratch, as if another car had bumped Silkwood's.

• Several years after the accident, family members filed a lawsuit against Kerr-McGee, claiming that the company intentionally contaminated Silkwood. In 1979, an Oklahoma jury ordered Kerr-McGee to pay Silkwood's estate more than $10.5 million in damages. The decision against Kerr-McGee was later overturned on appeal because the "award was ruled to have infringed on the U.S. government's exclusivity in regulating safety in the nuclear power industry" (*Encyclopedia of American Scandal*). Four years later, however, the U.S. Supreme Court ruled that "courts could impose punitive damages on the nuclear-power industry for violations of safety." Kerr-McGee eventually settled the suit for $1.3 million. Under the out-of-court agreement, the company admitted no guilt for the automobile accident.

## WAS IT A CONSPIRACY? #2

*If Silkwood was murdered, could agents of the U.S. government be responsible?*

### Suspicious Facts

• At least forty pounds of plutonium—the active ingredient in nuclear warheads—were missing from the Kerr-McGee plant. Silkwood was among the first to suggest this, and company officials later confirmed it.

• According to the *Progressive*, the Justice Department, "ignoring evidence that suggested the possibility of foul play at the accident site...shut down its investigation of Karén Silkwood's death early in 1974 with a four-and-a-half-page summary report dismissing the possibility of murder or any relationship of missing plutonium to the case."

• According to *Rebel* magazine, "Every attempt to get the government to release related intelligence files has been replied to by the Justice Department with claims of 'national security' and 'state secrets.' The FBI even tried to get a permanent gag order against Silkwood attorneys forbidding public disclosure of what they were finding."

• Attorneys working on the lawsuit brought by Silkwood's estate alleged that there was a relationship—and perhaps a conspiracy—between Kerr-McGee and the FBI. These attorneys said that Silkwood was being spied on and that transcripts of her private conversations were later passed from a Kerr-McGee official to both an FBI agent and an author (alleged to have CIA and Navy-intelligence links) who later wrote a disparaging book about Silkwood's activities.

• Attempting to clarify the relationship between Kerr-McGee, the FBI, and the author, Silkwood attorney Danny Sheehan repeatedly pressed the author in court to tell who had commissioned her book. The FBI objected 30 times, citing "national security." Finally, after conferring with FBI officials, the judge told Sheehan, "The information you seek is sinister and secret, and should never see the light of day." (*The Progressive*)

- The Oklahoma City Police Department (OCPD) also appears to have been involved in Kerr-McGee spying operations. "Silkwood estate investigators insist they found [OCPD] Intelligence Unit officers on Kerr-McGee's security payroll during the time Silkwood was being spied on," according to *Rebel* magazine. Moreover, "an FBI source claims OCPD's Intelligence Unit had been infiltrated by either CIA or [National Security Agency] undercover agents, and OCPD-gleaned FBI surveillance reports on Silkwood were transmitted via a NSA code classified top-secret."

- Sheehan, still trying to uncover possible CIA links to the case, pressed on until finally, he says, he was warned by a former Carter White House source to call his investigator off: "You're in way over your head. You don't have any idea how sensitive this issue is. You'd better contact your man...and tell him to stand down.... They'll kill him. And I promise you, no one will do anything about it." (*Rebel*)

- As for the missing plutonium, the English weekly *The New Statesman* suggests that "there is evidence that the material was sold on the black market to South Africa, Israel or Iran under the Shah. In our opinion, [Silkwood] had that kind of evidence—that's why she was killed."

## RECOMMENDED READING

- "The Real Enemies of Karen Silkwood," by Anthony Kimmery (*Rebel* magazine, Feb. 20, 1984)
- "Karen Silkwood: The Deepening Mystery," by Jeffrey Stein (*The Progressive* magazine, Jan. 1981)
- "The Case of Karen Silkwood," by B. J. Phillips (Ms. magazine)

# THE MAGIC BULLET

*The "magic bullet" theory is the linchpin of the Warren Commission's conclusion that one gunman killed President Kennedy.*
*But it defies the laws of physics and common sense.*

A ccording to the Warren Commission, there were "probably" three shots fired at Kennedy, all by Lee Harvey Oswald from a sixth-floor window of the Texas School Book Depository.

One bullet apparently missed. Another hit Kennedy in the head, killing him. That left one bullet. According to the commission, that single bullet caused seven wounds in JFK and Governor Connally, yet emerged virtually undamaged.

That bullet—dubbed the "magic bullet" by junior counselor Arlen Specter—became one of the most controversial findings of the Warren Commission.

## SUSPICIOUS FACTS

According to critics of the Warren Commission, there are some fatal flaws in the single-bullet theory:

• The Commission said the bullet entered "the back of President Kennedy's neck," moving downward at a seventeen-degree angle, then emerged out the front. But autopsy diagrams show that the bullet entered *between his shoulder blades*. Even the Commission reported that the bullet hole in Kennedy's jacket was "5-3/4 inches below the collar."

• The Commission reported that the exiting bullet "nicked the knot of the President's necktie." That means that the bullet somehow *reversed direction* and headed upward before exiting through the president's neck.

• From there, critics say, the bullet would have had to turn right and down in order to strike Connally in the back of his right armpit.

• Connally didn't react until 1.6 seconds after Kennedy was first hit, according to a film of the assassination taken by Abraham Zapruder with a home-movie camera. Was his reaction time that slow, did the bullet hang in mid-air, or was Connally struck by a different bullet?

• After entering Connally's body at a 27-degree angle downward, the "magic bullet" shattered his fifth rib and exited through the right side of his chest.

• It then hit Connally's right wrist, shattered his radius bone, and finally buried itself in his left thigh.

## THE "MAGIC BULLET"

• After Kennedy and Connally were rushed to Dallas's Parkland Hospital, a loose bullet was found on the stretcher that allegedly carried Governor Connally. The Warren Commission assumed that the bullet had fallen out of Connally's thigh wound.

• The bullet was largely intact, with its tip only slightly flattened. This condition baffled logistics experts, because the bullet supposedly caused seven wounds traveling through the bodies of Kennedy and Connally. (In reenactments, identical bullets fired into a cadaver's wristbone were grossly deformed.)

• Critics say more metal fragments were removed by doctors from Connally's wrist than were missing from this bullet.

• Several commissioners found the "magic bullet" theory so outlandish that they pressured Earl Warren to allow a minority (dissenting) opinion on the theory. But Warren, stressing the importance of unanimity, refused (see p. 95).

## WAS IT A COVER-UP?

In his controversial film, *JFK*, Oliver Stone suggests that the Commission knew the theory was implausible. Stone's Jim Garrison character calls Specter one of the "grossest liars in America" and says: "The single-bullet explanation is the foundation of the Warren Commission's claim of the lone assassin. And once you conclude that the magic bullet cannot create all seven of those wounds, you have to conclude that there was a fourth shot and a second rifle. If there was a second rifle, then by definition, there had to be a conspiracy."

## FOOTNOTES

• Commander James Humes, who headed Kennedy's autopsy team, may have actually found a fourth bullet, according to JFK conspiracy expert Mark Lane. An FBI memo that Lane obtained under the

Freedom of Information Act, dated November 22, 1963, was written to the commanding officer of the U.S. Naval Medical School at Bethesda by FBI agents Francis O'Neill and James Sibert, who attended the autopsy. It states, "We hereby acknowledge receipt of a missle [*sic*] removed by Commander James J. Humes, MC, USN on this date."

• Nowhere did Humes report removing a bullet from the president's body, and it certainly isn't mentioned in the Warren Report. If this "missile" was a fourth bullet, it most likely came from a second gun.

### OLLIE NORTH, PATRIOT
(from the Iran-Contra hearings, 1987)

Nields (chief counsel): "Where are these memoranda?"

North: "Which memoranda?"

Nields: "The memoranda that you sent up to Admiral Poindexter, seeking the President's approval."

North: "I think I shredded most of that. Did I get them all? I'm not trying to be flippant, I'm just..."

Nields: "Well, that was going to be my very next question, Colonel North. Isn't it true that you shredded them?"

North: "I believe I did."

# GOOD NEWS FOR HITLER

*After William Randolph Hearst's visit to a German spa, he had new respect for Hitler. Was there gold in the waters?*

I n September 1934, William Randolph Hearst went to the world-famous spa at Bad Nauheim to "take the waters." The Nazi government welcomed him. After a month of socializing with prominent Germans, Hearst was invited to meet the new chancellor, Adolph Hitler. According to German newspapers, "Hearst was charmed and converted by the Nazi leader."

The German newspaper may have been right. When he returned to the U.S., Hearst completely changed the editorial policy of his nineteen daily newspapers and began praising the Nazi regime. For example, a September 1934 editorial signed by Hearst began:

"Hitler is enormously unpopular outside of Germany and enormously popular in Germany. This is not difficult to understand. Hitler restored character and courage. Hitler gave hope and confidence. He established order and utility of purpose....And the Germans love him for that. They regard him as a savior."

Did Hearst offer his praise freely, or had he been paid?

## SUSPICIOUS FACTS

• Hearst's change in editorial policy came less than a month after the Nazi Ministry of Propaganda first subscribed to his International News Service (INS), a wire service that Hearst had created to compete against AP and UPI. INS was considered by journalists to be, by far, the worst of the three services.

• Even so, the Nazis paid Hearst more than $400,000 a year to subscribe to INS, at a time when other customers were only paying $50,000 to $70,000 for the same service. (The Nazis paid only $40,000 for their subscription to AP.)

• Hitler appears to have gotten what he paid for. According to legal papers filed in a lawsuit involving Hearst in the 1930s, "Promptly after the visit with Adolph Hitler and the making of...arrangements for furnishing INS material to Germany...William Randolph Hearst instructed all Hearst press correspondents in Germany, including those of INS, to report happenings in Germany only in a 'friendly' manner. All of such correspondents reporting happenings in Germany accurately and without friendliness, sympathy and bias for the actions of the then German government, were transferred elsewhere, discharged, or forced to resign." (*Even the Gods Can't Change History*)

• Week after week, Hearst papers ran pieces sympathetic to the Nazis. One article, which justified German rearmament to the American people, was written by Hitler's Minister of Aviation, Hermann Goering.

## WAS IT A CONSPIRACY?

*Was Hitler's payment a bribe to get Hearst to print pro-Nazi propaganda?*

The U.S. ambassador to Germany, William E. Dodd, thought so:

• According to Dodd, who was ambassador to Germany from 1933 to 1937, Hitler sent two of his chief propagandists to meet with Hearst at Bad Nauheim, to see how his image could be polished. When they found Hearst receptive, they set up a meeting and cut the deal.

• When Dodd found out about the arrangement, he "did not hesitate to tell the president that this was not a legitimate business deal; it was buying political support." (ibid.)

• Dodd noted that Hearst newspapers also began praising Italian dictator Mussolini after "Giannini, president of the Bank of America, had loaned Hearst some millions of dollars." Giannini was an avid Mussolini supporter. (ibid.)

• According to author George Seldes, Hearst's deals with the two dictators were widely rumored in the industry, but he was so powerful that "of the 1,730 daily newspapers" Hearst *didn't* own, "not 1 percent ever said a word about the situation." Hearst, untouched by the scandal, continued to smear the patriotism of "socialists, liberals and other un-Americans" until the day he died. (ibid.)

## RECOMMENDED READING

*Even the Gods Can't Change History*, by George Seldes (Lyle Stuart, 1976)

# WHO SAID IT?

*See if you can guess which of the schemers listed below made the following statements. Answers are at the bottom of the page.*

**1.** "You can't say Dallas doesn't love you."

**2.** "Truth will be the hallmark of the Nixon administration."

**3.** "Shouldn't someone tag [John] F. Kennedy's bold new imaginative program with its proper age? Under the tousled haircut it is still old Karl Marx—first launched a century ago."

**4.** "The police aren't here to create disorder. The police are here to preserve disorder."

**5.** "I'd rather have him inside the tent pissing out than outside pissing in."

**6.** "Don't get the idea that I'm one of those goddamn radicals. Don't get the idea that I'm knocking the American system."

**7.** "When information which properly belongs to the people is systematically withheld by those in power, the people soon become ignorant of their own affairs, distrustful of those who manage them, and—eventually—incapable of determining their own destinies."

**8.** "I have just received the following telegram from my generous Daddy. It says, 'Dear Jack: Don't buy a single vote more than is necessary. I'll be damned if I'm going to pay for a landslide.' "

**A.** Ronald Reagan, in a letter to Richard Nixon in 1960

**B.** Mayor Richard Daley, after the Chicago riots in 1968

**C.** President Lyndon Johnson, explaining why he kept J. Edgar Hoover as FBI director

**D.** Sen. John Kennedy, 1958

**E.** Herbert Klein, Nixon communications director, 1968

**F.** Mrs. John Connally to President John Kennedy, moments before he was shot

**G.** Richard Nixon

**H.** Al Capone

# THE S&L ROGUES' GALLERY

*The S&L scandal was the biggest rip-off in the U.S. ever.*
*Here are some of the conspirators who made it possible.*

S&Ls were traditionally one of the sleepiest sectors of the financial world; until the early 1980s, they took in the savings of middle-class depositors and lent them out as home mortgages to members of the community. Federal laws and regulations prevented S&Ls from doing much else. They didn't pay high interest, but their deposits were safe, because they were insured by the federal government.

Then, in 1982, came deregulation. Suddenly, S&L executives were free to lend money to whomever they wanted (even to themselves) and could spend it on whatever investments they pleased—no matter how risky.

Free from regulatory oversight, many S&Ls were bought up by real estate speculators, corrupt business people, and even the Mafia. The new owners spent depositors' money on exorbitant salaries, multimillion-dollar loans to their friends, wild parties, wildcat real estate deals, junk bonds, and other high-risk ventures. They didn't care if the S&Ls lost money: the deposits were insured, and the executives pocketed a huge transaction fee every time they made a loan—whether or not the loan was ever paid off.

Within two years of deregulation, however, the S&L industry was broke. In 1980, the industry was worth $32 billion; by 1982, it was worth less than $4 billion and falling fast; by 1990 it was more than $500 billion in the red.

Here are a few of the conspirators who stuck you with the bill for their multibillion-dollar spending spree:

**CHARLES KEATING,** Lincoln Savings and Loan
(Irvine, California)

Highlights: In 1984, Keating bought Lincoln Savings and Loan with cash he made with Michael Milken's junk bonds, "fired senior staff, and hired a slick crew of salespeople to push his worthless paper on elderly Southern Californians." He falsely claimed his bonds were guaranteed by the federal government and instructed his sales staff to focus on the "weak, meek, and ignorant. [They're] always good targets." (*Inside Job*)

Outcome: Within five years, Keating—and 11 of his relatives on the staff, who received more than $34 million in salaries and other perks—had run Lincoln into the ground. When Lincoln crashed in 1989, it lost the $230 million that had been invested in the bonds by some 23,000 people, most of them seniors. At least one of the victims (an 89-year-old who wrote, "There's nothing left for me.") committed suicide. Lincoln's end would have come much sooner, were it not for the help of "the Keating Five," U.S. Senators Cranston, DeConcini, Glenn, Riegle, and McCain, who pressured regulators to leave Lincoln alone. Their payoff was more than $1.3 million in campaign and other contributions. By the time regulators finally seized it in 1989, the bailout cost taxpayers $2.5 billion. Keating was sentenced to 10 years in prison.

## DON DIXON, Vernon Savings and Loan (Vernon, Texas)

Highlights: Dixon used Vernon depositors' money to buy a $2 million Swiss chalet, a $1 million San Diego beach house, a fleet of airplanes, a Rolls Royce/Ferrari dealership, and a $40,000 painting he eventually gave to Pope John Paul II. Dixon also bought the sister ship of the presidential yacht *Sequoia*, which he anchored in Washington, D.C. and used to entertain politicians.

Outcome: Vernon collapsed in 1987, with more than 97% of its loans in default. Convicted of 23 counts of fraud and "misapplication of funds," Dixon was sentenced to 5 years in prison. Cost to taxpayers: $1.3 billion. (*Savings & Loan Scandal Cards*)

## EDWIN "FAST EDDIE" McBIRNEY, Sunbelt Savings and Loan (Dallas, Texas)

Highlights: McBirney liked to spend Sunbelt's deposits entertaining business associates at a palatial suite at the Las Vegas Dunes. He flew them into town on a private 727, and provided them with prostitutes. At one lavish party, he fed his guests broiled lion and antelope; at a Halloween fiesta, he had a warehouse decorated as an African jungle and hired a magician to make an elephant disappear. McBirney also owned 7 airplanes.

**Outcome:** Sunbelt collapsed, and in the summer of 1990, the FSLIC sued McBirney for $500 million. He later pled guilty to four counts of bank fraud and tax evasion. The bailout of Sunbelt is expected to cost taxpayers $1.7 billion.

## DUAYNE CHRISTIANSEN, North American Savings and Loan (Santa Ana, California)

**Highlights:** Christiansen, a dentist who began wearing all-white suits after he bought North American, spent an enormous amount of depositors' money decorating his office: it was made completely of marble (including the desk), and the entrance boasted 14-foot-high copper doors.

**Outcome:** Christensen was killed in a mysterious car accident in June 1988—the day before regulators seized North American Savings and Loan. In broad daylight, he drove his Jaguar into a freeway abutment. Three days earlier he had rewritten his will, leaving everything to his girlfriend. Regulators estimate that he looted more than $40 million from North American; the money has not been recovered. North American's bailout is expected to cost taxpayers $209 million. (*Inside Job*)

## DONALD P. MANGANO and JOHN L. MOLINARO, Ramona Savings and Loan (Ramona, California)

**Highlights:** Some of Ramona's deposits were used to finance condos built by Magnano's construction company and carpeted by Molinaro's carpet store. Another portion of the depositors' funds were kept in the trunk of a car parked behind the S&L. According to one report, when regulators seized Ramona, they discovered an office with a fake wall and, behind that, "a secret passageway leading to the basement. From there it connected to a tunnel at the end of which, they said, was an alley behind the bank and a car packed with food, cash, and guns." Investigators speculate that Mangano and Molinaro were taking precautions, in case of a lightning raid by federal regulators. When FBI agents caught Molinaro "trying to get to the Cayman Islands on a dead man's passport," he told them "he had deposited $3 million in First Cayman Bank." (*Inside Job*)

**Outcome:** Ramona collapsed in 1986, more than $70 million in debt. The feds estimate that the two men alone looted more than $24 million from the S&L.

**ERWIN HANSEN,** Centennial Savings (Guerneville, California)

**Highlights:** Hansen invested a considerable amount of the S&L's money on his offices, including $48,000 on a desk and $98,000 on other decorations. He also liked cars. He bought a $77,000 Mercedes stretch limousine for Centennial and in one afternoon alone bought five cars for himself and his family. But his largest extravagance was The Stonehouse, an old stone building he refurbished into a $2 million corporate headquarters—only to abandon it after 4 months. He complained that the building was too cold and said, "It reminded me of a mortuary." (ibid.)

**Outcome:** Centennial collapsed in August 1985; Hansen died mysteriously two years later—one day before he was scheduled to begin cooperating with the Justice Department against other Centennial officials. The coroner ruled that he died from a cerebral aneurysm. Centennial's bailout could cost taxpayers as much as $165 million.

## RECOMMENDED READING
• *Savings & Loan Scandal Trading Cards*, by Dennis Bernstein and Laura Sydell (Eclipse Enterprises, Forestville, CA)

• *Inside Job: The Looting of America's Savings and Loans*, by Stephen Pizzo, Mary Fricker, and Paul Muolo (HarperCollins, 1991)

# DEALING WITH THE ENEMY

*America went to war in Southeast Asia to deal with the Communists. Little did the public know just what those deals were.*

I n the mid-1960s, President Lyndon Johnson and his military advisors decided that unless the United States made a stand in South Vietnam, all of Southeast Asia could fall to the Communists.

The subsequent military buildup in Vietnam happened so quickly that construction companies and arms makers couldn't keep up with the demand; they started running out of essential materials.

Even allies of the U.S. couldn't supply all the materials they needed. Where could America turn for help in its war against the Communists?

## LUCKY BREAKS

• In early 1966, a steel shortage slowed U.S. construction in South Vietnam. Suddenly, though, several thousand tons of steel unexpectedly turned up on the market in Singapore. Curiously, all the steel bars were either unmarked or had their markings filed off, so it was impossible to know where they had come from.

• Later that year, the Dow Chemical Co. desperately needed magnesium, whose lightweight alloys are used in military aircraft—but there wasn't any for sale in the free world. At the last minute, though, Dow also got lucky, receiving four mysterious shipments of magnesium via Holland, a country not known to have magnesium deposits. Dow eventually received several million pounds of the strategic metal.

• But perhaps the luckiest break for the U.S. war effort that year was finding a supply of cheap concrete. America needed it to pour miles of new highways, landing strips, bases, and ports in South Vietnam. But the bulky, heavy material is too expensive to ship very far. Fortunately, a steady supply of it suddenly became available from nearby Singapore.

## WAS IT A CONSPIRACY?
*Where did all of these mysterious materials come from, anyway?*

## SUSPICIOUS FACTS
• On December 18, 1966, the *Washington Post* ran a story headlined "Peking Sold Steel to Americans for Viet Bases." It said, "Communist China has sold several thousand tons of steel to Americans in South Vietnam for use in the construction of new Air and Army bases needed in the growing war against the Vietcong....The steel was sold through intermediaries in Singapore, who transshiped it to Saigon, and the Chinese Communists were paid through banks in Hong Kong....Reliable trading sources agree that all parties concerned, from Peking to the Pentagon, must have known both the origin and the destination of the bars."

• On February 12, 1967, the *Post* ran another story headlined, "U.S. Buying Magnesium from Russia." The newspaper noted, "An American firm has bought a reported $2.3 million worth of magnesium—a metal vital in military aircraft production—from the Soviet Union in the past two months. Officials of the Dow Chemical Co. said demand for magnesium has increased because of the Vietnam war." The total cost of the shipment included "a 100% U.S. customs tariff charge required on shipments from Communist nations."

• And the cement? It was so cheap because it didn't have far to travel: it apparently came from Haiphong, the main port of North Vietnam. "The Haiphong cement was very cheap," the *Post* pointed out, "even though the cost of shipping it from North Vietnam was increased by special insurance payments against the risk of American air attack in the Gulf of Tonkin."

## FOOTNOTE
In the mid-1960s, both public sentiment and U.S. law were strongly opposed to trading with the country's Communist enemies. Longshoremen in the U.S. refused to unload Russian ships, and the U.S. Battle Act specifically forbid most exports from communist nations. (China's goods were so tightly excluded that wig exporters from Hong Kong had to certify that they used no Red Chinese hair.)

# ELVIS LIVES

*Who really believes Elvis is still alive? Plenty of
people do. As RCA Records used to ask: Can millions
of Elvis fans be wrong? Judge for yourself.*

Early in the morning on August 16, 1977, Elvis Presley
and his girlfriend, Ginger Alden, returned to Graceland
from a late-night dentist appointment. The two stayed up
until about 7:00 a.m. Then Alden went to bed. But, according to
one source, "because he had taken some 'uppers,' Elvis was still
not sleepy."

So the King retired to his bathroom to read a book. That was the
last time anyone ever saw him alive.

## THE OFFICIAL STORY
• When Alden woke up at 2:00 in the afternoon, she noticed that
Elvis was still in his bathroom. So she decided to check up on him.
• When she opened the door, she saw Elvis sprawled face forward
on the floor. "I thought at first he might have hit his head because
he had fallen," she recalls, "and his face was buried in the carpet. I
slapped him a few times and it was like he breathed once when I
turned his head. I lifted one eyelid and it was just blood red. But I
couldn't move him." The King was dead.
• Elvis was rushed to Baptist Memorial Hospital in Memphis, but
doctors could not revive him. He was pronounced dead at 3:00
p.m. The official cause of death: cardiac arrhythmia brought on by
"straining at stool." (The actual cause of death: most likely a massive overdose of prescription drugs.)

That is what is supposed to have happened. Nevertheless, Elvis afi-
cionados across the country see a host of mysterious circumstances
that suggest that the King may still be alive.

## SUSPICIOUS FACTS
• The medical examiner's report stated that Elvis's body was found
in the bathroom in a rigor-mortised state. But the homicide report
said that Elvis was found unconscious in the bedroom. In *The Elvis*

*Files*, Gail Brewer-Giorgio notes: "Unconsciousness and rigor mortis are at opposite ends of the physical spectrum: rigor mortis is a stiffening condition that occurs after death; unconsciousness, a state in which a living body loses awareness. Bedroom and bathroom are two different places."

• The medical examiner's report lists Elvis's weight at the time of death as 170 pounds; he actually weighed about 250 pounds.

• Elvis's relatives can't agree on how Elvis died. His stepbrother Rick claims Elvis suffocated on the shag carpet; his stepbrother David thinks Elvis committed suicide. Larry Geller, Elvis's hairdresser and spiritual adviser, claims that Elvis's doctors told Vernon Presley (Elvis's father) that the King had leukemia, which may have contributed to his death. Some theorists charge that the confusion surrounding Elvis's death proves that the star faked his death—if the King is really dead, why can't his loved ones get their stories straight?

## UNANSWERED QUESTIONS
*Elvis's fans want the answers to the following mysteries:*

### Did Elvis Foresee—or Fake—His Death?
• Elvis didn't order any new jumpsuits—his trademark outfit—in all of 1977. Why not? Did he know he wasn't going to need any?

• On his last concert tour, Elvis was overheard saying, "I may not look good tonight, but I'll look good in my coffin."

• Was Elvis imitating his manager, Colonel Tom Parker? As a young man, Parker also faked his death. An illegal immigrant from Holland whose real name was Andreas Van Kujik, Parker left Holland without telling his relatives; they thought he was dead.

### Was the Corpse in Elvis's Coffin Really Elvis's?
• Country singer Tanya Tucker's sister LaCosta was at the King's funeral, and she was shocked at the body's appearance: "We went right up to his casket and stood there, and God, I couldn't believe it. He looked just like a piece of plastic laying there. He didn't look like him at all…he looked more like a dummy than a real person. You know a lot of people think it was a dummy. They don't think he was dead."

• Some observers said they thought the corpse's nose looked too "pugged" to be the King's. They speculated that even if the King had fallen forward and smashed his nose at the time of his death, it would have naturally returned to its original shape, or would at least have been fixed by the undertaker—if the body was really Elvis's. (*The Elvis Files*)

### Was the Corpse in Elvis's Coffin a Wax Dummy?

• Some theorists believe that Elvis's coffin weighed more than it was supposed to. Brewer-Giorgio reports receiving a letter from an Elvis fan who claimed to have "personally" known the man who made the King's coffin. The coffin maker revealed that the casket was a "rush" order—and that "there was no way" the coffin could have weighed 900 pounds, as the press reported—even with the King in it. So what was in the coffin with Elvis that made it so heavy?

• According to Brewer-Giorgio, the discrepancy between the coffin's actual weight with Elvis in it and its weight at the funeral is about 250 to 275 pounds, "the weight of a small air-conditioner." "Was there an air-conditioner in the coffin?" Brewer-Giorgio asks, "Wax dummy? Something cool to keep the wax from beading up?"

• To many witnesses, Elvis's corpse appeared to be "sweating" at the funeral. Brewer-Giorgio says she asked Joe Esposito, Elvis's road manager, about TV reports that there were "beads of sweat" on Elvis's body. "He said that was true, that everyone was sweating because the air-conditioner had broken down. Except that dead bodies do not sweat." *But wax melts*.

### Why Were the Mourners Acting So Strange at the Funeral?

• Parker wore a loud Hawaiian shirt and a baseball cap to Elvis's funeral and never once approached the casket to say farewell to the King. Elvis's fans argue that if Elvis were *really* dead, Parker would probably have shown a little more respect.

• Elvis's hairdresser claims that he saw Esposito remove Elvis's TCB (Takin' Care of Business) ring from the corpse's finger during the funeral services. Why would he remove one of Elvis's favorite pieces of jewelry—Elvis would surely have wanted to have been buried with it—unless the corpse being buried wasn't the King's?

### Is Elvis in the Federal Witness Protection Program?

• In 1970, Presley—a law enforcement buff—was made an honorary Agent-at-Large of the Drug Enforcement Administration by President Nixon after a visit to the White House. According to some theorists, Presley became more than just an honorary agent—he actually got involved in undercover narcotics work.

• In addition to his DEA work, Elvis may have been an FBI agent. During the same trip to Washington D.C., Elvis also wrote a letter to J. Edgar Hoover volunteering his confidential services to the FBI. Hoover wrote back thanking Elvis for his offer, but there is no record of him ever taking it up. Still, Brewer-Giorgio and other theorists argue, the government may have been keeping the King's government service a secret.

• According to Brewer-Giorgio, Elvis was also "a bonded deputy with the Memphis Police and was known to don disguises and go out on narc busts."

• Elvis took his law enforcement role seriously. More than one biography details the time that the King ran out onto the runway of the Las Vegas airport, flagged down a taxiing commercial airliner, and searched it for a man whom he believed had stolen something from him. Elvis looked around, realized his quarry wasn't aboard, and gave the pilot permission to take off.

• Some theorists believe that Elvis's extensive work in law enforcement made him a target for drug dealers and the Mob—and that he entered the Federal Witness Protection Program out of fear for his life. According to Brewer-Giorgio, when Elvis supplied the information that sent a major drug dealer to prison, the King and his family received death threats.

### Could Elvis Be in Hiding?

Hundreds of Elvis's loyal fans think they have spotted the King since his "death." He's been sighted at a Rolling Stones concert, working at a Burger King in Kalamazoo, buying gas in Tennessee, and shopping for old Monkees records in Michigan. One woman even claims that Elvis gave her a bologna sandwich and a bag of Cheetos during a 1987 visit to the Air Force Museum in Dayton, Ohio. Could so many people be lying or mistaken?

## OTHER MYSTERIES COLLECTED BY ELVIS FANS

• Vernon Presley never went to the hospital the night Elvis "died." If Elvis were really dead, some theorists speculate, he probably would have.

• According to some reports, within hours of Presley's death, souvenir shops near Graceland began selling commemorative T-shirts of his death. How could they have made so many T-shirts in so little time—unless Graceland had let them know about the "death" in advance?

• Elvis's middle name, Aron, is misspelled "Aaron" on his tombstone. If Elvis is really dead, why don't his relatives correct the mistake?

• Elvis is not buried next to his mother as he requested. Says Brewer-Giorgio: " 'Elvis loved his mother very much and always said he would be buried beside her,' many fans have noted. 'So why is he buried between his father and grandmother?' they ask."

• On a number of occasions after the King's death, Priscilla Presley referred to Elvis as a *living* legend—strange words for a woman who supposedly believes that Elvis is dead.

• Before he died, Elvis took out a multimillion-dollar life insurance policy. To date, no one in his family has tried to claim it. If Elvis's family really believes he is dead, why haven't they cashed in the policy?

## PASSING ON

• The people who were in Elvis's home when he died insist that he really *did* die. Joe Esposito, Elvis's road manager for 17 years, was one of the first people to see the body. "Believe me, the man that I tried to revive was Elvis."

• Elvis may even have committed suicide. According to his stepbrother David Stanley, "Elvis was too intelligent to overdose [accidentally]. He knew the *Physician's Desk Reference* inside and out." Why would Elvis take his own life? He was getting old, and the strain of his stagnating career may have become too much to bear. The pressure showed: in the last years of his life, Elvis's weight ballooned to more than 250 pounds, and his addiction to prescription drugs had gotten out of control.

• The impending publication of a book chronicling the King's erratic behavior and his drug problem may have been the final straw. In August 1977, the month of his death, two of his former aides were about to publish a book revealing much of his bizarre personal life to the public for the first time. He was already depressed, and the imminent public exposure of his drug habit may have pushed him over the edge.

## RECOMMENDED READING

*The Elvis Files*, by Gail Brewer-Giorgio (Shapolsky Publishers, 1990). *The fountain of Elvis conspiracies.*

## OLLIE NORTH, PATRIOT

In 1987, Oliver North testified to the Iran-Contra investigating committee that members of Congress couldn't be trusted with important secrets. As proof, he cited a case in which, he said, someone in Congress had leaked information to the press that "very seriously compromised intelligence activities" concerning the U.S. Air Force's interception of a plane carrying Arab terrorists.

But he was immediately discredited.

"*Newsweek* challenged North's assertion by revealing that members of Congress had not provided the interception story to Washington reporters. The actual source, the magazine reported, had been 'none other than North himself.' "

—Stephen Bates, *If No News, Send Rumors*
(St. Martin's Press, 1985)

# DOUBLE CROSS IN THE DESERT?

*Was Jimmy Carter just unlucky, or was his plan to rescue the Iranian hostages sabotaged?*

On November 4, 1979, mobs in revolutionary Iran stormed the U.S. Embassy in Teheran and took 53 Americans hostage. For the next six months, President Jimmy Carter tried to gain the hostages' release by negotiating with the Iranian government. Finally, frustrated with the lack of progress and concerned about deteriorating political conditions in Iran, Carter ordered a military rescue of the hostages on the night of April 24, 1980.

## THE RESCUE PLAN

• The mission, code-named Operation Eagle Claw, was spearheaded by roughly 100 members of Delta Force, a crack team chosen from all four U.S. military services.

• It was a complicated plan:

√ Four C-130 cargo planes with most of the Delta Force flew from a military base in Egypt to Desert One, a remote area in eastern Iran. There, they were to rendezvous with eight helicopters coming from an aircraft carrier stationed near the mouth of the Persian Gulf.

√ The commandos were to board the helicopters and fly to Desert Two, located fifty miles from Teheran. There they would meet with U.S. and Iranian operatives, then be transported by truck into the capital city.

√ At the embassy the team would storm the walled compound and free the hostages.

## PROBLEMS

• From the first, things went wrong. "Two of the helicopters experienced problems en route...and at the desert landing a third experienced a severe hydraulic malfunction." (*The New York Times*)

• Other sources claim that two other helicopters became "clogged with desert sand." (*Covert Action*)

• Since there weren't enough choppers to get the troops to Desert Two, the mission was aborted. But then, even more disaster struck: one of the helicopters collided with a cargo plane and exploded. The Americans fled, leaving behind wrecked aircraft and top-secret documents. There were eight American casualties.

• Carter was forced to admit failure. "The President has ordered the cancellation of an operation in Iran that was under way to prepare for a rescue of our hostages," the White House announced. "The mission was terminated because of equipment failure....The President accepts full responsibility."

## SUSPICIOUS FACTS

• According to *The New York Times*, "the breakdown of three of eight helicopters in a single operation is disturbing. Aircraft industry experts said they could not account for the high percentage of breakdowns and estimated the actuarial figures at 1 in 10,000."

• The manufacturer, Sikorsky, was also baffled: A company spokesperson said the helicopters were "routinely fitted with engine air-particle separators designed to exclude sand." Had the filters been removed?

• Many analysts thought the mission ill-conceived. "Ninety men, no matter how well trained and armed, could not storm a fortress, which is what the embassy has become, against a determined garrison of militants." (*The New York Times*)

• One of the support crew at Desert Two was a marine officer, Oliver North. He was later assigned to work with Major General Richard Secord on a second rescue mission.

## WAS IT A CONSPIRACY?

*Was the hostage rescue mission sabotaged?*

Some people suspect it was—possibly in a plot by Reagan supporters to discredit Carter. Conspiracy theorists point out that the helicopters could have been sabotaged by a single person removing engine filters or puncturing a hydraulic line. But as intriguing as it would be to link Oliver North to another conspiracy, so far there's no evidence either way. In fact, it's probably fortunate that the rescue failed where it did. Had Delta Force besieged the embassy, the hostages might well have been executed by their captors.

# KILLING MASS TRANSIT

*"Some people say that the people of Los Angeles chose the automobile over the trains, chose paved highways over palm trees, chose smog over clean air—all for the freedom and mobility associated with automobile travel. In fact, the people of L.A. had no say in the matter."* —Russell Mokhiber

Before the Second World War, nearly every major city in the U.S. had a network of low-polluting public transportation—streetcars, electric trains, or trolleys. Los Angeles, for example, had the largest electric train system in the world, which linked the 56 towns of greater Los Angeles and carried 80 million passengers a year.

Many of the public transit systems around the country were owned by electric companies. They had been built in the years before most homes were wired for electricity, to increase sales of electric power.

But in the mid-1930s, Congress began breaking up the utility monopolies. In 1935, it passed antitrust laws which forced them to sell their mass-transit holdings.

## MOTOR POOLS

• These mass-transit companies were put up for sale at a time when the nation's automakers, mired in the Great Depression, were looking for ways to increase sales.

• "The [auto] industry was in a vulnerable position," writes Russell Mokhiber in his book *Corporate Crime and Violence*. "It was not clear that the four-wheeled buggy would become the transportation method of choice for a nation in the midst of its worst economic depression...[but] the industry knew that without efficient rail systems, city-dwellers around the country would be forced to find alternative means of transportation. So General Motors, determined to sell more automobiles and buses, decided to destroy the rail systems."

## GM GOES TO WORK

• In 1932, GM formed a holding company called United Cities Motor Transit. Through UCMT, the auto maker bought three mass transit companies in Ohio and Michigan, converted them to buses, then sold them back to local companies with the stipulation that they buy only GM buses in the future. GM had hoped to use these "showcase" bus lines to persuade other companies to make the switch, but there was little interest.

• When GM tried to use the same technique in Portland, Oregon, it ran into trouble. The American Transit Association publicly exposed GM's plan and censured it. GM was forced to dismantle UCMT.

• But that didn't stop GM. In fact, it decided to skip the small companies and wipe out New York's trolley system, the largest in America. To protect itself from criticism, GM worked with an existing bus company, the Omnibus Corporation, rather than setting up its own. It took only 18 months to dismantle New York's massive public transportation system.

## THE SECOND STAGE

• GM was now ready to take on the rest of the country. Using a small Illinois bus company as a front, it began buying up dozens of mass-transit companies. "Tracks were literally torn out of the ground, sometimes overnight," writes journalist Jonathan Kwitny. "Overhead power lines were dismantled, and valuable off-street rights of way were sold." In East St. Louis, for example, "they discontinued operating streetcars in the city one night, and started operating modern buses...the next day." (Harper's)

• Soon the front company became too big for GM to finance. So GM transformed it into a holding company called National City Lines, Inc., and approached other companies that would also benefit from the destruction of electric transit. By 1937, Greyhound Bus Lines, the Firestone Tire and Rubber Company, Mack Manufacturing, Standard Oil of California, and Phillips Petroleum had also joined up, investing $10 million altogether.

• NCL finished dismantling transit systems after the end of World War II; by the time it was done, it had eliminated lines carrying hundreds of millions of passengers in more than 45 cities, including

New York, Philadelphia, Baltimore, St. Louis, Oakland, Salt Lake City, and Los Angeles. By 1955, only 5,000 streetcars remained nationwide out of a fleet that had numbered 40,000 in 1936.

## WAS IT A CONSPIRACY?

In 1949, GM and the other conspirators were indicted for violating antitrust laws. They defended themselves by claiming that their investments in the enterprise were small, that they had exerted no managerial control over National City Lines, and that a nationwide switch to buses had already begun.

## SUSPICIOUS FACTS

• The conspirators claimed that they had put money into National City Lines because transit lines were a good investment. But internal documents showed that they knew they were going to lose money. The real profits would come later, by selling products to the new *bus* lines. According to Kwitny, "a memo at Mack spoke of a 'probable loss' on the bus-line stock, but said it would be 'more than justified' by 'the business and gross profit flowing out of this move in years to come.'" (*Harper's*)

• The companies investing were very secretive about their involvement with National City Lines: Standard Oil of California invested its money through two other companies, because, a company official later admitted, "We didn't want to be criticized." Firestone channeled its investments through two of its employees who posed as independent investors.

• Though National City Lines was supposed to be independent, the agreements under which the conspirators provided money specified that all buses, tires, and petroleum products had to be purchased from the companies that owned stock in National City Lines. Moreover, NCL and its branches were run by employees of the stockholding companies.

• Furthermore, notes Kwitny, "the contracts also specified that the transit systems could never buy another streetcar or any other piece of equipment that would 'use any fuel or method of propulsion other than gasoline.' (In the early 1940s, when the diesel bus came into vogue as a replacement for the older, gasoline-engine models, the clause was changed to permit the purchase of diesel fuel.)"

## END OF THE LINE
• Once the light rail systems were gone, big business got out of the transit business: GM, Standard Oil, Firestone, Phillips, Mack, and Greyhound all dumped their stocks. Even the holding company itself, National City Lines, got entirely out of mass transit.

• Meanwhile, a federal court decided that the companies had engaged in an illegal conspiracy. GM, National City Lines, Firestone Tire and Rubber, Phillips Petroleum, Mack Manufacturing, and Standard Oil of California were all convicted of violating the Sherman Antitrust Act.

• Their penalty? A slap on the wrist. Each company was fined $5,000. Company officials that were found guilty were each fined a dollar.

## RECOMMENDED READING
• *Corporate Crime and Violence*, by Russell Mokhiber (Sierra Club Books, 1989). *Three dozen case studies of how big business has abused the public trust and fifty things citizens can do to prevent it from happening.*

• "The Great Transportation Conspiracy," by Jonathan Kwitny (*Harper's* magazine, Feb. 1981)

# ABBIE SPEAKS

*In the '60s many believed Abbie Hoffman was leading a hippie conspiracy to overthrow the establishment. And in a way he was. Here are some of the things this celebrated conspirator had to say.*

"Democracy is not something you believe in or a place to hang your hat, but it's something you do. You participate. If you stop doing it, democracy crumbles."

"I have never seen myself as anything more than a good community organizer. It was just the Vietnam War that made the community bigger, that's all."

"And so you ask, 'What about innocent bystanders?' But we are in a time of revolution. If you are a bystander, you are not innocent."

"Sacred cows make the tastiest hamburger."

"You measure democracy by the freedom it gives its dissidents, not the freedom it gives its assimilated conformists."

"Revolution is anything you can get away with."

"The Pentagon is a symbol of evil in most religions. You're religious, aren't you?"

"Kids, don't use needles. The only dope worth shooting is Richard Nixon."

"The Flower Brigade lost its first battle, but watch out, America. We were poorly equipped with flowers from uptown florists. Already there is talk of growing our own. Plans are being made to mine the East River with daffodils. Dandelion chains are being wrapped around [draft] induction centers. Holes are being dug in street pavements with seeds dropped in and covered. The cry of 'Flower Power' echoes through the land."

"The only way to support a revolution is to make your own."

"The first duty of a revolutionary is to get away with it."

# REEFER MADNESS

*After being widely cultivated for 10,000 years, marijuana was suddenly
outlawed in America in 1937. Was it because it was a threat to
the American public—or only to certain business interests?*

For thousands of years, hemp (*Cannabis sativa*) has been one of
the most useful plants known to man. Its strong, stringy fibers make durable rope and can be woven into anything from
sails to shirts; its pithy centers, or "hurds," make excellent paper; its
seeds, high in protein and oil, have been pressed for lighting and
lubricating oils and pulped into animal feed; and extracts of its
leaves have provided a wide range of medicines and tonics.

## HEMP & AMERICA
• Hemp also has a notable place in American history:

√ Washington and Jefferson grew it.

√ Our first flags were likely made of hemp cloth.

√ The first and second drafts of the Declaration of Independence
were written on paper made from Dutch hemp.

√ When the pioneers went west, their wagons were covered with
hemp canvas (the word "canvas" comes from *canabacius*, hemp
cloth).

√ The first Levis sold to prospectors were sturdy hemp coveralls.

√ Abraham Lincoln's wife, Mary Todd, came from the richest
hemp-growing family in Kentucky.

• After the Civil War, however, hemp production in the States declined steeply. Without slave labor, hemp became too expensive to
process. Besides, cotton ginned by machines was cheaper. Still,
hemp fabric remained the second most common cloth in America.

• The plant's by-products remained popular well into this century.
Maple sugar combined with hashish (a resin from hemp leaves) was
sold over the counter and in Sears Roebuck catalogs as a harmless
candy. Hemp rope was a mainstay of the navy. Two thousand tons
of hemp seed were sold annually as birdfeed. The pharmaceutical

industry used hemp extracts in hundreds of potions and vigorously fought attempts to restrict hemp production. And virtually all good paints and varnishes were made from hemp-seed oil and/or linseed oil.

## WHAT HAPPENED

• In the 1920s and '30s, the American public became increasingly concerned about drug addiction—especially to morphine and a "miracle drug" that had been introduced by the Bayer Company in 1898 under the brand name "Heroin." By the mid-1920s, there were 200,000 heroin addicts in the U.S. alone.

• Most Americans were unaware that smoking hemp leaves was intoxicating, however, until William Randolph Hearst launched a campaign of sensational stories that linked "the killer weed" to jazz musicians, "crazed minorities," and unspeakable crimes. Hearst's papers featured headlines like:

√ MARIJUANA MAKES FIENDS OF BOYS IN 30 DAYS: HASHEESH GOADS USERS TO BLOOD-LUST

√ NEW DOPE LURE, MARIJUANA, HAS MANY VICTIMS

• In 1930, Hearst was joined in his crusade against hemp by Harry J. Anslinger, commissioner of the newly organized Federal Bureau of Narcotics (FBN). Hearst often quoted Anslinger in his newspaper stories, printing sensational comments like: "If the hideous monster Frankenstein came face to face with the monster marijuana he would drop dead of fright."

• Not everyone shared their opinion. In 1930, the U.S. government formed the Siler Commission to study marijuana smoking by off-duty servicemen in Panama. The commission found no lasting effects and recommended that no criminal penalties apply to its use.

• Nonetheless, Hearst and Anslinger's anti-hemp campaign had results. By 1931, twenty-nine states had prohibited marijuana use for nonmedical purposes. In 1937, after two years of secret hearings—and based largely on Anslinger's testimony—Congress passed the Marijuana Tax Act, which essentially outlawed marijuana in America.

• Because Congress wasn't sure that it was constitutional to ban hemp outright, it taxed the plant prohibitively instead. Hemp growers had to register with the government; sellers and buyers had to fill out cumbersome paperwork; and, of course, it was a federal crime not to comply.

• For selling an ounce or less of marijuana to an unregistered person, the federal tax was $100. (To give some sense of how prohibitive the tax was, "legitimate" marijuana was selling for $2 a pound at the time. In 1992 dollars, the federal tax would be roughly $2,000 per ounce.)

• The Marijuana Tax Act effectively destroyed all legitimate commercial cultivation of hemp. Limited medical use was permitted, but as hemp derivatives became prohibitively expensive for doctors and pharmacists, they turned to chemically derived drugs instead. All other nonmedical uses, from rope to industrial lubricants, were taxed out of existence.

• With most of their markets gone, farmers stopped growing hemp, and the legitimate industry disappeared. Ironically, though, hemp continued to grow wild all over the country, and its "illegitimate" use was little affected by Congress.

## WAS IT A CONSPIRACY?
*Was a viable hemp industry forced out of existence because it was a threat to people's health or because it was a threat to a few large businesses that would profit from banning it?*

## THE HEARST CONSPIRACY
• Hemp was outlawed just as a new technology would have made hemp paper far cheaper than wood-pulp paper.

• Traditionally, hemp fiber had to be separated from the stalk by hand, and the cost of labor made this method uncompetitive. But in 1937—the year that hemp was outlawed, the *decorticator* machine was invented; it could process as much as 3 tons of hemp an hour and produced higher quality fibers with less loss of fiber than wood-based pulp. According to some scientists, hemp would have been able to undercut competing products overnight. Enthusiastic about the new technology, *Popular Mechanics* predicted that hemp would become America's first "billion-dollar crop." The magazine pointed out that "10,000 acres devoted to hemp will produce as much paper as 40,000 acres of average [forest] pulp land."

• According to Jack Herer, an expert on the "hemp conspiracy," Hearst, the du Ponts, and other "industrial barons and financiers knew that machinery to cut, bale, and decorticate (separate fiber from the stalk) and process hemp into paper was becoming available in the mid-1930s." (*The Emperor Wears No Clothes*)

• Hearst, one of the promoters of the anti-hemp hysteria, had a vested interest in protecting the pulp industry. Hearst owned enormous timber acreage; competition from hemp paper might have driven the Hearst paper-manufacturing division out of business and caused the value of his acreage to plummet. (ibid.)

• Herer suggests that Hearst slanted the news in his papers to protect his pulp investments. "In the 1920s and 30s," he writes, "Hearst's newspaper chain led the deliberate...yellow journalism campaign to have marijuana outlawed. From 1916 to 1937, as an example, the story of a car accident in which a marijuana cigarette was found would dominate the headlines for weeks, while alcohol-related car accidents (which outnumbered marijuana-related accidents by more than 1,000 to 1) made only the back pages." (ibid.)

• Herer says that Hearst was even responsible for popularizing the term "marijuana" in American culture. In fact, he suggests, popularizing the word was a key strategy of Hearst's efforts: "The first step [in creating hysteria] was to introduce the element of fear of the unknown by using a word that no one had ever heard of before...'marijuana.' " (ibid.)

## THE DU PONT CONSPIRACY

• The Du Pont Company also had an interest in the pulp industry. At this time, it was in the process of patenting a new sulfuric acid process for producing wood-pulp paper. According to the company's own records, wood-pulp products ultimately accounted for more than 80% of all of Du Pont's railroad car loadings for the next 50 years. (ibid.)

• But Du Pont had even more reasons to be concerned about hemp. In the 1930s, the company was making drastic changes in its business strategy. Traditionally a manufacturer of military explosives, Du Pont realized after the end of World War I that developing peacetime uses for artificial fibers and plastics would be more profitable in the long run. So it began pouring millions of dollars into research—which resulted in the development of such synthetic fibers as rayon and nylon.

√ Two years before the prohibitive hemp tax, Du Pont developed a new synthetic fiber, nylon, that was an ideal substitute for hemp rope.

√ The year after the hemp tax, Du Pont was able to bring another "miracle" synthetic fabric onto the market—rayon. Rayon, which became widely used for clothing, was a direct competitor to hemp cloth.

√ "Congress and the Treasury Department were assured, through secret testimony given by Du Pont, that hemp-seed oil could be replaced with synthetic petrochemical oils made principally by Du Pont." These oils were used in paints and other products. (ibid.)

• The millions spent on these products, as well as the hundreds of millions in expected profits from them, could have been wiped out if the newly affordable hemp products were allowed onto the market. So, according to Herer, Du Pont worked with Hearst to eliminate hemp.

• Du Pont's point-man was none other than Harry Anslinger, the commissioner of the FBN. Anslinger was appointed to the FBN by Treasury Secretary Andrew Mellon, who was also chairman of the Mellon Bank, Du Pont's chief financial backer. But Anslinger's relationship to Mellon wasn't just political; he was also married to Mellon's niece.

• Anslinger apparently used his political clout to sway congressional opinion on the hemp tax. According to Herer, the American Medical Association (AMA) tried to argue the medical benefits of hemp. But after AMA officials testified to Congress, "they were quickly denounced by Anslinger and the entire congressional committee, and curtly excused."

## FOOTNOTES

• Five years after the hemp tax was imposed, when Japanese seizure of Philippine hemp caused a wartime shortage of rope, the government reversed itself. Overnight, the U.S. government urged hemp cultivation once again and created a stirring movie called "Hemp for Victory"—then, just as quickly, it recriminalized hemp after the shortage had passed.

• While U.S. hemp was temporarily legal, however, it saved the life of a young pilot named George Bush, who was forced to bail out of his burning airplane after a battle over the Pacific. At the time, he didn't know that:

√ Parts of his aircraft engine were lubricated with hemp-seed oil.

√ 100% of his life-saving parachute webbing was made from U.S.-grown cannabis hemp.

√ Virtually all the rigging and ropes of the ship that rescued him were made of cannabis hemp.

√ The fire hoses on the ship were woven from cannabis hemp.

Ironically, President Bush has consistently opposed decriminalizing hemp grown in the United States.

• Does the hemp conspiracy continue today? In March 1992, Robert Bonner, the chief of the Drug Enforcement Agency, effectively rejected a petition to permit doctors to prescribe marijuana for patients as medication for chronic pain. Bonner said: "Beyond doubt the claims that marijuana is medicine are false, dangerous and cruel." But, according to a federal administrative law judge, Francis Young, "the record clearly shows that marijuana has been accepted as capable of relieving the distress of great numbers of very ill people and doing so with safety under medical supervision." (*The New York Times*)

## RECOMMENDED READING

Most of the quotes and some of the assertions in this chapter are from the book *The Emperor Wears No Clothes*, a virtual archive of hemp-related literature, including transcripts of the original congressional hearings. Well researched, personably written, and highly recommended, it is available from its author, Jack Herer of H.E.M.P. Publishing, 39 Park Avenue, Venice, CA 90291

# ALPHABET SNOOPS

*Spies like to talk in codes and acronyms. These agencies know your initials and what you stand for—what do you know about them?*

**ASA** (Army Security Agency): Monitors electronic transmissions.

**CIA** (Central Intelligence Agency): Created to gather and analyze foreign intelligence.

**CIAB** (Counter-Intelligence Analysis Branch): U.S. Army spycatchers

**COINTELPRO** (Counter-Intelligence Program): FBI program that illegally spied on and disrupted U.S. dissident groups

**DEA** (Drug Enforcement Agency): Heads U.S. war on drugs

**DIA** (Defense Intelligence Agency): Defense Department's CIA

**FBI** (Federal Bureau of Investigations): The nation's primary domestic law-enforcement agency

**IDIU** (Interdepartmental Information and Interdivisional Intelligence Unit); the ISD's intelligence unit

**IGRS** (Intelligence Gathering and Retrieval Service): Intelligence instrument of the IRS; used tax information to "neutralize" dissident political groups in the U.S.; suspended in 1975

**ISA** (Intelligence Support Activity): Supersecret operations group that even the CIA didn't know about; disbanded in 1985

**ISD** (Internal Security Division): Justice Department outfit that monitors "subversives"

**LEIU** (Law Enforcement Intelligence Unit): Highly secretive private intelligence network that gathers information about "radicals"

**MID** (Military Intelligence Division): Oversees military documents, personnel, and bases

**MIG** (Military Intelligence Group): Investigates military personnel

**NSA** (National Security Agency): Ultrasecret; monitors communications worldwide; can listen in on 450,000 phone calls simultaneously

**NSC** (National Security Council): "Originally intended to be a civilian advisory group, [it] has become a command post for covert operations run by the military." (*The Secret Government*)

**ONI** (Office of Naval Intelligence): The Navy's spies

# THE WARREN COMMISSION

*In 1964, the Warren Commission concluded that Lee Harvey Oswald was the lone gunman who killed JFK. Here are some of the reasons why few people believe it anymore.*

When Lee Harvey Oswald was murdered in police custody, many Americans began to suspect a conspiracy. Authorities in Dallas and Washington, D.C. immediately investigated the murder and concluded that neither Oswald nor Jack Ruby were involved in any conspiracy. They made their findings and much of their evidence public, but most Americans still had their doubts: a Gallup poll taken early in December 1963 found that 52% of Americans "believed that Oswald had not acted alone." (*Crossfire*)

There were calls for an independent congressional investigation. To forestall them, President Lyndon Johnson announced on November 29, 1963—just one week after JFK's death—that he had created a federal panel to "uncover all the facts concerning the assassination of President Kennedy and to determine if it was in any way directed or encouraged by unknown persons at home or abroad." The bipartisan panel was to be chaired by the Chief Justice of the U.S. Supreme Court, Earl Warren, and comprised of seven men "of unimpeachable integrity."

## COMMISSION MEMBERS
- Earl Warren, Chief Justice, U.S. Supreme Court
- Hale Boggs, Democratic representative from Louisiana
- John Sherman Cooper, Republican senator from Kentucky
- Gerald Ford, Republican representative from Michigan
- Richard Russell, Democratic senator from Georgia
- Allen Dulles, Wall Street lawyer, former director of the CIA
- John J. McCloy, post-WWII High Commissioner of Germany, former president of the World Bank

## THE FINDINGS

In September 1964, the Warren Commission presented a 26-volume report. Its findings included:

• "The shots which killed President Kennedy and wounded Governor Connally were fired from the sixth floor window of the Depository Building....There were three shots fired."

• "There is persuasive evidence from the experts to indicate that the same bullet which pierced the President's throat also caused Governor Connally's wounds."

• "The shots which killed President Kennedy...were fired by Lee Harvey Oswald."

• "The Commission has found no evidence that either Lee Harvey Oswald or Jack Ruby was part of any conspiracy, domestic or foreign, to assassinate President Kennedy."

## THE CONSPIRACY THEORY

• The FBI and the CIA prejudged the case, assumed Oswald to be the lone assassin, suppressed evidence to the contrary, and deliberately lied to the Warren Commission. The commissioners knew they weren't getting all the facts, but they went along.

• Senator Richard Schweiker, a member of the Senate Intelligence Committee's subcommittee that investigated the FBI's and CIA's role, said in 1976: "I believe the Warren Commission was set up at the time to feed pablum to the American people for reasons not yet known, and that one of the biggest coverups in the history of our country occurred at that time."

## SUSPICIOUS FACTS

• "Almost immediately after the assassination," said a 1976 Senate Intelligence Committee report, Lyndon Johnson rushed to wrap up the case; his aides pressed the FBI "to issue a factual report supporting the conclusion that Oswald was the lone assassin." At first, Johnson had wanted *no* investigation.

• In this, LBJ had the full support of J. Edgar Hoover. On November 24, 1963, Hoover said to Johnson's aide Walter Jenkins, "The thing I am concerned about...is having something issued so we can convince the public that Oswald is the real assassin."

• Once he realized that the public demanded a federal inquiry, LBJ hand-picked a panel. Chief Justice Warren wanted no part of it: he at first refused, saying that one branch of the government should not investigate another. But Johnson pressured him. Following the closed meeting in which LBJ convinced him to head the Commission, Warren emerged "with tears in his eyes."

## A Stacked Deck

• The CIA and the FBI, both potential suspects in the inquiry, were well represented on the Warren Commission. John J. McCloy had helped to establish the CIA. *Newsweek* called Gerald Ford "the CIA's best friend in Congress." Allen Dulles had been the director of the CIA for eight years before being fired by John Kennedy.

• According to *Crossfire*, "Dulles withheld CIA information from the Warren Commission, particularly concerning assassination plots between the Agency and organized crime." Had other Commission members known of the CIA's ties to the Mafia, mafioso Jack Ruby might have looked more like a "silencer" and less like a patriot distraught about the president's murder.

• Moreover, when he was asked in executive session about rumors tying Oswald to the agency, Dulles admitted that he and his agents "would lie about whether or not Oswald worked for the CIA." (*Coup d'Etat in America*)

• But the FBI's top "informant" may have been Gerald Ford, who, while supposedly conducting an impartial investigation, allegedly passed along information to the FBI. A memo from Cartha De-Loach, a close Hoover aide, said, "Ford indicated he would keep me thoroughly advised as to the activities of the Commission. He stated this would have to be on a confidential basis."

## Roads Not Taken

• Until commissioner John J. McCloy pointed out that the Secret Service and the FBI might be culpable and thus could not be counted on to provide an impartial investigation, Chairman Warren was not inclined to ask for subpoena powers or to hire independent investigators.

• Congress eventually did authorize the Warren Commission "to compel testimony by providing immunity from prosecution," but the Commission never once used this power.

• One striking failure: Although Commission members could have demanded to see the actual autopsy photos of the president's wounds, they settled for artists' drawings. Nor did they ask the Dallas doctors who'd attended the dying president if the drawings of his wounds were accurate.

• The Commission's interviews with Jack Ruby were superficial. Ruby, fearing for his life in Dallas, said he'd tell all if only the commissioners would take him to Washington. They refused.

### Ignored Witnesses
The Warren Commission questioned only 126 of the 266 witnesses to the killing, by testimony or affidavits. Among those it never called:

√ James Chaney, the motorcycle policeman who had been nearest Kennedy and saw the shot that killed him.

√ Senator Ralph Yarborough, part of the motorcade, who smelled gunpowder as he and LBJ drove past the infamous grassy knoll.

√ Bill and Gayle Newman, among the closest bystanders to JFK when he was hit, who insisted that the shot came from behind them on the grassy knoll.

√ Railroad employees Richard Dodd and James Simmons, who claimed that shots came from the picket fence behind the grassy knoll.

√ John Stringer and William Pitzer, medical technicians who photographed and X-rayed Kennedy's body.

√ Admiral George Burkley, Kennedy's personal physician, who attended the autopsy and allegedly passed on the medical evidence to the National Archives.

### Badgered Witnesses
• Several witnesses who offered views that contradicted the lone-assassin theory were badgered to change their accounts. Witness Jean Hill, who said she saw a rifleman on the grassy knoll, was interviewed by Warren Commission junior counsel Arlen Specter (later a U.S. senator from Pennsylvania). She also said she heard four to six shots.

• When she refused to change her story, she said Specter got "angrier and angrier and finally told me, 'Look, we can make you look as crazy as Marguerite Oswald [Lee's mother] and everyone knows how crazy she is. We could have you put in a mental institution if you don't cooperate with us.' " Specter promised Hill that he would not publish the interview until she had approved it. But according to Hill, she never got the chance: "When I finally read my testimony as published by the Warren Commission, I knew it was a fabrication from start to finish." (*Crossfire*)

**Dissenting Voices**

• Although all seven members eventually endorsed the Warren Report in 1964, the Commission had its doubters. As author Anthony Summers points out in his book *Conspiracy*: "Three of the seven members of the Warren Commission did not fully believe the theory of the magic bullet, even though it appeared in their report. The commissioners wrangled about it up to the moment their findings went to press. Congressman Hale Boggs had 'strong doubts.' Senator Sherman Cooper was, as he told me in 1978, 'unconvinced.' Senator Richard Russell did not want to sign a report which said definitely that both men were hit by the same bullet and wanted a footnote added indicating his dissent. Warren declined to put one in."

• In 1970, Russell became the first to question the Commission's findings publicly. He told the *Washington Post* that he had come to believe Kennedy's death was caused by a conspiracy. He also called the report "a sorrily incompetent document." He died shortly after, of natural causes.

• Within a year, Representative Hale Boggs, the majority leader of the House, also expressed doubts about the Commission's findings, especially the "magic bullet" theory. He followed that on April 1, 1971, with a stinging attack on J. Edgar Hoover, whom he accused of Gestapo tactics. Because Boggs was likely to become Speaker of the House, rumors flew that he was going to reopen the JFK assassination investigation. But it never happened: On October 16, 1972, while on a junket to Alaska, Boggs's plane disappeared and was never found, despite a massive search.

# SUSPICIOUS DEATH #3: JIM MORRISON

*Did Jim Morrison really leave the land of the living in 1971...*
*or did he just slip out of the limelight?*

T
he deceased: Jim Morrison, the lead singer of the Doors, one of the most popular rock bands of the 1960s.

How he died: In the summer of 1971, Morrison and his girlfriend, Pamela Courson, went to Paris on vacation. On July 5, Courson allegedly found him dead in the bathtub. Two days later, he was buried in a quiet service attended by five close friends. The official cause of death was listed as a heart attack. He was 27.

## SUSPICIOUS FACTS

• Nobody but Courson ever saw Morrison's dead body; neither Morrison's friends nor his family were given the opportunity to view it. After Morrison died, Courson asked Bill Siddons, the Doors' road manager, to come to Paris. He said that when he arrived on July 6, he "was met at the flat by Pamela, a sealed coffin, and a signed death certificate." He never saw Morrison's body.

• When asked the name of the doctor who signed the death certificate, Siddons said he didn't know, and Courson said she didn't remember. Moreover, according to *No One Here Gets Out Alive*, a 1980 biography of Morrison, "There was no police report, no doctor present. No autopsy had been conducted."

• When Courson filed the death certificate at the U.S. Embassy on July 7, the day of the funeral, she claimed there were no living relatives—which meant that since there was no one to be notified, Morrison could be buried quickly. In fact, Jim's family lived in Arlington, Virginia.

• Morrison's friends kept the story of his death a secret for almost a week. Siddons told his story to the media six days after Morrison died, two days after the funeral. Beyond noting that Morrison had died of "natural causes," Siddons had no more to add.

## POSSIBLE CONCLUSIONS

• **Morrison is really dead.** His friends say they hushed up his death to protect his privacy. A statement prepared for the public said, "The initial news of his death and funeral was kept quiet...to avoid all the notoriety and circus-like atmosphere that surrounded the deaths of such other rock personalities as Janis Joplin and Jimmy Hendrix."

• **Morrison is hiding out.** At the time of his death, Morrison's life was a mess. He had been convicted on two counts of profanity and indecent exposure in Miami and faced a jail sentence if his appeal failed; he faced a possible 10-year sentence after being busted by the FBI for being drunk and disorderly on an airplane; and more than *twenty* paternity suits were pending against him.

Morrison was sick of his life as a rock star and had been saying so for years. He said he wanted to start over anonymously, so he could just write. With Courson's help, he could easily have faked his own death to give himself a fresh start.

√ For years, Courson had urged Morrison to quit the band and develop himself as a poet.

√ She, or someone else, started a rumor that Morrison may have visited a Paris hangout earlier in the evening and obtained some heroin. That, mixed with alcohol, is what supposedly killed him. Yet for all the drugs he ingested, no friends ever mentioned heroin, and Morrison was afraid of needles.

√ The absence of an autopsy and police report is very suspicious, and the lie about his parents and the quick "burial" forestalled any further inquiries. A doctor could have been bribed to fake a death certificate.

√ Finally, Morrison had repeatedly talked about Paris. According to one close friend of the singer, "he thought it was a place where he could be himself and not have people hounding him and making a circus out of his life, making him something he wasn't."

## RECOMMENDED READING

All of the quotes in this chapter are from *No One Here Gets Out Alive*, by Jerry Hopkins and Danny Sugerman (Warner Books, 1980).

# SUPPRESSING SARKHAN

*Here's a story that should make you wonder
about free speech in America.*

I n the early 1960s, *The Ugly American*, a controversial novel
written by William Lederer and Eugene Burdick, shot to the
top of the bestseller lists.

This unflattering portrait of the American foreign service in
Southeast Asia infuriated the State Department...but it also made
friends in high places. It was praised by President Kennedy, for example—and his mother, Rose Kennedy, liked it so much that she
sent a copy to every member of Congress.

In 1962, *The Ugly American* was made into a movie starring Marlon Brando. And in 1965, coauthors Lederer and Burdick published
their next work, a novel called *Sarkhan*.

### LEDERER'S STORY

*Here's William Lederer's account of what happened.*

"*The Ugly American*, written by Eugene Burdick and myself, was
published in the fall of 1958. At first it had a modest success; however, it became a great success after it became public knowledge
that the U.S. government had taken steps to suppress the sale of
the book in foreign countries. We learned about this by chance. A
bookstore owner from Manila happened to be sitting next to me on
a plane, and he angrily informed me that USIS [United States Information Service], by cutting off funds, was suppressing *The Ugly
American* in the Philippines.

"Later, when George Englund and Marlon Brando were making
the book into a motion picture, the government once more attempted to abort the growing popularity of the book. The Agency
for International Development sent 'Asian experts' to persuade the
producer that some of the things in our book were not only untrue
but impossible. (For one entertaining small example, the 'experts'
said it was impossible to use hollow bamboo as a pipe for water. Of
course, this method has been used in Southeast Asia for thousands
of years and is still being used today.)

"When the American public began asking questions regarding the ineffectiveness of our foreign policies (Burdick and I received an average of 2,000 letters a week during that time), the State Department gave evidence of concern. The Department of State had a speech prepared which was read from the legal sanctuary of the Senate floor by Senator William J. Fulbright. He challenged the validity of the book's premises and suggested that Burdick and I were tantamount to traitors.

"We wrote Senator Fulbright and offered to take him—at our expense—on a tour through Southeast Asia and show him what we had seen. All we requested from him was that he go incognito so that we'd have no official meddling.

"The only reply we received was a short paragraph from the senator's secretary. She said the senator was too busy.

"There were many other attempts to belittle and indirectly to suppress *The Ugly American*. But these attempts were micro-efforts compared to what happened later to our follow-up novel, *Sarkhan*."

## THE SARKHAN STORY

"We published *Sarkhan* in the fall of 1965. In writing the book we had several objectives. First, we wanted to produce a book which was exciting and entertaining, the first requirement for a novel. Second, we wanted to use that narrative quality to show what was happening eight years after *The Ugly American*; and that things probably would get even worse unless the U.S. foreign relations process improved.

"However, showing the eruptions and stupidities in the field was not sufficient. The cause was in Washington. Among the major characters in our book were officials who made foreign relations policy and whose departments implemented these policies. The crux was that many officials were more skilled at perpetuating their own personal power and the funding of their agencies than they were knowledgeable about the true welfare and well-being of the United States.

"At publication time it seemed as if the book would be a tremendous success. There were advance orders of several tens of thousands in the bookstores. *Sarkhan* was the choice of the Literary Guild. This represented an additional 100,000 at least. It was also the choice of the Reader's Digest Book Club, which had a circulation of several hundred thousand.

"However, some strange things began happening even before books were available in the stores. First, it was reviewed in *Time* several days before the books were on sale. Although this sometimes happens, it seemed odd to me. My previous book, *A Nation of Sheep*, had been on the best-seller list for forty weeks before *Time* reviewed it. Now came a review before *Sarkhan's* publication. The review itself was done in a way (bearing in mind the political climate of the time) which seemed to be aimed at discrediting *Sarkhan* rather than reviewing the contents and grading the book's quality. It was so off-center that I wondered whether or not the *Time* reviewer had read the book.

"I was sufficiently curious about this to mention it to an old friend, an editor of *Time*. Several days later my friend and I met at lunch in an obscure uptown restaurant (at his request). After looking about the room, he leaned over and whispered that if I ever quoted him he would deny he had spoken to me. If it became known he had supplied me with information it would cost him his job. He told me this: 'About a month ago two men came up from Washington and called on the publisher. These two men told the publisher "that it is against the interest of the United States that *Sarkhan* be a success." ' This startled me, because we had written the book not only to be entertaining, but also to help the United States."

## SARKHAN DISAPPEARS

"Shortly after publication date, I was scheduled to be on a television show in New York. On the way to the studio I stopped in at Brentano's bookstore. It pleased me to see two large stacks of *Sarkhan* in a primary display location. From the store I went to the studio, arriving early. The receptionist was kind, bringing me coffee, telling me the broadcast would be easy, and so forth. I felt grateful, and after the broadcast I thought the least I could do was to buy a copy of *Sarkhan* and present it to the thoughtful receptionist. However, when I returned to Brentano's, the two big stacks of *Sarkhan* no longer were there. I knew it was improbable that so many books would have sold so quickly. I asked the clerk for a copy of the book.

She couldn't find one. She said, 'That's funny, there were a lot of them out front this morning.'

"I urged her to look about the store. She did. In a few minutes she returned and told me, 'We received a phone call and all the books have been sent back.'

"Previous to this, we had been receiving vigorous interest from various Hollywood studios. Soon after publication that vigorous interest abruptly stopped. A studio executive told me that his studio had received a telephone call from Washington informing the studio that if *Sarkhan* were made into a motion picture, the studio might have grave problems in obtaining their export licenses. My Hollywood informant told me he would get into much trouble if it were known that he had given me information."

## FOOTNOTES

*Sarkhan's* sales dried up and the book went out of print, but for more than a decade, Lederer continued looking for answers: Why had the book been suppressed, and by whom? Several years later, while discussing the subject with an acquaintance who worked for the CIA, Lederer learned that the Agency had done it.

• According to Lederer, his CIA source told him that the plot of *Sarkhan* was "almost a blueprint of an Agency operation in Thailand at the time." Assuming that the authors had somehow gotten classified documents and based the book upon them, the source explained, the CIA suppressed it. Lederer was incredulous when he heard this explanation. He denied ever having had privileged information. "This is bullshit," he told his source. "Burdick and I just made it up. You know I would never compromise the United States."

• Assuming that the CIA did suppress *Sarkhan*, could there have been another reason? Maybe. The CIA often implements State Department policy. Given the State Department's displeasure with *The Ugly American* and the impact the book had on public opinion, the department may have been eager to squelch any further criticism.

• Finally, in 1977, long after the Vietnam War—and, presumably, the CIA's covert operation in Thailand—had ended, *Sarkhan* was reissued as *The Deceptive American*.

# THE JFK ROGUES' GALLERY

*Here are some of the characters who play pivotal
roles in JFK assassination theories.*

**ARLEN SPECTER.** Junior counselor, Warren Commission

**JFK connection:** Championed the "magic bullet" theory, in which one bullet strikes JFK in the throat, waits in midair for 1.6 seconds, then causes five wounds in Governor John Connally (see p. 63).

**Further adventures:** When impeachment loomed in 1974 for Richard Nixon, he asked Specter to head his defense team. Specter later became a Republican senator for Pennsylvania, and aggressively interrogated Anita Hill at the Clarence Thomas Supreme Court hearings.

**E. HOWARD HUNT.** Veteran CIA agent, novelist, spook

**JFK connection:** In *Plausible Denial*, attorney Mark Lane says Hunt was the CIA's "paymaster" in the Kennedy assassination—that Hunt paid off JFK's killers. When a magazine article written by renegade CIA agent Victor Marchetti linked Hunt to JFK's killing, Hunt sued for libel. But the jury decided against Hunt. Many conspiracy theorists also believe that Hunt was one of the "three tramps" arrested in Dealey Plaza right after the assassination.

**Further adventures:** Hunt is famous as one of the Watergate "plumbers"; on the White House tapes Nixon discussed paying Hunt a million dollars to keep him quiet. What was Nixon trying to hush up?

**GERALD FORD.** Republican representative from Michigan; House minority leader; described by *Newsweek* as "the CIA's best friend in Congress."

**JFK connection:** Appointed to the Warren Commission at the suggestion of Richard Nixon. J. Edgar Hoover's close aide Cartha DeLoach said, "Ford indicated he would keep me advised to the activities of the Commission...on a confidential basis" (even though the FBI was a potential suspect). Ford denies any impropriety and says DeLoach exaggerated.

**Further adventures:** When Vice President Spiro Agnew resigned in 1973, Ford was appointed vice president. When President Nixon resigned in 1974, Ford became the first unelected President—and pardoned Nixon of all crimes.

**J. LEE RANKIN.** General counsel of the Warren Commission.

**JFK connection:** According to *Crossfire* author Jim Marrs, "Rankin appeared more concerned with wrapping up the Commission's investigation swiftly than fully probing each issue."

**Further adventures:** Ten years later, Nixon considered appointing Rankin Watergate special prosecutor, but instead had him "prepare" the presidential tapes for the Watergate investigation.

**SAM GIANCANA.** Chicago Mob boss—supposedly the "godfather" of the American Mafia.

**JFK connection:** According to *Double-Cross*, the Mafia helped elect JFK by rigging votes in Chicago. In return, JFK promised to ease up on the Mob. When the president broke his promise, Giancana "put out a contract" on JFK. (Giancana and Kennedy also allegedly shared a mistress, Judith Campbell.)

**Further adventures:** Before Kennedy became president, the CIA had asked Giancana to help assassinate Fidel Castro, and the mobster continued to work for the Agency. In 1975, shortly before he was slated to talk to a Senate committee about Mob-CIA assassination plots, Giancana was shot in the head while cooking sausages in his basement.

**LEON JAWORSKI.** Texas attorney; member of the prosecution team in the Nuremberg trials after World War II.

**JFK connection:** Special counsel on the Warren Commission who, according to Kennedy biographer John Davis, was "instrumental in preventing the Warren Commission from investigating, in depth, an alleged connection between Oswald and the FBI."

**Further adventures:** After Richard Nixon fired Watergate special prosecutor Archibald Cox, Jaworski was picked to replace him.

**RICHARD NIXON.** Former vice president; attorney for Pepsi Cola in 1963.

**JFK connection:** Opponent in 1960 election. Was in Dallas on November 22, 1963—supposedly on business for Pepsi. Some people think he was involved with the assassination.

**Further adventures:** Became president of the U.S. in 1968; and, in 1974, became the first president forced to resign, after the Watergate scandal.

# THE TONKIN INCIDENT

*Lyndon Johnson claimed that the U.S. was forced into the Vietnam War by an unprovoked North Vietnamese attack. Did it really happen that way—or was it a phony story to get the U.S. into the war?*

L ate in the evening on August 4, 1964, President Lyndon Johnson interrupted television programs on all three national networks with grim news. He announced that American destroyers off the coast of North Vietnam in the Gulf of Tonkin had been attacked twice by the North Vietnamese—without provocation.

He promised reprisals; in fact, he declared that U.S. planes were on their way to bomb North Vietnam as he spoke.

Three days later, President Johnson asked Congress to pass an emergency resolution that would authorize him to "take all necessary measures to repel any armed attack against the forces of the United States and to prevent further aggression."

Congress obliged: the Gulf of Tonkin Resolution passed 98-2 in the Senate, and Johnson used it to launch the longest war in American history—a war that cost more than $400 billion, killed 58,000 U.S. service people, and divided the country more than any other conflict since the Civil War.

Yet, as incredible as it seems, evidence now suggests that LBJ and his advisors wanted that war in Vietnam—and conspired to start it with a lie.

## THE OFFICIAL STORY

**First attack: August 2, 1964.** According to government reports, three North Vietnamese PT boats, unprovoked and without warning, fired torpedoes and shells at the *Maddox*, a United States destroyer on patrol about 30 miles off the coast of North Vietnam. The destroyer and support aircraft fired back and drove them off.

**Second attack: August 4, 1964.** North Vietnamese PT boats made another "deliberate attack" on two United States destroyers —the *Maddox* and the *Turner Joy*—which were patrolling international waters about 65 miles off the coast of North Vietnam. This attack was described as "much fiercer than the first one," lasting about three hours in rough seas, with bad weather and low visibility. The government said that American destroyers and aircraft fired on the vessels and sank at least two of them.

## SUSPICIOUS FACTS

### The First Attack

• The government lied about where the *Maddox* was and what it was doing on the night of the first attack:

√ The *Maddox* wasn't in international waters. According to numerous reports, it was no farther than 10 miles—and possibly as close as 4 miles—from the North Vietnamese coast.

√ It wasn't on a "routine patrol." The *Maddox* was providing cover for South Vietnamese gunboats attacking North Vietnamese radar stations in the Gulf of Tonkin. According to former CIA station chief John Stockwell, those gunboats were "manned with CIA crew" and had been raiding North Vietnam all summer.

• The government said the attack on the *Maddox* was "unprovoked." However, the *Maddox*'s log showed that it had fired first while North Vietnamese boats were still 6 miles away.

### The Second Attack

• Many people doubt that the alleged August 4 attack ever occurred. They include:

√ The *Maddox*'s captain, John Herrick. He radioed that reports of an enemy attack "appear very doubtful" and said there were "no actual sightings by *Maddox*." (*Manufacturing Consent*)

√ Commander Jim Stockdale, a Navy pilot who responded to the *Maddox*'s distress calls. According to an October 1988 article in *The New American*, Stockdale "found the destroyers sitting in the water firing at—nothing....Not one American out there ever saw a PT boat. There was absolutely no gunfire except our own, no PT boat wakes, not a candle light, let alone a burning ship. No one could have been there and not have been seen on such a black night."

√ Pentagon planners who analyzed the information from Vietnam. "There was a great amount of uncertainty as to whether there was such an attack," recalls Daniel Ellsberg, who was working with the Pentagon at the time. (*The 10,000-Day War*)

√ President Lyndon Johnson. "Johnson privately expressed doubts only a few days after the second attack supposedly took place, confiding to an aide, 'Hell, those dumb sailors were just shooting flying fish.' " (*Vietnam: A History*)

• According to investigative reporter Jonathan Kwitny in his book *Endless Enemies*: "At one point things were so confused that the *Maddox* mistook the *Turner Joy* for a North Vietnamese ship and a gunner was ordered to fire at her point blank—which would have sunk her—but he refused the order pending an identity check. That was the closest that a U.S. ship came to being hit that night."

## The Resolution
Although the Gulf of Tonkin Resolution was supposedly submitted "in response to this outrageous incident" (the second attack), the document had actually been drafted by William Bundy, Johnson's assistant secretary of state, three months earlier.

## WAS IT A CONSPIRACY?
*Did our government intentionally draw the U.S. into war?*
Kwitny writes: "What we know is entirely consistent with the possibility that the Tonkin Gulf Incident was a put-up job, designed to sucker the North Vietnamese into providing justification for a planned U.S. expansion of the war....The North Vietnamese had every reason to believe they were under attack before they approached a U.S. ship, and they certainly were under attack before they fired a shot. The press was lied to, and so misinformed the public. We were all lied to."

## FOOTNOTE
The Tonkin Resolution was passed a few months before the 1964 presidential election between Johnson and Barry Goldwater. According to Kenneth Davis in his book *Don't Know Much About History*, "the Resolution not only gave Johnson the powers he needed to increase American commitment in Vietnam, but allowed him to blunt Goldwater's accusations that Johnson was 'timid before Communism.' "

## RECOMMENDED READING
• *Don't Know Much About History*, by Kenneth C. Davis (Avon Books, 1990)
• *Endless Enemies: The Making of an Unfriendly World*, by Jonathan Kwitny (Congdon & Weed, Inc., 1984)
• *Manufacturing Consent: The Political Economy of the Mass Media*, by Edward Herman and Noam Chomsky (Pantheon, 1988).

## TAKING LIBERTIES
In July 1984, the Knight-Ridder News Service broke a chilling story: In response to growing public unrest over U.S. policy in Nicaragua, the Reagan White House had developed a plan that "called for the suspension of the Constitution, turning control of the government over to the Federal Emergency Management Agency (FEMA)...and the declaration of martial law." The plan, code-named REX 84, was allegedly drafted by National Guard Colonel Louis Giuffrida, the director of FEMA, and Oliver North.

REX 84 was created to crush "national opposition to a U.S. military invasion abroad." North, a Vietnam veteran, was obsessed with making sure that a Nicaraguan war—or any other future war—did not end stalemated as the Vietnam War did. REX 84 called for the declaration of martial law and the immediate arrest and internment in concentration camps of more than 100,000 "illegal immigrants and political dissidents." According to columnist Jack Anderson, FEMA had draft legislation ready to go; its Defense Resources Act "would suspend the Constitution and the Bill of Rights...and generally clamp Americans in a totalitarian vise."

REX 84 was uncovered and sidetracked during investigations into the Iran-Contra affair. But the executive orders that made it possible are still on the books. According to Professor Diana Reynolds of Northeastern University, America is "a presidential directive away from a civil security state of emergency, which, if ever enacted, could create a constitutional crisis equal in severity to the American Civil War."

# NIXON'S THE ONE?

*Did Richard Nixon undermine LBJ's peace talks and keep the Vietnam War going in 1968, just to get elected?*

Although President Lyndon Johnson wasn't running for re-election in 1968, he was still obsessed with ending the war in Vietnam. His decision was partly political, since any resolution would help the Democrats hold on to the White House. But more important, by finding an "honorable" settlement to the conflict, Johnson could avoid becoming the first American president to lose a foreign war.

In June, Johnson came up with a plan: he proposed a halt to the U.S. bombing of North Vietnam, to be followed by negotiations with all parties. At first the proposal was rejected by the Communists. Then, after several months of secret meetings, the North Vietnamese suddenly agreed to his terms. The U.S. allies, the South Vietnamese, also accepted the plan—in fact, they insisted that talks begin immediately after the cease-fire went into effect.

Peace talks were scheduled to begin on November 2, three days before the presidential election. Democrats were sure the talks would help defeat Richard Nixon.

## WHAT HAPPENED

• Suddenly, on October 29, South Vietnam—whose defense had already cost 29,000 American lives—backed out of the peace talks. According to former Defense Secretary Clark Clifford, South Vietnamese President Nguyen Van Thieu "reneged on everything he had previously agreed to," saying the peace talks were "too soon."

• Thieu said he would need "materially more time" to prepare for talks in Paris, and that he "needed to consult the South Vietnamese National Security Council again."

• Johnson and his aides were livid. But they could do nothing to bring Thieu back to the negotiating table. When the peace talks were aborted, so was Democratic nominee Hubert Humphrey's bid for the presidency. On November 2, Richard Nixon won by 510,645 votes, or less than 1 percent of the total votes cast.

## SUSPICIOUS FACTS

• On July 12, 1968, Nixon, Bui Diem (the South Vietnamese ambassador to the U.S.), and Anna Chennault (a prominent right-wing Republican) met secretly in New York City.

• Chennault was an important figure in both Asian and American politics and had access to highly placed officials on the two continents. She was one of the mainstays of the China Lobby, a Taiwan-based group that fought to keep Red China out of the United Nations, and was the chairwoman of Republican Women for Nixon.

• At Nixon's request—perhaps made at the July 12 meeting—Ambassador Diem began regular and secret communications with Nixon's campaign manager, John Mitchell, and other senior members of the Nixon team.

• The White House knew what was going on. "Gradually," Defense Secretary Clark Clifford wrote later, "we realized that President Thieu's growing resistance to the agreement in Paris was being encouraged—indeed, stimulated—by the Republicans, and especially by Anna Chennault." (*The New Yorker*)

• According to former Assistant Secretary of State William Bundy: "Johnson and his inner circle...learned through intercepted South Vietnam Embassy cables, particularly one of October 27, that Anna Chennault was conveying via Bui Diem apparently authoritative 'Republican' messages urging Mr. Thieu to abort or cripple the deal by refusing to participate. That 'smoking gun' cable included promises of later favor from Mr. Nixon, including a possible visit to Saigon before the inauguration if he were elected." (*The New York Times*)

• Bundy also said that "on November 3, two days before the election, Mr. Johnson [confronted] Mr. Nixon with Mrs. Chennault's activities, and Mr. Nixon categorically denied any connection or knowledge—almost certainly a lie in light of later disclosures." (ibid.)

• Clifford reported that, on the day after the election, South Vietnamese Vice President Nguyen Ky "almost contemptuously" told

U.S. Ambassador Ellsworth Bunker "that it might take two months—just about the length of time left to the Johnson administration—to resolve his government's problems with the negotiating format." President Thieu finally agreed to resume peace negotiations on January 25, 1969—just days after Richard Nixon's inauguration.

## WAS IT A CONSPIRACY?

Clark Clifford thought so. He said the secret Republican effort was "a plot—there is no other word for it—to help Nixon win the election by a flagrant interference in the negotiations."

• Clifford adds: "No proof...has ever turned up linking Nixon [himself] directly to the messages to Thieu....On the other hand, this chain of events undeniably began with Bui Diem's meeting with Richard Nixon in New York, and Nixon's closest adviser, John Mitchell, ran the Chennault channel personally, with full understanding of its sensitivity." (*The New Yorker*)

• "The activities of the Nixon campaign team," Clifford wrote, "went far beyond the bounds of justifiable political combat. They constituted direct interference in the activities of the executive branch and the responsibilities of the Chief Executive—the only people with authority to negotiate on behalf of the nation. [They] constituted a gross—and potentially illegal—interference in the national-security affairs by private individuals." (ibid.)

## FOOTNOTE

Why didn't LBJ or Hubert Humphrey turn Nixon's alleged interference with peace talks into a campaign issue? Bundy says that "in the circumstances, Mr. Johnson and Mr. Humphrey decided, separately, not to raise what would surely have been a highly divisive issue so late in the campaign."

## RECOMMENDED READING

• "Annals of Government: The Vietnam Years," by Clark Clifford and Richard Holbroke (*The New Yorker* magazine, May 6, May 13, and May 20, 1991). *A three-part article.*

# LITTLE NAYIRAH'S TALE

*Praise Allah and pass the press releases. Here's how Americans were bamboozled into fighting the Kuwaiti oil sheiks' war by a multimillion-dollar public relations campaign.*

W ho could forget the pretty young Kuwaiti refugee with tears running down her cheeks? While America was deciding whether to go to war against Iraq, on October 10, 1990, little "Nayirah" testified before a televised congressional hearing. Quietly sobbing at times, the teenager told how she had watched Iraqi troops storm a Kuwait City hospital, snatch fifteen infants from their incubators, and leave "the babies to die on the cold floor." Americans were appalled. People across the country joined George Bush in citing the story as a good reason why America should go to war.

## THE TRUTH OF THE MATTER

• As it turns out, Nayirah's story was a lie. Doctors at the Al-Adan Hospital in Kuwait City, where the incident allegedly took place, said it never happened.

• Congressional representatives conducting the hearing took pains to explain that Nayirah's last name was withheld "to protect her family from reprisals in occupied Kuwait." Also untrue. In fact, the young woman was not a refugee at all: she was the daughter of the Kuwaiti ambassador to the United States, and she likely wasn't in Kuwait at all when the atrocities supposedly happened.

• Actually, Nayirah had been coached by Hill and Knowlton, an American public relations firm headed by George Bush's former chief of staff, Craig Fuller. Hill and Knowlton selected her wardrobe, wrote her a script to memorize, and rehearsed with her for hours in front of video cameras.

## DISINFORMING THE WORLD

"Nayirah" was just one of many media stunts that sold a dubious war to the American people. According to "Nightline" reporter

Morgan Strong in an article he wrote for *TV Guide* in 1992:

• A second Kuwaiti woman testified before a widely televised session of the U.N. while the world body was deciding whether to sanction force against Iraq. She was identified as simply another refugee. But it turns out that she was the wife of Kuwait's minister of planning and was herself a well-known TV personality in Kuwait. Strong asked a Kuwaiti exile leader why such a high-profile person was passed off as just another refugee. "Because of her professional experience," the Kuwaiti replied, "she is more believable." In her testimony, she indicated that her experience was firsthand. "Such stories...I personally have experienced," she said. But when interviewed later, in Saudi Arabia, she admitted that she had no direct knowledge of the events.

• Hill and Knowlton personnel were allowed to travel unescorted through Saudi Arabia at a time when news reporters were severely restricted by the U.S. Army. The PR firm's employees interviewed Kuwaiti refugees, looking for lurid stories and amateur videos that fit their political agenda. Kuwaitis with the most compelling tales were coached and made available to a press hamstrung by military restrictions. Happy for any stories to file, reporters rarely questioned the stories of Iraqi brutality that the refugees told them.

• Hill and Knowlton also supplied networks with videotapes that distorted the truth. One Hill and Knowlton tape purported to show Iraqis firing on peaceful Kuwaiti demonstrators...and that's the way the news media dutifully reported it. But the incident on tape was actually Iraqi soldiers *firing back* at Kuwaiti resistance fighters.

## WAS IT A CONSPIRACY?
Says Strong: "These examples are but a few of the incidents of outright misinformation that found their way onto network news. It is an inescapable fact that much of what Americans saw on their news broadcasts, especially leading up to the Allied offensive against Iraqi-occupied Kuwait, was in large measure the contrivance of a public relations firm."

## RECOMMENDED READING
• "Fake News: Video Press Releases," by David Lieberman and Morgan Strong (*TV Guide*, Feb. 22, 1992)

# JOE McCARTHY'S LIST

*In the early 1950s, Senator Joseph McCarthy had Americans believing that Red Agents had infiltrated the U.S. government. But were the real conspirators the Communists—or McCarthy and his allies?*

On February 9, 1950, Joe McCarthy, a rumpled, ill-shaven junior senator from Wisconsin, made a Lincoln's Birthday speech to a Republican women's club in Wheeling, West Virginia. No one—not even McCarthy—considered it an important appearance. Yet that speech made Senator Joseph McCarthy the most feared man in America.

Waving a piece of paper before the group, McCarthy declared, "I have here in my hand a list of 205 names made known to the Secretary of State as being members of the Communist party, who are nevertheless still working and shaping policy in the State Department."

Republicans had been calling Democrats Communists for years. But before this, no one had ever claimed to know exactly how many Communists were in the government. McCarthy's speech made headlines. By the time he had given a similar speech in Salt Lake City and returned to Washington, newspapers from coast to coast had repeated his charges. The country was in an uproar.

The McCarthy Era—an American inquisition that ruined the lives of thousands of innocent citizens accused of being Communists, Communist dupes, or Communist sympathizers—had begun.

## THE McCARTHY ERA

• McCarthy's influence grew rapidly. As chairman of the Permanent Investigations Sub-Committee of a Senate Committee on Government Operations, he presided over a witch-hunt for Communists.

• Fear became his most potent weapon. "Many of those who came before McCarthy, as well as many who testified before the powerful House Un-American Activities Committee (HUAC), were willing to point fingers at others to save their own careers and reputations. To fight back was to be tarred with McCarthy's 'Communist sympathizer' brush....In this cynical atmosphere, laws of evidence and constitutional guarantees didn't apply." (*Don't Know Much About History*)

• For four years, McCarthy was as powerful as anyone in Washington. He forced President Eisenhower to clear appointments through him; the president even instituted loyalty programs for those working for the government, to prove that he, too, was tough on Communism.

## WAS IT A CONSPIRACY ? #1
*Did McCarthy and his cronies really believe there was a Communist conspiracy, or was it just an attempt to gain power?*

## SUSPICIOUS FACTS
• Early in 1950, McCarthy told friends he needed a gimmick to get reelected. He was in political hot water with voters because he had introduced no major legislation and had been assigned to no important committees. Newspaper correspondents in the capital had voted him "the worst in the Senate."

• According to Frederick Woltman, a friend of the senator's, McCarthy had made up the number of Communists on the spur of the moment during his Lincoln's Birthday speech—and had just as promptly forgotten it. Caught off-guard by the outcry, McCarthy and his advisors wracked their brains for some lead as to what he had said in the Wheeling speech. "He had no copy...he could not find the notes....The Senator's staff could find no one who could recall what he'd said precisely." (*Senator Joe McCarthy*)

• That may be why every time McCarthy counted Communists, he came up with a different number. The day after the Wheeling speech, he changed the number from 205 to 57 "card-carrying Communists." A week later, he stated before a Senate Foreign Relations subcommittee that he knew of "81 known Communists." The number changed to 10 in open committee hearings, 116 in an executive session, 121 at the end of a four-month investigation, and 106 in a June 6 Senate speech.

• Privately, friends say he treated the list of Communists as a joke. When asked, "Joe, just what did you have in your hand down there in Wheeling?" McCarthy gave his characteristic roguish grin and replied, "An old laundry list." (*The Nightmare Decade*)

• He was able to keep up the charade for so long because he would attack anybody who questioned his accuracy. For example: When the Majority Leader of the Senate, unable to get a firm number from McCarthy, asked if the newspaper accounts of his Wheeling speech were accurate, McCarthy replied indignantly, "I may say if the Senator is going to make a farce of this, I will not yield to him. I shall not answer any more silly questions of the Senator. This is too important, too serious a matter for that."

## WAS IT A CONSPIRACY? #2

*Was top lawman J. Edgar Hoover a co-conspirator—even though it meant he was breaking the law? (The FBI's charter prohibits it from getting involved in domestic politics.) Evidence suggests he was. In fact, without Hoover's covert support, McCarthy couldn't have kept up his attacks.*

## SUSPICIOUS FACTS

• McCarthy and Hoover were friends. They often dined together, and played the ponies frequently.

• According to Curt Gentry in his definitive study, *J. Edgar Hoover, the Man and the Secrets:* "On returning home from his speaking tour, McCarthy called J. Edgar Hoover and told him he was getting a lot of attention on the Communist issue. But, he frankly admitted, he had made up the numbers as he talked...and he asked if the FBI could give him the information to back him up." William Sullivan, who later became third in command at the FBI, protested that the Bureau didn't have sufficient evidence to prove that there was even *one* Communist in the State Department.

• Hoover—completely ignoring the FBI's charter—assigned FBI agents to gather domestic intelligence on his ideological enemies, poring over hundreds of Bureau security files to help support McCarthy's charges.

• According to Gentry, Hoover did even more: "He supplied speechwriters for McCarthy...[One Hoover aide] personally took McCarthy in hand and instructed him how to release a story just before press deadline, so that reporters wouldn't have time to ask for rebuttals. Even more important, he advised him to avoid the phrase 'card-carrying Communist,' which usually couldn't be proven, substituting instead 'Communist sympathizer' or 'loyalty risk,' which required only some affiliation, however slight."

• As McCarthy's star rose, Hoover helped the senator pick his staff. In fact, McCarthy hired so many ex-FBI agents that his office was reportedly nicknamed "the little FBI."

• Hoover was concerned about McCarthy's reckless charges—but not because they were untrue. A Hoover crony once noted: "I've spoken to J. Edgar Hoover about McCarthy. He said the only trouble with Joe is that he's not general enough in his accusations. He'll give some number like '274 Communists.' And then the FBI has to account for them. It makes the job a whole lot tougher."

## McCARTHY'S DOWNFALL

When McCarthy began attacking President Eisenhower and the Army in 1954, Hoover sensed that his own job might be in danger and ordered FBI aides not to help the senator further. Poorly prepared, McCarthy tried to bluff his way through the televised Army hearings, but this time he failed. Americans saw him as a bully and a liar, and the press turned on him. In December 1954, McCarthy became the fourth member in history to be censured by the U.S. Senate. In May 1957, he died of alcohol-related ailments.

## FOOTNOTE

Apparently, McCarthy depended on his co-conspirators at the FBI for more than information—he also needed their silence. Curt Gentry's painstaking research suggests that:

• J. Edgar Hoover had several fat FBI files on McCarthy that could have destroyed his career. Much of the information they contained eventually became known: that McCarthy was a boozer and a chronic gambler; that he had exaggerated and lied about his military record during World War II; "that as a Wisconsin judge he had granted quickie divorces for a price"; and that he had used campaign contributions to speculate in the stock market.

• Gentry adds that there was another, more secret file on McCarthy that only Hoover and a handful of other agents had ever seen: "It concerned McCarthy's involvement with young girls. Very young girls....Former close personal friends of the senator were quoted in the memorandum as cautioning other friends that they should never leave McCarthy alone in a room with young children, that there had been 'incidents'...involving girls under ten years of age."

## RECOMMENDED READING

• *J. Edgar Hoover: The Man and the Secrets*, by Curt Gentry (Norton, 1991). *An extraordinary book.*

• *The Life and Times of Joe McCarthy*, by Thomas Reeves (Stein & Day, 1982)

• *The Nightmare Decade: The Life and Times of Senator Joe McCarthy*, by Fred Cook (Random House, 1971)

• *Senator Joe McCarthy*, by Richard Rovere (Harcourt, Brace, Jovanovich, 1959)

## TALES OF THE CIA

"The CIA was never meant to do its own spying. And it certainly wasn't meant to conduct clandestine operations. The original purpose of the CIA was to summarize and analyze information turned up by other intelligence operations. It was a report-writing department.

"The CIA's one loophole is a fuzzy phrase in the 1947 law [that created the agency]. According to the bill signed by Truman, the Central Intelligence Agency would perform 'other functions' at the discretion of the National Security Council. The language of the act is fairly specific. Those 'other functions' relate only to intelligence. Nowhere does it mention clandestine operations. Even so, the 'other functions' clause has been the rationale for what has become...a fully functioning, government-sanctioned, secret society."

—Jonathan Vankin,
*Conspiracies, Cover-ups, and Crimes*

# ROCK 'n' REVOLUTION

*Positive proof that rock 'n' rollers are agents of the Communist conspiracy*

"Rock 'n' roll [is] Communist music...aiding and abetting demoralization among teenagers, in producing artificial neurosis and preparing them for riot and ultimately revolution to destroy the American form of government and the basic Christian principles governing our way of life.

—**David Noebel,
Rhythm, Riots & Revolution**

"Rock and roll is a means of pulling the white man down to the level of the Negro. It is part of a plot to undermine the morals of the youth of our nation."

—*The North Alabama
White Citizens Council*

"Adolf Hitler, ancient Greek orators, the Beatles and African witch doctors all practice a similar type of brainwashing....The primitive rhythms of a Stone Age tribe in Kenya and a band at a London ball produce the same trancelike emotions.... This method can be used for good or evil. Hitler used it and killed 20 million people."

—*Dr. William Sargant,
Royal Society of Medicine*

"The reason the Beatles and other folk-rock groups received such success was because they were backed by the Entertainment Section of the Communist Party....Paul McCartney of the Beatles was a member of the Young Communist League."

—*Chicago Police Undercover
Operative David Gumaer*

"The loud sounds and bright lights of today are tremendous indoctrination tools....If the right kind of beat makes you tap your foot, what kind of beat makes you curl your fist and strike?"

—*Frank Zappa*

"Some of the newer Beatles songs show an acute awareness of the principles of rhythm and brainwashing. Neither Lennon nor McCartney...had technical training in music. For them to have written some of their songs is like someone who has not had physics or math inventing the A-bomb...it is possible that this music is put together by behavioral scientists in some 'think tank.' "

—*Dr. Joseph Crow,
American Opinion magazine*

# HELPING HITLER

*Without help from U.S. industrialists, Hitler might never have been able to wage World War II.*

W hile most Americans were appalled by the Nazis and the rearming of Germany in the 1930s, some of America's most powerful corporations were more concerned about making a buck from their German investments. Here are a few examples of how U.S. industrialists supported Adolf Hitler and Nazi Germany.

### GENERAL MOTORS

**The Nazi connection:** GM, which was controlled by the du Pont family during the 1930s, owned 80% of the stock of Opel AG, which made 30% of Germany's passenger cars.

**Helping Hitler:** When Hitler's panzer divisions rolled into France and Eastern Europe, they were riding in Opel trucks and other equipment. Opel earned GM a hefty $36 million in the 10 years before war broke out, but because Hitler prohibited the export of capital, GM reinvested the profits in other German companies. At least $20 million was invested in companies owned or controlled by Nazi officials.

• GM may have even been plotting against the Roosevelt administration. According to Charles Higham in his book *Trading with the Enemy*, GM representatives met secretly with Baron Manfred von Killinger, Nazi Germany's West Coast chief of espionage, and Baron von Tippleskirsch, the Nazi consul general and Gestapo leader, in Boston on November 23, 1937. The group "signed a joint agreement showing total commitment to the Nazi cause for the indefinite future," and proclaimed that "in view of Roosevelt's attitude toward Germany, every effort must be made to remove him by defeat at the next election. Jewish influence in the political, cultural, and public life of America must be stamped out. Press and radio must be subsidized to smear the administration," and a führer, perhaps Sen. Burton Wheeler of Montana, should be in the White

House. Although the group tried to keep the agreement secret, Representative John M. Coffee of Washington found out about it and had the entire text of the agreement printed in the Congressional Record in August 1942.

### HENRY FORD, founder of the Ford Motor Company

**The Nazi connection:** Ford, an outspoken anti-Semite, was a big donor to the Nazi party.

**Helping Hitler:** Ford allegedly bankrolled Hitler in the early 1920s, at a time when the party had few other sources of income. In fact, the Party might have perished without Ford's sponsorship. Hitler admired Ford enormously. In 1922, *The New York Times* reported, "The wall beside his desk in Hitler's private office is decorated with a large picture of Henry Ford. In the antechamber there is a large table covered with books, nearly all of which are translations of books written and published by Henry Ford." (Hitler actually borrowed passages from Ford's book *The International Jew* to use in *Mein Kampf*). The same year, the German newspaper *Berliner Tageblatt*, a Hitler foe, called on the American ambassador to investigate Ford's funding of Hitler, but nothing was ever done. Ford never denied that he had bankrolled the führer. In fact, Hitler presented Nazi Germany's highest decoration for foreigners, the Grand Cross of the German Eagle, to Ford.

### THE CURTISS-WRIGHT AVIATION COMPANY

**The Nazi connection:** Employees of Curtiss-Wright taught dive-bombing to Hitler's *Luftwaffe*.

**Helping Hitler:** When Hitler's bombers terrorized Europe, they were using American bombing techniques. The U.S. Navy invented dive-bombing several years before Hitler came to power, but managed to keep it a secret from the rest of the world by expressly prohibiting U.S. aircraft manufacturers from mentioning the technique to other countries. However, in 1934, Curtiss-Wright, hoping to increase sales of airplanes to Nazi Germany, found a way around the restriction: instead of *telling* the Nazis about dive-bombing, it *demonstrated* the technique in air shows. A U.S. Senate investigation concluded, "It is apparent that American aviation companies did their part to assist Germany's air armament."

## STANDARD OIL

**The Nazi connection:** The oil giant developed and financed Germany's synthetic fuel program in partnership with the German chemical giant, I.G. Farben.

**Helping Hitler:** As late as 1934, Germany was forced to import as much as 85% of its petroleum from abroad. This meant that a worldwide fuel embargo could stop Hitler's army overnight. To get around this threat, Nazi Germany began converting domestic coal into synthetic fuel using processes developed jointly by Standard Oil and I.G. Farben.

• Standard taught I.G. Farben how to make tetraethyl-lead and add it to gasoline to make leaded gasoline. This information was priceless; leaded gas was essential for modern mechanized warfare. An I.G. Farben memo stated, "Since the beginning of the war we have been in a position to produce lead tetraethyl solely because, a short time before the outbreak of the war, the Americans had established plants for us ready for production and supplied us with all available experience. In this manner we did not need to perform the difficult work of development because we could start production right away on the basis of all the experience that the Americans had had for years." Another memo noted that "without tetraethyl-lead, present methods of warfare would not be possible." (*Trading with the Enemy*)

• Still another I.G. Farben memo chronicled Standard's assistance in procuring $20 million worth of aviation fuel and lubricants to be stockpiled for war: "The fact that we actually succeeded by means of the most difficult negotiations in buying the quantity desired by our government...and transporting it to Germany, was made possible only through the aid of the Standard Oil Co." (Note: According to a 1992 article in the *Village Voice*, Brown Brothers Harriman was the Wall Street investment firm that "arranged for a loan of tetraethyl lead to the Nazi *Luftwaffe*" in 1938. A senior managing partner of the firm was George Bush's father, Prescott Bush.)

• Standard Oil may also have undermined U.S. preparations for war. A congressional investigation conducted after World War II found evidence that Standard Oil had conspired with I.G. Farben to block American research into synthetic rubber, in exchange for a promise that I.G. Farben would give Standard Oil a monopoly on its rubber-synthesizing process. The investigation concluded that "Standard fully accomplished I.G.'s purpose of preventing the United States production by dissuading American rubber companies from undertaking independent research in developing synthetic rubber processes."

• Standard Oil may have also helped distribute pro-Nazi literature in Central America. According to Charles Higham in *Trading with the Enemy*, "on May 5, 1941, the U.S. Legation at Managua, Nicaragua, reported that Standard Oil subsidiaries were distributing *Epoca*, a publication filled with pro-Nazi propaganda. John J. Muccio, of the U.S. Consulate, made an investigation and found that Standard was distributing this inflammatory publication all over the world."

## INTERNATIONAL TELEPHONE AND TELEGRAPH

**The Nazi connection:** IT&T owned substantial amounts of stock in several German armaments companies, including a 28% stake in Focke-Wolf, which built fighter aircraft for the German army.

**Helping Hitler:** Unlike General Motors, IT&T was permitted to repatriate the profits it made in Germany, but it chose not to. Instead, the profits were reinvested in the German armaments industry. According to Anthony Sutton, author of *Wall Street and the Rise of Hitler*: "IT&T's purchase of a substantial interest in Focke-Wolf meant that IT&T was producing German planes used to kill Americans and their allies—and it made excellent profits out of the enterprise." IT&T also owned factories in the neutral countries of Spain, Portugal, Switzerland, and Sweden, which continued selling products to Axis countries.

• The relationship with the Nazis continued even after the U.S. entered the war. According to Charles Higham in *Trading with the Enemy*, the German army, navy, and air force hired IT&T to make "switchboards, telephones, alarm gongs, buoys, air raid warning devices, radar equipment, and 30,000 fuses per month for artillery shells used to kill British and American troops" *after* the bombing of Pearl Harbor. "In addition," Higham writes, "IT&T supplied ingredients for the rocket bombs that fell on London…high frequency radio equipment, and fortification and field communication sets. Without this supply of crucial materials, it would have been impossible for the German air force to kill American and British troops, for the German army to fight the Allies in Africa, Italy, France, and Germany, for England to have been bombed, or for Allied ships to have been attacked at sea."

## CHASE NATIONAL BANK (later Chase Manhattan Bank)

**The Nazi connection:** Chase operated branches in Nazi-occupied Paris and handled accounts for the German embassy as well as German businesses operating in France.

**Helping Hitler:** As late as 6 months before the start of World War II in Europe, Chase National Bank worked with the Nazis to raise money for Hitler from Nazi sympathizers in the U.S.

• According to Higham in *Trading with the Enemy,* "In essence, the Nazi government through the Chase National Bank offered Nazis in America the opportunity to buy German marks with dollars at a discount. The arrangement was open only to those who wished to return to Germany and would use the marks in the interest of the Nazis." Americans who were interested had to prove to the Nazi embassy that they supported Hitler and his policies.

• Cooperation with the Nazis continued even after America entered the war. For example, Higham says, Chase offices in Paris remained open long after other American banks had shut down, and even provided assistance to the Nazis: "The Chase Bank in Paris was the focus of substantial financing of the Nazi embassy's activities throughout World War II with the full knowledge of [Chase headquarters in] New York. In order to assure the Germans of its loyalty to the Nazi cause…the Vichy branch of Chase at Chateauneuf-sur-Cher were strenuous in enforcing restrictions against Jewish property, even going so far as to refuse to release funds belonging to Jews because they anticipated a Nazi decree with retroactive provisions prohibiting such a release." (*Trading with the Enemy*)

## RECOMMENDED READING

• *Facts and Fascism,* by George Seldes (out of print; check your public library)
• *Trading with the Enemy: An Exposé of the Nazi-American Money Plot 1933-1949,* by Charles Higham (Delacorte Press, 1983)

# OSWALD'S GUN?

*If Oswald really did leave his palm print on the alleged murder weapon, was it before or after he died?*

An hour after President Kennedy was killed in Dealey Plaza, Dallas police searching the sixth floor of the Texas School Book Depository reportedly found a rifle with a telescopic sight. It was flown to Washington that night. The next day, the FBI declared that it was the weapon used to kill the president.

Although the gun was a central part of the case against Lee Harvey Oswald, there was actually no physical evidence that he fired it that day. Paraffin tests taken by the Dallas police showed no nitrate residue from gunpowder on Oswald's cheek, which normally would have shown up if he had fired a rifle. And on November 23, 1963, after a fingerprint test, the FBI issued a report signed by J. Edgar Hoover that reported "No latent prints of value on...the clip in the rifle or the inner parts of the rifle."

Yet two days after Oswald was killed, the rifle was retested for prints, and his palm print was unexpectedly discovered on the rifle stock. This discovery became a critical part of the government's conclusion that Oswald was the sole assassin.

## WAS IT A CONSPIRACY?
*Did the U.S. government fabricate physical evidence to connect Oswald to the gun allegedly used in the assassination?*

## SUSPICIOUS FACTS
• On the afternoon of November 24, 1963—the day Oswald was killed—an FBI agent took the rifle back to Dallas.

• Very early the next morning, men identifying themselves as "agents" visited the Miller Funeral Home in Fort Worth, where Oswald's body lay. According to Paul Groody, director of the funeral home, "the agents asked us if they might have the room to themselves. After it was all over we found ink on Lee Harvey's hands, showing that they had fingerprinted and palm-printed him." He added: "We had a heck of a time getting the black fingerprint ink off."

• The next day, November 26, reporters asked Dallas District Attorney Henry Wade for proof of Oswald's guilt. He replied offhandedly, "Let's see…his fingerprints were found on the gun." It was the first mention of any such prints.

• Three days later, after the rifle and other physical evidence had been sent to Washington, D.C. again, the FBI reported that Oswald's palm print had been found on the stock of the rifle.

• According to Jim Marrs's book *Crossfire*, Dallas police Lieutenant John Carl Day claimed that he had "discovered the palm print shortly before turning the rifle over to the FBI about midnight on November 22." Yet the FBI reported no such evidence.

• In August 1964, Warren Commission general counsel J. Lee Rankin told the FBI that "there was a serious question in the minds of the Commission as to whether or not the palm impression that has been obtained from the Dallas Police Department is a legitimate… impression." He asked for more proof. The FBI responded by asking Lieutenant Day to sign an affidavit verifying that he had found Oswald's palm print on November 22, as he had asserted. Day declined.

• Nonetheless, the Warren Commission accepted the FBI's finding that the rifle had been used by Oswald to kill President Kennedy.

## PARTING SHOTS
• The rifle was a Mannlicher-Carcano, an Italian-made gun of WWII vintage. Some of its moving parts were rusty. No sharpshooter has been able to duplicate Oswald's three shots in 5.6 seconds with that bolt-action weapon.

• Ronald Simmon, chief of a U.S. Army ballistics lab, told the FBI and the Warren Commission that the rifle could not be accurately sighted—which made it unlikely that Oswald, or anyone else, could have used it to kill Kennedy. He explained that he had to "adjust the telescopic sight by the addition of two shims, one which tended to adjust the azimuth and one which adjusted an elevation." What's more, the sight was adjusted for a left-handed shooter; Oswald was right-handed.

# MARILYN

*According to her autopsy, Marilyn Monroe committed suicide.*
*But were John and Robert Kennedy fatal attractions?*

At 4:25 a.m. on August 5, 1962, Sergeant Jack Clemmons of the West Los Angeles Police Department received a call from Dr. Hyman Engelberg. "I am calling from the house of Marilyn Monroe," he said. "She is dead."

When Clemmons arrived at 12305 Helena Drive, he found the body lying face down on the bed. The coroner investigating the case ruled that Monroe, 36, had died from "acute barbiturate poisoning due to ingestion of overdose...a probable suicide."

## THE OFFICIAL STORY

• The night before, Monroe had gone to bed at about 8:00 p.m., too tired to attend a dinner party at actor Peter Lawford's beach house. A few hours later, Monroe's housekeeper, Eunice Murray, knocked on the star's bedroom door when she noticed a light was on inside, but got no response. Assuming that Monroe had fallen asleep, Murray turned in.

• When Murray awoke at about 3:30 a.m. and noticed the light still on in Monroe's room, she went outside to peek into the window. She saw Monroe lying nude on the bed in an "unnatural" position. Alarmed, Murray called Dr. Ralph Greenson, Monroe's psychiatrist, who came over immediately and broke into the bedroom. She also called Dr. Engelberg, Monroe's personal physician. After Engelberg pronounced her dead, they called the police.

## SUSPICIOUS FACTS

*From the start, there were conflicting versions of what had happened.*

### When Did Monroe Die?

Although Murray told the police she'd found the body after 3:30 a.m., there's evidence that Monroe died much earlier.

• Murray first told the police that she'd called Dr. Greenson at midnight; she later changed her story and said it had been 3:30

a.m. Sgt. Clemmons claims that when he first arrived on the scene, Engelberg and Greenson agreed that Murray had called them at about midnight. But in their official police statements, the doctors said they were called at 3:30 a.m.

• According to Anthony Summers in his book *Goddess*, Monroe's press agent, Arthur Jacobs, may have been notified of Monroe's death as early as 11:00 p.m., when he and his wife were at a Hollywood Bowl concert. According to Jacob's wife, Natalie, "We got the news long before it broke. We left the concert at once."

• In 1982, Peter Lawford admitted in a sworn statement that he learned of Monroe's death at 1:30 a.m., when her lawyer, Milton Rudin, called from the house to tell him about it.

• The ambulance crew summoned by the police noticed that Monroe's body was in "advanced rigor mortis," suggesting that she had been dead for 4 to 6 hours. That would mean she died about midnight.

### Where Did Monroe Die?

*Monroe supposedly died in her bedroom. But did she?*

• Monroe's body was stretched out flat on the bed, with the legs straight—not typical for a person who had overdosed on barbiturates. According to Sgt. Clemmons, barbiturate overdoses often cause a body to go into convulsions, leaving it contorted: "You never see a body with the legs straight. And I've seen hundreds of suicides by drug overdose." He speculated that she had been moved. (*The Marilyn Conspiracy*)

• William Shaefer, president of the Shaefer Ambulance Service, insists that "in the very early morning hours"—well before 3:00 a.m.—one of his ambulances was called to Monroe's house. She was comatose; the ambulance took her to Santa Monica Hospital, where she died. "She passed away at the hospital. She did not die at home." And he was certain it was Monroe: "We'd hauled her before because of [earlier overdoses of] barbiturates. We'd hauled her when she was comatose." (ibid.)

### How Did Monroe Die?

• Though Deputy Medical Examiner Thomas Noguchi speculated that Monroe had swallowed roughly 50 Nembutal pills, a common barbiturate, he found "no visual evidence of pills in the stomach or the small intestine. No residue. No refractile crystals." Yet, as Noguchi recounted in his book *Coroner*, toxicological reports of Monroe's blood confirmed his suspicions of an overdose.

• Why was there no pill residue in Monroe's body? Noguchi said that some "murder theorists" have suggested that an injection of barbiturates would have killed her without leaving pill residue. Other theorists have suggested that a suppository with a fatal dose of barbiturates would also leave no residue in her stomach. Or, at some point after the overdose, Monroe's stomach may have been pumped.

## MISSING EVIDENCE

*Why has so much evidence pertaining to Marilyn Monroe's case disappeared or been destroyed?*

### Phone Records

• Did Monroe try to call anyone the night she died? When a reporter for the *Los Angeles Herald Tribune* tried to get her phone records and find out, a phone company contact told him, "All hell is breaking loose down here! Apparently you're not the only one interested in Marilyn's calls. But the tape [of her calls] has disappeared. I'm told it was impounded by the Secret Service....Obviously somebody high up ordered it." (*Goddess*)

• In 1985, a former FBI agent claimed: "The FBI did remove certain Monroe records. I was on a visit to California when Monroe died, and became aware of the removal of the records from my Los Angeles colleagues. I knew there were some people there, Bureau personnel, who normally wouldn't have been there—agents from out of town. They were there on the scene immediately, as soon as she died, before anyone realized what had happened. It had to be on the instruction of somebody high up, higher even than Hoover...either the Attorney General or the President." (ibid.)

### Monroe's Diary

• Monroe supposedly kept a detailed diary. According to Robert Slatzer, a longtime friend of the actress, "For years, Marilyn kept scribbled notes of conversations to help her remember things." What things? Slatzer said the diary included her intimate discussions with people like Robert Kennedy. Monroe supposedly told Slatzer, "Bobby liked to talk about political things. He got mad at me one day because he said I didn't remember the things he told me." (*The Marilyn Conspiracy*)

• After Monroe's death, Coroner's Aide Lionel Grandison claimed that the diary "came into my office with the rest of Miss Monroe's personal effects" during the investigation. But by the next day the diary had vanished—and, according to Grandison, someone had removed it from the list of items that had been brought in for investigation. (ibid.)

### The Original Police Files

• In 1974, Captain Kenneth McCauley of the Los Angeles Police Department contacted the Homicide Department to ask about the files. They wrote back that the department had no crime reports in its files pertaining to Monroe's death. Even the death report had vanished.

• The files on Monroe may have disappeared as early as 1966. That year, Los Angeles Mayor Sam Yorty requested a copy of the files from the police department. The police declined, saying that the file "isn't here."

• What happened to the files? Lieutenant Marion Phillips of the Los Angeles Police Department claimed that he was told in 1962 that a high-ranking police official "had taken the file to show someone in Washington. That was the last we heard of it."

### MONROE AND THE KENNEDYS

• As part of his research for *Goddess*, the most authoritative book on Marilyn Monroe, Anthony Summers interviewed more than 600 people linked to her. He quotes friends, acquaintances, reporters, and politicians who confirm what many Americans already suspected—that Monroe had affairs with both John and Robert Kennedy.

• Apparently, John Kennedy met her through his brother-in-law, Peter Lawford. According to Lawford's third wife, Deborah Gould, "Peter told me that Jack...had always wanted to meet Marilyn Monroe; it was one of his fantasies." Quoting Lawford, Gould says Monroe's affair with John Kennedy began before he became president and continued for several years. (*Goddess*)

• According to Gould, JFK decided to end his affair with Monroe early in 1962. He sent his brother Robert to California to give her the news. "Marilyn took it quite badly," says Gould, "and Bobby went away with a feeling of wanting to get to know her better. At the beginning it was just to help and console, but then it led into an affair between Marilyn and Bobby." (ibid.)

• It didn't last long. By the summer of 1962, RFK began having second thoughts and decided to break off the affair. Monroe, already severely depressed, began acting erratically after being dumped by Bobby. She began calling him at home; when he changed his unlisted phone number to avoid her, she began calling him at the Justice Department, the White House, and even at the Kennedy compound in Hyannisport. When Bobby still refused to take her calls, Monroe threatened to go public with both affairs.

## WAS IT A CONSPIRACY?

**THEORY #1:** Monroe was distraught about her affairs and committed suicide. To protect the Kennedys from scandal, someone tried to cover up the suicide and cleaned up Monroe's house.

• Monroe may have become frantic when Robert Kennedy cut her off, perhaps—as some theorists guess—because she was pregnant.

• Fred Otash, a Hollywood private detective, claimed that a "police source" told him that weeks before her death Monroe had gone to Mexico to have an abortion. According to Otash, "An American doctor went down to Tijuana to do it, which made Monroe safe medically, and made the doctor safe from U.S. law," since at that time abortion was illegal in the U.S. But author Summers disagrees, noting: "There was no medical evidence to support the theory that Monroe had been pregnant." (*Goddess*)

• In any event, if Monroe was threatening to embarrass the Kennedys by going public about their affairs, it was cause for alarm. According to several reports, Robert Kennedy—who was vacationing with his family north of San Francisco—flew to Los Angeles on August 4 to meet with Monroe and try to calm her down. It didn't work.

• Terribly depressed, Monroe took a massive dose of sleeping pills, but not before calling Peter Lawford and saying, in a slurred voice,

"Say goodbye to Pat [Lawford's wife], say goodbye to Jack [JFK], and say goodbye to yourself, because you're such a nice guy."

• The call may have frightened Lawford so badly that he—and perhaps RFK—drove to Monroe's home. There he may have found her comatose and called an ambulance. (This would explain the Shaefer Ambulance claim of having taken Monroe to the hospital that night.) If Monroe had been taken to a hospital emergency room because of an overdose, her stomach would almost certainly have been pumped—which would account for the coroner's finding no "pill residue" in her stomach. When even the hospital's best attempts could not save Monroe, perhaps her body was returned to her bedroom in an effort to avoid controversy.

### The Cleanup

• No suicide note was ever found, nor was Monroe's personal phone book. Someone had probably "sanitized" her bedroom before the police came. The most likely person was Peter Lawford. His former wife Deborah Gould claimed, "He went there and tidied up the place, and did what he could, before the police and the press arrived." She also claimed that Lawford had found a suicide note and destroyed it. (*Goddess*)

• Lawford may also have hired detective Fred Otash to finish the cleanup. According to a security consultant who worked with Otash, Lawford hired him on the night of the death to "check her house, especially for papers or letters, that might give away her affairs with the Kennedys."

**THEORY #2: The Mob killed Monroe to embarrass—or even frame—Attorney General Robert Kennedy.**

• The Mob almost certainly knew of Monroe's affairs with the Kennedys: in fact, several reputable accounts claim that the star's house had been bugged by the Mob. By recording intimate moments between Monroe and Robert Kennedy, the syndicate may have hoped to blackmail the attorney general and thus end his prosecution of Teamsters boss Jimmy Hoffa and other gangsters.

• In their book *Double Cross*, Chuck and Sam Giancana—the brother and godson of Mob godfather Sam "Mooney" Giancana—allege that the Mafia eventually decided to kill Monroe and make it look like a suicide. Once the press learned of her recent affair with RFK, they figured, the public would decide that Monroe had killed herself over him. They figured a sex and suicide scandal would force him to resign in disgrace. So, the Mob waited for Kennedy to visit Monroe, in response to her increasingly desperate phone calls.

• Finally, Kennedy took the bait. According to the authors of *Double Cross*, when Sam Giancana learned that Bobby would be in California the weekend of August 4, he arranged the hit on Marilyn. The authors allege he chose Needles Gianola, an experienced killer, for the mission. Needles selected three men of his own to help him. Together they traveled to California "under Mooney's orders, to murder Marilyn Monroe."

• According to *Double Cross*, the mob had already bugged Marilyn's home, and the hit men were waiting at their secret listening post nearby when Kennedy arrived late Saturday night. They heard Bobby and another man enter the home and begin talking to Marilyn, who was extremely upset. Marilyn, the authors report, "became agitated—hysterical, in fact—and in response, they heard Kennedy instruct the man with him, evidently a doctor, to give her a shot to 'calm her down.' Shortly thereafter, the attorney general and the doctor left."

• *Double Cross* claims that the four killers waited until nightfall and then sneaked into Monroe's home to make the hit. Marilyn resisted, but was easily subdued because of the sedatives: "Camly, and with all the efficiency of a team of surgeons, they taped her mouth shut and proceeded to insert a specially 'doctored' Nembutal suppository into her anus. According to the authors, the killers waited for the lethal combination of barbiturates and chloral hydrate to take effect. Once she was totally unconscious, the men carefully removed the tape, wiped her mouth clean, and placed her across the bed. Their job completed, they left as quietly as they had come."

• Unfortunately for the conspirators, however, Kennedy's close friends and the FBI so thoroughly cleaned up Monroe's house and commandeered her phone records that any proof of the romance was eliminated. The Giancanas say that J. Edgar Hoover protected the Kennedys because, after keeping their secrets, he knew that they'd never fire him. *Double Cross* also alleges that the CIA was also in on the hit, but its reasoning is not convincing.

## FOOTNOTE

In 1982, after reinvestigating Marilyn Monroe's death, the Los Angeles District Attorney's Office released the following statement: "Marilyn Monroe's murder would have required a massive, in-place conspiracy covering all of the principals at the death scene on August 4 and 5, 1962; the actual killer or killers; the Chief Medical Examiner-Coroner; the autopsy surgeon to whom the case was fortuitously assigned; and almost all of the police officers assigned to the case, as well as their superiors in the LAPD...our inquiries and document examination uncovered no credible evidence supporting a murder theory."

## RECOMMENDED READING

- *Goddess*, by Anthony Summers (Macmillan, 1985)
- *The Marilyn Conspiracy*, by Mario Spiriglio (Pocket Books, 1986)
- *Double Cross*, by Sam and Chuck Giancana (Warner, 1992)

## MEDIA CONSPIRACIES

Historians now generally concede that the August 4, 1965, Gulf of Tonkin attack that LBJ used to escalate the Vietnam War never happened (see p. 108). But that didn't stop *Time* magazine's writers from whipping up a swashbuckling tale of the phantom battle:

> The weather in the gulf turned bad. Thunder rumbled across the water. Sporadic storms churned waves, and the two U.S. destroyers pitched and rolled....Through the darkness, from the west and south the intruders boldly sped. There were at least six of them, Russian-designed "Swatow" gunboats....At 9:52 p.m. they opened fire on the destroyers with automatic weapons....
>
> For 3-1/2 hours the small boats attacked in pass after pass. Ten enemy torpedoes sizzled through the water. Each time the skippers, tracking the fish by radar, maneuvered to evade them. Gunfire... smells and shouts stung the air. Two of the enemy boats went down. Then, at 1:30 a.m., the remaining PTs ended the fight, roared off through the black night to the north.
>
> **—*Time*, August 14, 1964**

# LAW & ORDER

*Many of our most prominent conspirators think of themselves as extremely patriotic citizens. So how do they justify illegal, unconstitutional actions? Here are some thoughts on the subject.*

"Justice is incidental to law and order."
—J. Edgar Hoover

"When the president does it, that means it is not illegal."
—Richard Nixon

"You don't have many suspects who are innocent of a crime. That's contradictory. If a person is innocent of a crime, then he is not a suspect."
—Attorney General Ed Meese

(*Testimony in the Iran-Contra hearings, 1987*)
**John Nields** (House chief counsel): "What was the reason to withhold information from Congress when they inquired about it?"
**Admiral Poindexter:** "I simply didn't want any outside interference."
**Nields:** "Now, the outside interference you're talking about was Congress, and I take it the reason they were inquiring was precisely so that they could fulfill...their constitutional function, to pass legislation one way or another, isn't that true?"
**Poindexter:** "Yes, I suppose that's true."

(*Iran-Contra hearings, 1987*)
**Sen. George Mitchell:** "During your discussions with Mr. Casey, Mr. McFarlane, and Mr. Poindexter about the plan, did a question ever rise among you as to whether what was being proposed was legal?"
**Oliver North:** "Oh, no, I don't think it was—I mean, first of all, we operated from the premise that everything we do is legal."

"Sometimes you have to go above the written law, I believe."
— *Fawn Hall,*
*Oliver North's Secretary*

"I think it's a neat idea."
—*Oliver North, commenting on illegally funding the contras with profits from arms deals with Iran*

# YELLOW RAIN

*Biochemical weapons are so repugnant to the American public that the Reagan White House needed a powerful excuse to resume producing them. It found the excuse in an old scapegoat—the Soviet Union.*

I n September 1981, Secretary of State Alexander Haig derailed arms talks with the Soviet Union when he accused it of producing and stockpiling biological weapons in violation of international accords. The U.S. had "physical evidence," said Haig, "that the Soviets and its allies have been using lethal chemical weapons in Laos [Cambodia] and Afghanistan." (*The New Yorker*)

Haig's charges reopened an area of arms control most people thought was closed for good: biochemical weapons. America hadn't produced any new chemical weapons since 1969, when President Nixon renounced them as "repugnant to the conscience of mankind."

### HAIG'S CHARGES

• In March 1982, Haig issued a report to Congress in which he claimed that 251 toxic-gas attacks in Laos had killed more than 6,000 people—mostly Hmong tribe members.

• Based on testimony from Hmong refugees, the report concluded that the toxic clouds—usually sprayed from aircraft—resembled a "yellow rain" and caused "nausea, dizziness, rapid heartbeat, chest pain...and a feeling of intense heat and burning on the skin." Victims of the attacks also suffered from "intense reddening of the eyes, bleeding gums, convulsions, and vomiting of blood" within hours of being exposed. (ibid.)

• Haig's report claimed that the yellow rain contained a deadly group of mycotoxins—fungal poisons—called *trichothecenes*. Scientists who analyzed the yellow-rain samples said that the toxins were mixed with a sticky base very much like pollen—in fact, all the samples actually contained levels of insect pollen. It seemed diabolically simple: by sticking to a victim's skin, the toxins could penetrate more easily. One government scientist called the samples "a very clever, clever mixture."

## WHAT HAPPENED

• The Soviet press called the Haig report "a dirty lie." President Reagan and his advisors, meanwhile, pushed Congress to provide funds to renew U.S. production of chemical weapons.

• Despite heavy pressure from the Pentagon, however, Congress refused. But the administration persisted, reintroducing legislation to resume production of chemical weapons in 1983, 1984, and 1985.

• Finally, in 1985, after three tie-breaking votes by Vice President Bush in the Senate, the Reagan administration got what it wanted. In December 1987, the United States began producing its first chemical weapons in 18 years and became the only country making binary chemical weapons.

## SUSPICIOUS FACTS

### Physical Evidence

• Haig's "physical evidence" was scant. In fact, the largest piece of evidence was a single leaf and stem allegedly found at an attack site in Cambodia. It was forwarded in July 1981 from the Armed Forces Medical Intelligence Center at Fort Dedrick, Maryland, to Dr. Chester Mirocha at the University of Minnesota. Dr. Mirocha reported that it contained various combinations of trichothecenes.

• But in 1982, scientists at the U.S. Army's Chemical Systems Laboratory at Edgewood Arsenal analyzed eighty samples of what was purported to be yellow rain—including remnants of the sample Dr. Mirocha tested—and found "no traces of any trichothecenes in this or any of the samples."

### Anecdotal Evidence

• The U.S. government's evidence of chemical warfare in southeast Asia was mostly anecdotal. Most of it came from interviews with Hmong tribespeople in Thai refugee camps. Journalists familiar with the Hmong people called them unreliable witnesses. A former editor of *National Geographic* who had traveled widely in Southeast Asia explained the problem in *The New Yorker*:

> If you go into a Thai refugee camp, the Hmong will give you horror stories about yellow rain because they know it's the kind of thing that gets attention and maybe a visa out. They want to come to the United States, and we want to hear about yellow rain—[so] they'll tell

us about it....I guarantee that the Hmong are some of the best storytellers on earth. They can make up stories faster than you and I can write them down.

## Field Reports

• For two years a team of chemical- and biological-warfare specialists cabled reports back to Washington from Southeast Asia. Their reports—which were never made public—suggest that U.S. government claims of Russian chemical warfare may have been deliberate lies. For example:

√ One report said that when the team started to question a Khmer Rouge guerrilla who had allegedly been gassed he replied, "Why do you want to interview me? I will tell you the same story as the rest, since we have been ordered to do so by our leader." (*The New Yorker*)

√ Another cable said: "Neither the team chief nor the Thai... interpreter found [names of Hmong deleted] to be credible witnesses of CBW attacks, they seem to be fabricating their accounts during the interviews....The question is not whether Hmong refugees lie but whether Hmong refugees are accurate reporters of reality." (ibid.)

## Sticky Business

• So what was the yellow rain mentioned in so many Hmong accounts? Noting that the Army's few samples of "sticky yellow material" contained large amounts of pollen, a group of scientists investigated. In Southeast Asia, they found and collected their own "yellow rain" from natural sources and found that it matched government samples exactly.

• Matthew Meselson, a professor of biochemistry and molecular biology at Harvard University was among the first to suggest that yellow rain was really bee poop. Local bees, "confined to their nests for the winter...take part in what are known as mass cleansing flights. In those flights, the bees release waste matter that has built up in their abdomens during their winter confinement." (*The New Yorker*)

• Any toxins found in the samples seemed to simply have been mold that grew on the bee droppings. The government apparently knew that, but chose to discredit the scientists who advanced the bee-poop hypothesis by attacking their patriotism and professionalism. Several leading national newspapers also disparaged them.

• *The Wall Street Journal*, for example, declared that "among men of affairs the 'yellow rain' debate is closed." But no one ever disproved the bee-poop hypothesis.

## WAS IT A CONSPIRACY?

*Did the government knowingly spread the phony "yellow rain" story to resume production of chemical weapons?*

• The Reagan administration never looked for *scientific* proof that the Soviets had violated chemical warfare agreements. The prestigious journal *Foreign Policy* noted that "the president's science adviser, the Department of Defense Scientific Board, and the National Academy of Sciences were not asked to evaluate the evidence before policy [to resume production of chemical weapons] was set. The Secretary of State's dramatic announcement...locked the administration into a political position."

• Then the Reagan White House pressured the press to spread its fabricated claims of Soviet violations: "The Administration asked the *Wall Street Journal* to play up the story, and the *Journal* ran some 50 articles in the 18 months following the initial U.S. accusation." (*Z Magazine*, February 1991)

• The administration committed itself to an expanded chemical arsenal that had no military justification. According to the *Defense Monitor*, the U.S. *already* had stockpiles of "enough chemical weapons to kill everyone in the world 5,000 times over."

• The Reaganites' public statements against the proliferation of chemical weapons contradicted their public policies in the Middle East. The *Defense Monitor* pointed out that "while condemning the use of chemical weapons, the Reagan Administration opposed congressional efforts to punish Iraq with economic sanctions."

• Why was the White House so anxious to resume production of chemical weapons? Perhaps because the chemical industry was among the biggest political action committees to contribute to Reagan's victories in 1980 and 1984. The *Columbia Journalism*

*Review*, for one, observed that chemical industry executives got preferred treatment from the administration: "Industry executives have periodically met secretly with officials of the White House's Office of Management and Budget to discuss EPA regulations that would affect their profits…and suggest revisions in these regulations to reduce costs to their industry." Making chemical weapons is a high-volume business with potential profits as high as $50 billion, worldwide.

## FOOTNOTES

• Historically, the U.S. chemical industry has fought international controls on chemical weapons. The United States praised the 1925 Geneva Protocol to ban wartime use of chemical weapons…but did not sign it until 1974. It was the last major nation to do so.

• Although George Bush called for a United Nations chemical-weapons treaty that allowed inspections "anywhere, anytime, [with] no right of refusal," he reversed himself shortly after production resumed. The turnabout, according to *The New York Times*, "was based on fears that other nations might…pry into extremely sensitive military intelligence under the guise of looking for clandestine stocks of chemical weapons."

## RECOMMENDED READING

• "Annals of the Cold War: The Yellow-Rain Complex," by Thomas Whiteside (*The New Yorker*, Feb. 11 and Feb. 18, 1991)

• *Z Magazine*, 116 St. Botolph St., Boston, MA 02115. (Feb., 1991)

"People who shut their eyes to reality simply invite their own destruction."
—James Baldwin

# FOOD FOR THOUGHT

"The environmental movement is one of the subversive element's last steps. They've gone after the military and the police and now they're going after our parks and playgrounds."
—*Mrs. Clarence Howard, Daughters of the American Revolution*

"Gosh, we're awed at how a story can be told and retold by the anti-cigarette people, and how little attention is given in the press to claims *for* cigarettes."
—*James C. Bowling, assistant to the president, Philip Morris Co.*

"How can we account for our present situation unless we believe that men high in this government are concerting to deliver us to disaster? This must be the product of a great conspiracy, a conspiracy on a scale so immense as to dwarf any previous venture in the history of man. A conspiracy of infamy so black that, when it is finally exposed, its principals shall be forever deserving of the maledictions of all honest men."
—*Senator Joseph McCarthy, 1951*

"The West created James Bond to soften up the world for the gas wars in Vietnam, the murder of civil rights demonstrators in America, and the blackmailing of young African nationalist states."
—Junge Welt, *the East German youth paper*

"We have stated repeatedly …that the trouble in the South over integration is Communist contrived; that Communist agents, working largely behind the scenes, are using every trick and skill in the Communist repertoire to foment bitterness between blacks and white members of communities where no bitterness existed before and that the Communists thoroughly intend to fan…flames of 'civil disorder' into…civil war."
—*American Opinion* magazine, 1958

"The more solid the information from a defector, the more you should not trust him, and the more you should suspect he has something to hide."
—*James Angleton, CIA Counter-Intelligence*

# SUSPICIOUS DEATH #4: ROBERT MAXWELL

---

*Found bobbing in the Atlantic, Robert Maxwell left behind*
*an ocean of debt. Did he fall, did he jump—or was he pushed?*

The deceased: Robert Maxwell, self-made billionaire, newspaper baron, and World War II hero. Maxwell has been described as "the Citizen Kane of his time."

How he died: On November 5, 1991, Maxwell was sailing off the coast of the Canary Islands on his 180-foot yacht, *Lady Ghislane*. Sometime during the night, he went for a stroll on the deck. He was never seen alive again. Seven hours after the crew reported him missing, the body of the 68-year-old publisher was found floating in the Atlantic. The preliminary autopsy report, prepared by Spanish authorities, stated that he had probably died of a heart attack while on board and fallen over the side of the ship.

## SUSPICIOUS FACTS

• According to one witness on the *Lady Ghislane* that night, the boat had been shadowed by "another unidentified yacht" the evening before Maxwell died.

• The Spanish autopsy was unusually quick. According to newspaper reports, "in less than 30 hours after a helicopter brought it ashore, the body had been subjected to an autopsy and was released to the undertakers, a process that usually takes seven to ten days." And although the coroner speculated that Maxwell died of a heart attack, he found "no evidence of such an attack."

• A second autopsy, conducted only hours before burial by Israeli doctors, came to a different conclusion. It found that "the late press baron suffered serious injuries to the head, shoulder, abdomen, and spinal cord." One of the doctors involved in the autopsy concluded that Maxwell suffered from "traumatisms before his death."

• A French expert who viewed the Israeli autopsy photographs speculated that Maxwell "was struck by a violent blow to the back of the skull, no doubt with the aid of a blunt instrument." Another expert suggested that he died "either from a fall following a collapse or malaise, or from a blow to the face leading to a fall and a loss of consciousness."

## POSSIBLE CONCLUSIONS

• **He committed suicide.** In the months before his death, Maxwell had engaged in a desperate pyramid scheme to keep his business empire afloat. Maxwell looted pension funds, took out fraudulent loans, and manipulated stocks, but to no avail; by November 1991, his companies were more than $4.4 billion in debt. Unable to face the bankruptcy and ruin that were only weeks away, he may have killed himself by jumping off his boat.

• **He had a heart attack.** Maxwell was a sick man. He was grossly overweight, had severe hardening of the arteries and lung tissue, and had had half of his left lung removed 30 years earlier. He ignored his health problems, which only made them worse. According to one report, "the overweight entrepreneur apparently followed no diet or regular treatment, and appeared to be as impulsive and disorderly in caring for his health as he was in his business dealings." The stress of his collapsing business empire may have proved too great a stress: while on deck he could have suffered a massive heart attack, slumped over the rail, and fell into the sea.

• **He was murdered.** A few months before Maxwell died, journalist Seymore Hersh, in his book *The Sampson Option*, linked the press baron to Mossad, the Israeli spy agency, and its secret weapons deals with Iran. Ari Ben-Menashe, a self-proclaimed Iran-Contra conspirator, was even more specific, stating that "the publisher had been the money launderer in Israel's shipment of arms to Iran and may have been murdered for his knowledge."

"Why shouldn't the truth be stranger than fiction? Fiction, after all, has to make sense."

—Mark Twain

# IRAN-CONTRA ROGUES' GALLERY

*Many of the key players in the Iran-Contra scandal were seasoned CIA operatives. Was the whole operation, in fact, an Agency job?*

When the Iran-Contra scandal hit the news, it looked like the Reagan administration might come crashing down.

It was bad enough that presidential aides in the White House had been selling arms to America's avowed enemy, Iran. But even worse, profits from those sales were illegally diverted to fund the secret contra army in Nicaragua.

Some people were talking impeachment. But in the nick of time, a special commission appointed by President Reagan reassured the public that government still heeded the will of the people.

The commission, headed by Senator John Tower of Texas, found that the Iran-Contra scandal was "a rogue operation" run by "reckless cowboys" within the National Security Council. In other words, the people who ran Iran-Contra were just a few misguided individuals. Or were they? Was the scandal a rare look at the way our government really works behind the scenes? Look closely and you'll find the men who ran—and may still be running—the biggest CIA operations in the last 45 years:

## WILLIAM CASEY

**CIA connection:** Casey was a spy in the OSS, the precursor of the CIA, during World War II. While making his fortune as a securities lawyer, Casey kept up his ties with the Agency until 1981, when he was named its director by Ronald Reagan.

**Role in Iran-Contra:** Architect of the CIA's war against the Sandinista government. When Congress cut off funds for the war, Casey masterminded illegal efforts to keep it going. When Congress voted to end the CIA's arms shipments to the contras, for example, Casey got the Pentagon to *give* the contras $12 million in "surplus" military equipment. And when Congress next prohibited *all* military aid to the contras in 1984, Casey suggested to Colonel Oliver North that he hire ex-CIA agent Richard Secord to keep the war alive.

## MAJOR GENERAL JOHN SINGLAUB, U.S. ARMY (RET.)

**CIA connection:** "An OSS veteran and then CIA Officer responsible for China and Korea, Singlaub later directed secret CIA-linked infiltration into North Vietnam, Laos, and Cambodia, during the Vietnam War—provocative raids conducted with no consultation of Congress" (*The Iran-Contra Connection*).

Richard Secord and Oliver North worked with Singlaub in Southeast Asia. (ibid.)

**Role in Iran-Contra:** As chairman of the World Anti-Communist League (WACL), an association that includes "Latin American dictators, death squad leaders and neo-fascists," Singlaub helped Oliver North raise $1 million a month in 1984 and 1985, after Congress cut off aid to the contras. (*Iran-Contra Scandal Cards*)

He may also have advised North how to run the secret war in Nicaragua. Singlaub's specialty was reportedly unconventional warfare, including "sabatoge, terrorism, assassination, guerilla warfare... psychological warfare, economic sabotage, and disinformation." (ibid.)

## MAJOR GENERAL RICHARD SECORD, USAF (RET.)

**CIA connection:** Between 1963 and 1968, Secord flew more than 285 combat missions in Southeast Asia. As the airwing commander for the CIA's secret war in Laos, he was in charge of all tactical air operations. Secord allegedly resigned from the Agency in 1983 when he was linked to renegade CIA officer Edwin Wilson, who had been convicted of smuggling explosives to Libya.

**Role in Iran-Contra:** Secord set up the complicated network that moved high-tech weapons to Iran, put profits from the arms sales into secret bank accounts, and eventually got equipment to the contras. This private, for-profit network was called "The Enterprise." "Within two years," says one report, "the 'Enterprise' had five airplanes, twenty pilots on contract, two airfields, a boat, a stockpile of guns and military equipment, and numerous shell companies and secret bank accounts—all for the purpose of conducting covert military actions for [Oliver North's] National Security Council." Secord also reportedly "shook down the government of Saudi Arabia for funds for the contras." (ibid.)

## THEODORE SHACKLEY ("THE BLONDE GHOST")

**CIA connection:** After the CIA-planned Bay of Pigs invasion failed, says one account, "Shackley became CIA station chief in Miami. There he directed Operation Mongoose, which conducted sabotage and assassination raids on Cuba." From 1966 to 1968, Shackley was Station Chief in Laos; he then "spent four years in Saigon directing Operation Phoenix, a program designed to 'neutralize' communist sympathizers." More than 40,000 civilians were reportedly killed. During the Laotian operations, Shackley worked closely with Singlaub, Secord, Tom Clines, and Felix Rodriguez.

Director of the CIA's worldwide covert operations under George Bush from 1976 to 1977, Shackley reportedly would have become director of the agency if Gerald Ford had been reelected in 1976.

**Role in Iran-Contra:** A crucial yet mysterious figure in the operation. Some researchers think that Shackley's contacts with Iranian-born arms dealers paved the way for arms-for-hostages trades with Teheran and that Shackley also helped assemble the secret team that ran the contra war.

## THOMAS CLINES

**CIA connection:** Shackley's deputy in Laos. Clines reportedly supervised the creation of a secret army of Hmong tribesmen to fight Laotian Communist forces. Interesting sidelight: The CIA's secret Laotian operations—which fielded a 30,000-man army—"were partially financed with opium profits." (*Iran-Contra Scandal Cards*)

**Role in Iran-Contra:** In 1986, Clines "helped Secord arrange clandestine arms deliveries to the contras out of Portugal, recruited ex-CIA pilots for the supply operation and helped Oliver North obtain a ship used in the attempt to rescue American hostages in Lebanon." (*Iran-Contra Connection*)

## FELIX RODRIGUEZ

**CIA connection:** His CIA ties go back to the Bay of Pigs invasion. He was a member of the CIA's Operation 40 Assassination Unit, also called "the shooter team," led by E. Howard Hunt, which was formed to assassinate Fidel and Raul Castro and Che Guevera. He next went to Vietnam where "he flew hundreds of missions for the CIA in Vietnam as a helicopter pilot and counter-insurgency expert. His superior officer was Donald Gregg." (*Iran-Contra Scandal Cards*)

**Role in Iran-Contra:** Rodriguez was one of North's key people in the field, managing secret contra supply operations from an air base inside El Salvador.

## DONALD GREGG

**CIA connection:** Gregg served in Saigon under Shackley and Clines. A seasoned agency veteran, in 1979 he was appointed to Jimmy Carter's National Security Council as a CIA liaison.

**Role in Iran-Contra:** National Security Advisor to Vice President George Bush during the Iran-Contra operation. According to *Covert Action* magazine, Gregg worked closely with Oliver North and Felix Rodriguez, acting as an NSC-CIA liaison. "Between 1983 and 1986, Felix Rodriguez had 17 meetings with Gregg, three of which included Vice President George Bush." (ibid.)

Gregg introduced Rodriguez to Oliver North. Nonetheless, he asserted that he knew nothing of Rodriguez's involvement in the contra supply network until August 8, 1986. Gregg did admit, however, that he and Rodriguez were "fast friends."

## OLIVER NORTH

**CIA connection:** No formal ties known. However, he was involved in "counterinsurgency activities in Vietnam, where he allegedly served at least briefly with Singlaub and Secord," according to *The Iran-Contra Connection*.

North and Secord also worked together during Jimmy Carter's ill-fated attempt to rescue the hostages in Iran (see p. 81).

**Role in Iran-Contra:** National Security Council coordinator, fundraiser, and self-described "fall guy" to protect the president (and the CIA) when the operation was exposed to the public.

## RECOMMENDED READING

• *The Iran-Contra Connection: Secret Teams and Covert Operations in the Reagan Era*, by Jonathan Marshall, Peter Dale Scott, and Jane Hunter (South End Press, 1987)

• *Iran-Contra Scandal Trading Cards*, by Salim Yaqub and Paul Brancato. Available from Eclipse Enterprises, P.O. Box 1099, Forestville, CA 95436.

# JUST SAY NO

*When officials deny that a conspiracy has occurred, can you believe them? Here are a few examples to consider.*

"The charge has been made that the United States has shipped weapons to Iran as ransom payment for the release of American hostages in Lebanon, that the United States undercut its allies and secretly violated American policy against trafficking with terrorists. Those charges are utterly false."
—*Ronald Reagan, 1986*

"The CIA had nothing to do with the [Chilean] coup, to the best of my knowledge and belief, and I only put in that qualification in case some madman appears down there who, without instructions, talked to somebody."
—*Henry Kissinger,
denying U.S. involvement
in the overthrow of Chile's
President Allende*

"There was no blacklist....That was a lot of horseshit....The only thing our side did that was anywhere near blacklisting was just running a lot of people out of the business..."
—*John Wayne,
unclear on the concept*

"U.S. military exercise activities have no connection with anti-Sandinistas."
—*The Pentagon,
responding to questions from
the House Committee on
Appropriations in 1984*

"We did not—repeat, did not —trade weapons or anything else for hostages, nor will we."
—*Ronald Reagan, 1986*

"The nation must to a degree take it on faith that we who lead the CIA are honorable men, devoted to the nation's service."
—*CIA Director Richard
Helms, denying that the CIA
gave U.S. citizens LSD*

"We are not telling lies or doing any of these disinformation things."
—*Ronald Reagan,
discussing Iran-Contra*

"Your President is not a crook."
—*Richard Nixon*

"The agency does not violate U.S. law."
—*CIA spokesperson*

# MARTIN LUTHER KING, JR.

*And they said to one another, "Behold, this dreamer cometh.*
*Come now, therefore, and let us slay him...and we shall see*
*what will become of his dreams." —Genesis 37: 19-20*

Martin Luther King, Jr. was one of the most charismatic leaders of the civil rights struggle. By successfully organizing nonviolent boycotts, marches, strikes, and voter-registration drives, he unified the African American community and demonstrated its economic and political power. Beatings, police dogs, fire hoses, prison—none of them stopped him. In October 1964, the world honored his commitment to peaceful change by making him the youngest person ever to receive the Nobel Peace Prize.

Dr. King was deeply troubled when a March 28, 1968, protest he organized on behalf of Memphis sanitation workers turned violent, injuring 60 people and killing one youth. But he was not deterred. He returned to Memphis a week later, intending to lead another, peaceful, march.

At 6 p.m. on April 4, King stood on the second-floor balcony of the Lorraine Motel smoking a cigarette and talking to aides in the parking lot below. Suddenly, a shot rang out and King was struck by a single fragmenting bullet, which tore open his throat and severed his spine. He lost consciousness almost immediately and was declared dead an hour later.

King's killer escaped. According to the police, as the assailant fled from a cheap rooming house across the street from King's motel, he dumped a bundle onto the sidewalk and then sped off in a white Mustang. The bundle, wrapped in a green bedspread, contained personal items and the 30.06 Remington rifle allegedly used to kill King.

## THE OFFICIAL STORY

• For more than two weeks, law enforcement agencies didn't know whom they were chasing. The flophouse room had been rented in the name of "John Willard." It was an alias—as were "John L. Rayns," "Eric Starvo Galt," "Harvey Lowmyer," and "Ramon George Sneyd"—all names used by the fugitive.

• Finally, on April 19, the FBI announced that the fugitive was James Earl Ray, a prisoner who had escaped from Missouri State Prison the year before. Supposedly Ray had killed King because he hated blacks. He was finally arrested on June 8, 1968, at London's Heathrow Airport—just two days after Robert Kennedy's murder in Los Angeles. Ray was extradited and returned home to a country teeming with conspiracy theories and anxiously awaiting answers at his trial.

• There was no trial. At a March 1969 hearing, which lasted 144 minutes, Ray pled guilty, waived all rights to a future trial, and was sentenced to 99 years in prison. But the outcome satisfied no one, least of all Ray, who quickly recanted his guilty plea and accused his lawyer of cutting a deal with the judge. (Ray said he had pleaded guilty solely to avoid the electric chair.) To this day, Ray calls for the trial he never got. And questions that should have been answered in 1969 still remain unanswered.

## UNANSWERED QUESTIONS
*Ray's aborted trial was just one of many bizarre events connected to King's slaying.*

### Was King Tricked into Staying at the Lorraine Motel?
• King had never stayed at the Lorraine before. Because of the many death threats he had received in Memphis, he usually stayed downtown at the Claridge, a relatively secure hotel across from City Hall. The Lorraine was in a run-down part of town.

• King's fatal decision to stay there was probably prompted by hostile newspaper editorials mocking his "hasty exit" to a white-owned Holiday Inn when the March 28 protest turned violent. The editorials called King "a Judas" for not staying at the "fine Motel Lorraine...owned and patronized exclusively by Negroes," and said, "There will be no boycott of white merchants for King, only for his followers." Sensitive to its community image, King's group booked his next stay at the Lorraine.

• In hindsight, those editorials look suspicious. According to

Michael Newton in his book *The King Conspiracy*, these taunting quotes were taken verbatim from a press release written by the FBI's Domestic Intelligence Division and sent to Memphis newspapers.

- Was King set up?

  √ Certainly the Lorraine Motel, with its balconies facing the street, was less secure than the Claridge.

  √ The second-story rooms, which could be watched from farther away, were even less secure than the ground-floor rooms.

  √ Yet, two days before King's arrival, a man introducing himself as an "advance security man for Dr. King showed up at the Lorraine and insisted that King's reservation be changed from a ground-floor room to one on the second floor....In the wake of the assassination, it was determined that no such advance man had been dispatched to Memphis for King's visit, and no one in his entourage matched the description." (*The King Conspiracy*)

  √ Finally, anyone wanting to find King would have had an easy time of it. Memphis TV stations and newspapers not only announced that King would be staying at the Lorraine, they also broadcast and printed his room number.

### Where Was King's Police Protection?

- The FBI knew of at least 50 serious threats made against King's life. And the Memphis Police normally provided police protection for him. But suddenly, at 5 p.m. on April 3, the day before the shooting, "King was stripped of police security; the [officers assigned to protect him] departed...never to return." (*The Martin Luther King Assassination, New Revelations on the Conspiracy and Cover-Up, 1968-1991*, by Philip Melanson)

- In hindsight, withdrawing security was unwise, but the police offered a credible reason for doing so: Dr. King's aides were not cooperating. More than once, for example, King's drivers tried to give the slip to police cruisers assigned to follow them. (King's people suspected undercover police agents of sparking the March 28 riot.) And even if the security detail had been in place, it could have done little to protect King from a long-range sniper.

- According to Melanson, a more serious—and suspicious—security lapse was the Memphis Police Department's decision to pull special TACT (tactical) units five blocks away from the Lorraine Motel. Supposedly "an unnamed member of Dr. King's entourage" had asked that the TACT units be withdrawn. But, as Melanson points out, those TACT units were not there to protect King in the first place. Rather, the anti-riot squads were there "to protect the city of Memphis from King," whom they considered an outside agitator. It's not likely that the units would have pulled back at Dr. King's request. The pullback was critical, however: "Had the TACT vehicles remained in place, swarming around the Lorraine, it would have been extremely difficult for anyone to escape the crime scene." (*The Martin Luther King Assassination*)

• Some theorists who think King was killed by a conspiracy cite as evidence the allegations of Edward Reddit, one of two black police officers stationed in a firehouse near King's motel to keep an eye on the black leader. The day of the assassination, Reddit was removed from duty and placed under protective custody because of a mysterious threat against his life. Reddit subsequently appeared on a number of TV shows and suggested that his removal from "security duty" was part of a plot to kill King. But when he was questioned by the House Select Committee on Assassinations, Reddit admitted that his assertion that he was providing security was "absolutely false." Reddit's job, as it turned out, "was not to protect King but to surveil him." He could not have prevented the shooting. (ibid.)

### Did Somebody Help the Assassin Escape?

• Shortly after the Memphis Police broadcast word of a suspect fleeing the murder scene in a white Mustang, a CB broadcaster established radio contact with the police and kept up a running description of a chase involving a white Mustang, a blue Pontiac, and gunfire. Various police units attempted to intercept the cars, while the police dispatcher frantically tried to keep up with conflicting accounts of the chase's progress.

• Later the CB broadcast was reported to be a hoax. It was allegedly perpetrated by two teenagers whose identities were never released, and who were never prosecuted. Whether the phony broadcast was part of a conspiracy or not, it succeeded in diverting police pursuers to northeastern parts of Memphis while Ray made his escape to the southwest.

• Even more inexplicable, a "Signal Y"—an all-points bulletin— was never issued by the police department for Memphis. Had one been issued, police cars would have driven immediately to preassigned locations, thus blocking all the main exits from the city. Nor did Lieutenant Frank Kallaher, the "shift commander of communications," issue an all-points bulletin describing the suspect to the neighboring states of Alabama, Mississippi, and Arkansas.

• Kallaher blamed his failure to issue a citywide Signal Y on "the massive confusion and huge volume of radio traffic which erupted immediately following the assassination." Asked why he also failed to alert neighboring states, Kallaher said that he had mistakenly thought that once a fugitive crossed a state line, it was the FBI's responsibility to spread the word. He added that he wouldn't have notified Mississippi in any event, "due to a past history of noncooperation from that state."

### Was the Eyewitness Testimony Unreliable?

• Because two bullet fragments taken from King's body were so distorted that ballistics tests were inconclusive, the state's case rested heavily on the eyewitness testimony of Charles Stephens, who lived in the boardinghouse from which Ray allegedly shot King. Stephens said that shortly after hearing a rifle shot, he saw Ray run down the hall, away from the second-floor bathroom. But in his introduction to Ray's 1992 book, *Who Killed Martin Luther King?*, attorney Mark Lane says that Stephens's testimony was disputed almost immediately by his wife:

√ Mrs. Stephens claimed that on the morning of April 4, 1968, her husband was drunk, and was actually urinating in the bushes in front of the boardinghouse at the time he claimed to have seen the assassin run down the hallway. Mrs. Stephens claims that *she* saw the killer, carrying a package in his hand, as he walked past her door moments after the shots were fired.

√ Lane asserts that Charles Stephens was probably "oblivious" to the shooting, and never knew that a stranger had been in the building at all. "Very likely," Lane says, "the only eyewitness of value in the rooming house was Mrs. Stephens." But when she was shown photographs of James Earl Ray, "she unequivocally stated" that he was *not* the man she saw in the hallway that day.

• According to Lane, however, the authorities tried first to shake Mrs. Stephens's testimony and then to shut her up. "She was threatened by FBI agents and local police and told to cooperate." They even offered to pay her a reward for identifying Ray, but she refused, promising instead to identify the man she believed was the real assassin as soon as he was caught. In violation of Tennessee law, Lane alleges, Mrs. Stephens was "surreptitiously" sent to a mental institution; although she had no history of mental illness, she was held there for 10 years. (*Who Killed Martin Luther King?*)

• About the same time, cabdriver James McCraw, who corroborated Mrs. Stephens's account that her husband was dead drunk, saw two white Mustangs parked at the curb outside the rooming house. The police never determined who owned the second one.

## WAS IT A CONSPIRACY?
**THEORY #1: James Earl Ray's story is true: "I personally did not shoot Dr. King, but I may have been partially responsible without knowing it."**

• Ray admits renting the room in Memphis and leaving a number of his personal effects there, but says he was not in the rooming house when King was killed.

• Ray claims that in July 1967, not long after he had escaped from Missouri State Prison, he met a fair-haired man in Montreal known as "Raoul." (Ray was seen in Toronto after the assassination in the company of a fair-haired man.) Raoul paid Ray several thousand dollars for his help in a few small drug-smuggling and gun-running deals; they met 12 to 15 times in the nine months preceding the assassination—in Birmingham, Mexico, New Orleans and, finally, in Memphis on April 3 and 4.

• Ray contends that Raoul directed every move that would later incriminate Ray in King's slaying: he told Ray to buy the rifle, allegedly to show gun-running clients what they'd be getting; had Ray rent the boardinghouse room so they'd have a place to cut deals; and had Ray buy binoculars to keep an eye out for police.

• Ray's account of his whereabouts during the shooting is a little sketchy, however. He claims that he left Raoul alone in the rented room and went to change a flat tire on the Mustang. As he drove back toward the rooming house, Ray says, he saw the street blocked by squad cars, learned of King's assassination on the radio, and realized that he would be implicated. Then he left town.

**THEORY #2: James Earl Ray did it, and he acted alone.**

• Ray admits that he rented the room and bought the gun and white Mustang in which he escaped. Ray's mystery accomplice, "Raoul," has never been located or conclusively identified.

• And the telltale bundle left on the sidewalk? The House Select Committee on Assassinations concluded that Ray saw a police squad car as he was leaving the boardinghouse, panicked, and dumped the stuff. It would have been typical: Ray had bumbled every crime he had ever undertaken.

• The weak point of this theory, though, is Ray's motivation to kill King. Ray had no history of racial extremism and was unlikely to risk his freedom by such a daring act unless he would gain directly from it. As one person who knew him well put it, "Jimmie wouldn't cross the street unless there was a dollar in it."

**THEORY #3: The CIA planned the assassination and set up Ray as the patsy.**

• One of the most implausible parts of the Ray-as-sole-assassin theory is his escape. He fled to Canada, England, Portugal, then back to England, where he was arrested while awaiting a flight to Belgium. Where did he get the money to do all of that traveling, and who gave him the phony passports he carried? Although he had no known source of income between the time he escaped prison in April 1967 and was arrested at Heathrow Airport in June 1968, Ray may have spent as much as $25,000 on plane fares, lodging, and other expenses.

• Moreover, where did Ray get the sophistication to zip around the world, eluding international authorities hot on his trail? He was a poor man from backwater towns who had spent most of his adulthood in jail because he was a bumbler. According to one account, Ray's first burglary ended in a jail sentence because he dropped his army discharge notice in the building he'd just burgled.

• Researchers John Edginton and John Sergeant assert in a recent *Covert Action* magazine article that they have met the man who may have set Ray up. Jules R. Kimble, they say, "claims to have flown Ray to Montreal, where he brought him to a CIA identities specialist who provided Ray with his aliases." The article further alleges that Kimble had ties to New Orleans Mob boss Carlos Marcello "and admits to having done mob-related work in New Orleans, Montreal, and Memphis during the late sixties—three key cities in Ray's odyssey."

• Kimble says that Ray was a decoy and that the actual assassins were two snipers who flew into Memphis "using a West Memphis airfield belonging to a CIA front company." Kimble asserts that while members of the Memphis Police Department cooperated in the plot, "the actual operation was coordinated by a high-ranking intelligence official based in Atlanta." ("The Murder of Martin Luther King Jr.," by John Edginton and John Sergeant, *Covert Action*, Summer 1990)

**THEORY #4: At the prompting of J. Edgar Hoover, rogue elements within the FBI conspired to kill King and cover up the crime. Ray was a conspirator, in it for the money, but he didn't personally kill King.**

• Hoover hated King, calling him the "the most dangerous man in America," "the most notorious liar in the country," and a "moral degenerate." And Hoover didn't stop with name-calling. He illegally bugged the civil rights leader's hotel rooms and then circulated tapes of King's extramarital affairs to King's wife, members of King's Southern Christian Leadership Conference (SCLC), and the press.

• When King was about to be awarded the Nobel Peace Prize in 1964, the FBI tried to get him to kill himself. Assistant Director William Sullivan sent King a composite tape recording of several of his hotel-room indiscretions along with an anonymous blackmail note, which read in part: "You are done. King, there is only one thing left for you to do....There is but one way out for you. You better take it before your filthy, abnormal fraudulent self is bared to the nation." (*J.Edgar Hoover: The Man and the Secrets*)

• Convinced that King was a Communist, Hoover also had the FBI infiltrate King's SCLC staff: "James A. Harrison joined the SCLC in 1964 and was recruited almost immediately to spy for the Bureau." He received a weekly stipend from the FBI, to whom he reported every week about the SCLC and King's activities. (*The FBI and Martin Luther King, Jr.*)

• Former Atlanta FBI agent Arthur Murtagh recalled in an interview that when he and a fellow FBI agent heard the news of MLK's death over the radio, "My colleague leapt up, clapped his hands and said 'Goddamn, we got him! We finally got him.' " Murtagh also noted that evidence of a King assassination plot was "washed out consistently and deliberately" by the Atlanta G-men. (*Covert Action*)

• The House Select Committee on Assassinations concluded "that the Bureau [the FBI] had contributed to a moral climate conducive to the murder of Dr. King, but it stopped short of accusing the Bureau of actual involvement in the killing." (ibid.)

• However, J. B. Stoner, former chairman of the National States Rights Party and an admitted racist and white supremacist, said in an interview in the 1970s, "several years ago the FBI, through an undercover agent, offered me $25,000 to kill King." Though Stoner says he declined, he believes that the Bureau got someone to accept. In an interview with journalist William Bradford Huie, Stoner said, "Ray was a pawn, a decoy, in a conspiracy planned and carried out by agencies of the United States Government. And the conspirators were using some of King's own people." Huie pressed Stoner: "Specifically, do you mean that the FBI was responsible for Dr. King's death?—Stoner: Yes." (*Esquire*, March 1972)

## SIMILARITIES BETWEEN MLK'S AND JFK'S KILLINGS

*Ex-FBI agent William Turner noted these disturbing similarities between King's murder and that of John F. Kennedy* (Ramparts *magazine*, July 13, 1968):

• An artist's sketch of the man eyewitnesses allegedly saw fleeing the flophouse looks startling like the "third tramp" photographed leaving Dealey Plaza after JFK was shot. "The sketch and the photograph both portray a man with a sharp, pronounced nose,...a wide mouth with thin lips, and a firm set to the jaw."

• A rifle with a telescopic sight was conveniently dropped at the crime scene in both cases.

- Following both killings, the local police radio networks were "penetrated," interfering with police efforts to catch the suspects.

- In both cases, high law-enforcement officials alleged that the slayings were done by lone assassins, even before investigations were well under way. Within 24 hours of King's death, Attorney General Ramsey Clark said there was no evidence of a conspiracy.

- In both assassinations, Turner alleges, there was official falsification of evidence.

- In both cases, the assassins allegedly killed for "political" reasons. Oswald's "fervent communism" was likely a cover.

- Investigative files for both investigations were sealed for a long time: JFK's for 75 years, and King's for 50.

- Both Kennedy (see p. 222) and King tried to cut short the Vietnam War. Four days before his death, King gave this speech:

  Our involvement in the war in Vietnam has...strengthened the military-industrial complex....played havoc with our domestic destiny. This day we are spending $500,000 to kill every Vietcong soldier...While we spend only $53 a year for every person trying to rise in...so-called poverty programs...here we are ten thousand miles away from home, fighting for the so-called freedom of the Vietnamese people, when we do not even put our own house in order.

## RECOMMENDED READING

- "Are You Sure Who Killed Martin Luther King?" by Bynum Shaw (*Esquire*, March 1972)

- *The King Conspiracy*, by Michael Newton (Holloway House Publishing Co., 1987)

- *The Martin Luther King Assassination: New Revelations on the Conspiracy and Cover-Up, 1968-1991*, by Dr. Philip H. Melanson (Shapolsky Publishers, 1991)

- "The Murder of Martin Luther King Jr.," by John Edginton and John Sergeant (*Covert Action*, Summer 1990)

- "Some Disturbing Parallels," by William Turner (*Ramparts*, July 13, 1968)

- *Who Killed Martin Luther King? The True Story By The Alleged Assassin*, by James Earl Ray (National Press Books, 1992)

# WHO SAID IT?

*See if you can guess which of the schemers listed below made the following statements. Answers are at the bottom of the page.*

**1.** "There's one difference between the Reds and the Pinks. The Pinks want to socialize America. The Reds want to socialize the world and make Moscow the world capital. Their paths are similar; they have the same bible—the teachings of Karl Marx."

**2.** "I'm a Groucho-Marxist"

**3.** "No, sir, I didn't kill anybody. I'm just the patsy in this deal."

**4.** "I am a man who sees life in terms of missions. Missions defined, and missions completed."

**5.** "I never saw myself as being above the law, nor did I ever intend to do anything illegal."

**6.** "Communism is knocking at our gates, and we can't afford to let it in....We must keep America whole and safe and unspoiled."

**7.** "The minute the FBI begins making recommendations on what should be done with its information, it becomes a Gestapo."

**8.** "We must guard against the acquisition of unwarranted influence...by the military-industrial complex. The potential for a disastrous rise of misplaced power exists and will persist."

**9.** "Left-wingers are incapable of conspiring because they are all egomaniacs."

**10.** "You'd be surprised how much [being] a good actor pays off."

---

**A.** Abbie Hoffman

**B.** Oliver North

**C.** Ronald Reagan

**D.** Norman Mailer

**E.** Lee Harvey Oswald

**F.** Dwight D. Eisenhower

**G.** J. Edgar Hoover

**H.** George Bush

**I.** Richard Nixon

**J.** Al Capone

Answers: 1–I; 2–A; 3–E; 4–H; 5–B; 6–J; 7–G; 8–F; 9–D; 10–C.

# MORGAN'S SWINDLE

*"Great is Mr. Morgan's power, greater in some respects even than that of Presidents or kings," wrote a British journalist about financier J.P. Morgan in the late 1800s. Did the journalist know that Morgan got his start as a petty swindler?*

I n May 1861, the Civil War had just begun...and the U.S. Army desperately needed rifles. It was paying top dollar to anybody who had guns to sell. So when the commander of the Union Army in St. Louis received a telegram from a man in New York offering to sell "5,000 new carbines in perfect condition" for $22 each, the commander accepted—sight unseen.

When the rifles arrived in St. Louis, the commander found that they had a serious defect: they often misfired, blowing off soldiers' thumbs. The Army refused to pay for them.

But 24-year-old J. P. Morgan, who was selling the guns, insisted on full payment. When he sued, the Army tried to compromise, offering $13.31 per rifle. Morgan refused to settle. The case went to court, and the judge ruled in Morgan's favor; the government was instructed to pay Morgan in full—$109,912.

Was it a legitimate business deal? Or had Morgan and his cronies conspired to bilk the U.S. government?

## SUSPICIOUS FACTS

• The guns had been bought from an army arsenal in New York City for $3.50 apiece. They were the last of a batch that had been there since 1857, when they were condemned as "thoroughly unserviceable, obsolete, and dangerous."

• The deal was arranged by a speculator named Simon Stevens, who knew exactly what he was buying. Court records later showed that Stevens was working for J. P. Morgan.

• After the commander agreed to buy the guns, Morgan borrowed money to purchase them—using the Army voucher as collateral for the loan. So the U.S. Army was buying its own unusable rifles—at a profit to Morgan of roughly 500% per rifle.

• Morgan never even took possession of the guns. When the loan came through, he had the defective rifles shipped directly from the New York arsenal to St. Louis.

## WAS IT A CONSPIRACY?

A U.S. congressional committee investigating J. P. Morgan's arms swindle in 1862 found that Morgan had engaged in a conspiracy to defraud the U.S. government. It reported:

> The proposal actually was to sell the Government at $22 each 5,000 of its own arms, the intention being, if the offer was accepted, to obtain these arms from the Government at $3.50 each....The Government not only sold one day for $17,486 arms which it had agreed the day before to repurchase for $109,912—making a loss to the United States of $92,426—but virtually furnished the money to pay itself the $17,486 which it received.

• Morgan's case set an unfortunate precedent for the thousands of "dead horse claims" that followed, in which wartime swindlers were paid in full for putrid meat, rotting ships, flimsy tents, shoes that fell apart, and weapons that maimed the soldiers who used them.

## GULF WAR QUIZ

**1.** A Census Bureau employee discovered that more Iraqis died in the Gulf War than the government had previously announced. So she...

    **A)** Kept her mouth shut.    **B)** Made the information public.

**2.** To show its appreciation, the Census Bureau:

        **A)** Promoted her.        **B)** Fired her.

**3.** The U.S. command gave the American public the impression that there was "an awesome display of high-tech precision" going on. But it never mentioned that:

**A)** American planes often bombed the same targets over and over, "after they had already been destroyed."

**B)** Some planes couldn't find their targets and had to return with full bomb loads.

**C)** Spy satellite photographs were so detailed that they were worthless—commanders needed broad views of the battlefields, not close-ups.

Answers: 1—B; 2—B; 3—all of them

# THE CIA & LSD

*In the 1950s, the CIA spent millions developing mind-control techniques. But whose minds were CIA officials trying to control?*

During World War II, Nazi scientists tested hallucinogenic drugs (like mescaline) on inmates at the Dachau concentration camp. The Nazis were ostensibly trying to find a new "aviation medicine," but what they were really looking for was the secret to "mind control."

After dosing inmates for years, the Nazi scientists concluded that it was "impossible to impose one's will on another person...even when strong doses had been given." But they found they *could* extract "even the most intimate secrets" from subjects under a drug's influence.

After the war, U.S. military intelligence officers found out about the Nazi experiments and wondered if hallucinogenic drugs might be used for espionage. Could such drugs be sprayed over enemy armies to disable them? Could the drugs be used in covert actions—to confuse or discredit leaders in hostile countries? The possibilities seemed endless. So, in 1950, the CIA took over where the Nazis had left off.

## THE CIA ON DOPE

• In 1953, the CIA initiated a full-scale mind-control program called Operation MK-ULTRA. Its experiments included hypnosis, sensory deprivation, electroshock, ESP, lobotomy, subliminal projection, sleep teaching—and drugs. The operation is said to have lasted 20 years and cost $25 million.

• According to the book *Acid Dreams: The CIA, LSD and the Sixties Rebellion:* "[N]early every drug that appeared on the black market during the 1960s—marijuana, cocaine, heroin, PCP, amyl nitrate, mushrooms, DMT, barbiturates, laughing gas, speed, and many others—had previously been scrutinized, tested, and in some cases refined by the CIA and army scientists. But...none received as much attention or was embraced with such enthusiasm as LSD-25 [lysergic acid diethylamide]. For a time CIA personnel were completely infatuated with the hallucinogen. Those who first tested LSD in the early 1950s were convinced that it would revolutionize the cloak-and-dagger trade."

But how could the CIA find out if the drug was an effective secret weapon unless it was first tested on people?

## WAS IT A CONSPIRACY? #1

*Was testing LSD part of an MK-ULTRA conspiracy? Did the CIA give American citizens psychedelic drugs, using them as human guinea pigs without their knowledge?*

In 1973, the CIA destroyed most of its files on the MK-ULTRA project; however, some files escaped destruction. When the contents of the files were revealed, the Senate held hearings on MK-ULTRA and human drug testing by the CIA.

## THE ACID TEST

• To test LSD, the CIA had set up both clandestine operations and academic fronts. For instance, it established a "Society for the Investigation of Human Ecology" at the Cornell University medical school, which dispensed "grants" to institutions in the U.S. and Canada to conduct experiments with LSD.

• The LSD project was administered by the CIA's Technical Services Staff. A freewheeling atmosphere developed in which anyone was likely to be dosed without warning in the name of research. Before the program concluded, thousands of people had been involuntarily dosed.

• Not only the CIA, but also the U.S. Army was involved in LSD experiments. *Acid Dreams* reports that in the 1950s, "nearly fifteen hundred military personnel had served as human guinea pigs in LSD experiments conducted by the U.S. Army Chemical Corps." The Army even made a film of troops trying to drill while stoned on acid.

## WHAT HAPPENED

• The government admitted giving LSD to about 1,000 unsuspecting people from 1955 to 1958 and has paid millions of dollars to settle lawsuits that were filed when subjects given drugs became permanently incapacitated or committed suicide.

A few examples:

√ In a San Francisco operation code-named "Midnight Climax," prostitutes brought men to bordellos that were actually CIA safe houses. There, as reported in *Acid Dreams*, they would "spike the drinks of unlucky customers while CIA operatives observed, photographed, and recorded the action."

√ In one experiment, black inmates at the Lexington Narcotics Hospital were given LSD for 75 consecutive days in gradually increasing doses.

√ In 1953, a civilian working for the Army was slipped LSD at a CIA party. He jumped to his death from a 10th-story window. It was ruled a suicide until 1975, when the government revealed the truth. The CIA apologized and Congress awarded his family $750,000.

√ A CIA-funded psychiatrist in Canada dosed patients with LSD and used other mind-control techniques, trying to "reprogram" them. Nine of the patients sued the CIA for damages. The case was settled out of court in 1988.

## WAS IT A CONSPIRACY? #2

*Did the CIA use LSD and other psychedelics deliberately to take the steam out of a rebellious generation? It's something a number of counterculture heroes have considered:*

"Am I the product of one of the CIA's lamentable, ill-advised, or triumphantly successful experiments in mind control? [Has the CIA] by conscious plan or inadvertent Pandora's Box, let loose the whole LSD fad on the U.S. and the world?"
—**Allen Ginsberg, writing while high on LSD in 1977**

"The LSD movement was started by the CIA. I wouldn't be here now without the foresight of the CIA scientists."
—**Timothy Leary**

"We must always remember to thank the CIA and the army for LSD. That's what people forget.... They invented LSD to control people and what they did give us was freedom."
—**John Lennon**

## SUSPICIOUS FACTS

• Not all of the CIA drug experiments had been done without the participants' consent—volunteers in experiments at universities were also being dosed. While many of them had negative experiences, some actually enjoyed the experiments, and began turning their friends on. (LSD was still legal then.)

• The CIA had something big in mind. According to a November 16, 1953, document, the CIA ordered ten kilos of LSD—enough for *30 million doses*—from the Swiss manufacturer Sandoz.

• When Sandoz got suspicious in 1954 and refused to supply the drug, the CIA asked the Eli Lilly Company to crack Sandoz's formula for LSD. Shortly, Lilly scientists assured the Agency, "LSD would be available in tonnage quantities." One ton would yield more than *2.5 billion* doses. What did the CIA intend to do with all that acid?

• In 1967, the CIA's formula for STP (a psychedelic even more powerful than LSD) was released to the scientific community. Within a few weeks, the drug was available all across America.

• According to *Acid Dreams*: "A former CIA contract employee [reported that] CIA personnel actually helped underground chemists set up LSD laboratories in the San Francisco Bay area."

## FOOTNOTE: THE OSWALD CONNECTION

• Was Lee Harvey Oswald given LSD by the CIA? In 1957, Oswald—then a 17-year-old marine—was assigned to the U.S. naval air base in Atsugi, Japan. According to *Rolling Stone*, this base "served as one of two overseas field stations where the CIA conducted extensive LSD testing."

• Two years later, Oswald was discharged and moved to the USSR, supposedly as a defector. "If Oswald was sent to Russia as a pseudo-defector, performing some covert task for the U.S., then it's quite possible he was given LSD as part of his training." (*Rolling Stone*)

## RECOMMENDED READING

*Acid Dreams: The CIA, LSD and the Sixties Rebellion*, by Martin Lee and Bruce Shlain (Grove Press, 1985)

# BOBBY

*"I now fully realize that only the powers of the presidency
will reveal the secrets of my brother's death."*
—Robert Kennedy, June 1968, two days before he was killed

On June 5, 1968, Senator Robert Kennedy won the Democratic Primary in California—and seemed poised to win the presidency that fall. Savoring his victory, Bobby turned to one of his brother John's former aides, Kenneth O'Donnell, and said, "You know, Kenny, I feel now that for the first time I've shaken off the shadow of my brother."

That evening Kennedy gave a brief victory speech to campaign workers in Los Angeles's Ambassador Hotel. Then, around midnight, he and his entourage began leaving, shaking hands and chatting as they exited through the hotel pantry. As RFK pressed through the crowd, a man suddenly stepped in front of him and began firing a pistol. Kennedy staggered backward and fell.

Several men wrestled with the gunman, but he continued firing until his revolver was empty, wounding another five people. Kennedy was rushed to a hospital, bleeding profusely from three wounds, including a massive hole in the back of his head. He died the following day at 1:44 p.m.

## THE OFFICIAL STORY

• According to press accounts the following day, a Palestinian refugee named Sirhan Sirhan shot Kennedy; reportedly he was "furious over the plight of Palestinian Arabs" and resented "Senator Kennedy's recent support for the sale of 50 Phantom jets to Israel."

• The Los Angeles Police Department (LAPD) investigated the murder for a year and produced a ten-volume illustrated report that said that "Sirhan fired the shots which killed Kennedy and wounded five others; that his act was premeditated; that he was not under the influence of any drug or intoxicant; that he was legally sane; and that there was no evidence of conspiracy." (*Harper's Magazine*)

• To this day, Sirhan maintains that he assassinated Kennedy for political reasons and acted entirely alone. But two dead Kennedys and dozens of suspicious facts make many Americans wonder if there was a conspiracy to kill RFK and then cover up the crime.

## SUSPICIOUS FACTS: THE SCENE OF THE CRIME
*Inconsistencies in the official story of RFK's slaying start with the alleged murder weapon.*

### How Many Bullets?
• Sirhan's revolver held eight bullets. According to Dr. Phillip Melanson, an expert on the RFK assassination, "seven bullets were recovered from the bodies of Senator Kennedy and the five surviving shooting victims; one was allegedly lost in the ceiling interspace.... Thus with all of Sirhan's eight bullets otherwise accounted for, if but one bullet was recovered from the crime scene, it constitutes a ninth bullet—too many for one gun." Yet police photographs of the scene appear to show several slugs lodged in doorjambs, and one eyewitness, Lisa Urso, said she saw "at least four bullet holes in ceiling tiles."

• The LAPD supported its single-gun theory by claiming that some bullets did "double duty" by striking more than one person and/or ricocheting elsewhere. But here, as in JFK's assassination, bullet trajectories and official versions of who stood where are inconsistent with eyewitness accounts. However, we'll never be able to tell exactly how many bullets were fired because the LAPD destroyed the bullet-riddled woodwork and tiles (as described in "Missing Evidence," below.)

• In his book *The Assassination of Robert F. Kennedy*, former FBI agent William Turner hypothesized that as many as fifteen bullets were fired. Several eyewitnesses said that the shots sounded like a string of firecrackers going off, with shots spaced more closely together than would have been possible from a single gun.

### The Fatal Shot
• When he fired, Sirhan stood in front of Kennedy. Yet, according to Los Angeles County Coroner Dr. Thomas Noguchi, the shot that killed Kennedy "struck his head just *behind* his right ear and fragmented in the right-hand side of his brain." Moreover, Noguchi calculated that the muzzle of the gun was fired "at point-blank

range," roughly *three inches* from the back of Kennedy's head.

• The LAPD report attempted to explain this contradiction by saying that RFK had made a ninety-degree turn to the left to shake a waiter's hand, thus "presenting his right and hinder side" to the muzzle of Sirhan's gun. If true, this would explain the direction of the shots relative to RFK's body, but it does not account for a gunshot just inches away. The closest *any* witnesses thought Sirhan's gun got to RFK was about two feet—and most witnesses placed the gun at four feet. But *none* saw the weapon as close as the LAPD explanation required.

### Who Was the "Polka-Dot Woman?"

• Sirhan claimed that he acted alone. Maybe so. But more than a dozen witnesses reported seeing him with a woman about 25 years old, wearing a dress with dime-sized black or navy blue polka dots.

• For example, Sandy Serrano, co-chair of the Pasadena-Altadena Youth for Kennedy Committee, told investigators she was sitting on a stairway outside the Ambassador Hotel at 11:30 p.m., when two men and a woman in a polka-dot dress climbed the stairs.

• Serrano "sat there for about a half hour, she estimated, and saw no one else. Then, she heard what she thought were six car 'backfires,' four of which seemed close together. Moments later a man and a woman (two of the trio she had seen previously) came running down the stairs toward her. The woman said, 'We shot him! We shot him!' Serrano asked: 'Who did you shoot?' The woman replied, 'Kennedy.' " (*The Robert F. Kennedy Assassination*)

• When she later saw photographs of Sirhan, Serrano realized that he was "the man who had earlier been with the couple she saw fleeing" (ibid.). Although her account of a woman in a polka-dot dress was corroborated by other witnesses, the LAPD simply denied that Sirhan had been accompanied by a woman before the assassination and failed to mention the "polka-dot woman" in its final report.

### Blacked Out

• LAPD Seargent Paul Scharaga, the first supervising officer to arrive at the Ambassador Hotel after the shooting, set up a command post and—in response to the eyewitnesses who ran up to him in the hotel parking lot—attempted to put out an all-points bulletin

(APB) on the polka-dot woman. Yet for some unknown reason, Scharaga encountered a 15- or 20-minute police radio blackout during which he could not communicate with other cars or head-quarters.

• At 2:30 a.m., Detective Inspector John Powers showed up at the command post and ordered Scharaga to cancel the APB. "Let's cancel that description," Powers reportedly said. "We don't want to make a federal case out of it. We've got the suspect in custody." Scharaga refused to cancel the APB, but Powers went over his head and ordered the APB discontinued. (*The Assassination of Robert F. Kennedy*)

• Scharaga's subsequent reports mentioning the APB were confis-cated, and their existence was denied by Scharaga's superiors. Though a veteran with an excellent record, Scharaga's "efficiency ratings spiralled downward" and in 1969 he left the force. (*The Robert F. Kennedy Assassination*)

## SUSPICIOUS FACTS: THE TRIAL AND BEYOND
### The Gun
• No one disputed that Sirhan had fired a gun at Senator Kennedy. But "at [Sirhan's] trial—as at the grand jury—nobody introduced any evidence which scientifically, or even demonstrably, linked Sirhan's gun to the bullets and fragments that made up the other relevant exhibits." (*Harper's Magazine*)

• LAPD criminologist DeWayne Wolfer initially told the grand jury that he had test-fired Sirhan's .22 revolver into a tank of wa-ter, retrieved the unharmed slugs, and compared them to an intact bullet taken from RFK's neck wound. He said the bullets matched.

• But later, Wolfer was not so sure. Noting that he had also done test-firings with a *similar* .22 pistol, he admitted that he might have mixed up those bullets with the ones fired from Sirhan's gun. In fact, the gun that Wolfer had labeled as Sirhan's and brought into the courtroom as "the proven murder weapon" (serial no. H53725) might have actually been the "similar gun" (serial no. 18602) that Wolfer had used for his tests. We'll never know. The "similar gun" was destroyed by the LAPD a month after it was tested, while Sirhan's case was still being appealed. (*Harper's Magazine*)

## A Dissenting Opinion

• William Harper, a veteran criminologist who had "conducted thousands of examinations for both prosecution and defense, and testified as a firearms expert in more than three hundred criminal trials around the nation," criticized Wolfer's competency. So, in 1970—after Sirhan's trial was over—Harper "obtained permission from Sirhan's attorney to examine the evidence bullets that were stored in the County Clerk's office." (*The Assassination of Robert F. Kennedy*)

• Harper concentrated on two of the bullets: one taken from Kennedy's body, and one taken from the body of ABC reporter William Weisel, who had been injured in the attack. The bullets were in good enough shape for Harper to compare them to one another. (ibid.)

• He concluded that the two bullets had "no individual characteristics in common," and proposed that they had been fired from different guns—one used to kill Kennedy, the other to injure the bystanders. (ibid.)

• In August 1971, the day before Harper presented his findings to a grand jury, two men "wearing workmen's caps pulled down over their foreheads" shot at Harper's car and narrowly missed killing him. He testified anyhow. (ibid.)

## Missing Evidence

• The .22 revolver *similar* to Sirhan's was not the only piece of evidence destroyed by the LAPD. The police also removed physical evidence from the hotel pantry and, on June 27, 1969, improperly destroyed it while Sirhan's case was still being appealed.

• Some of the other evidence that was destroyed: 2,400 photographs, including 3 rolls of film "confiscated by the police from an eyewitness who took pictures of Senator Kennedy" *as he was shot.* More than 3,000 of the 3,470 tapes of interviews that the LAPD conducted in its investigation were also burned—including *all* of the tapes made of the 51 witnesses that the FBI and the LAPD considered most important to the case. "Somehow not *one* of their testimonies has survived." (*The Robert F. Kennedy Assassination*)

• Material evidence is missing as well—including the ceiling tiles and a pantry doorframe that had been hit with bullets, as well as the x-ray and spectrographic tests that had been made on these items. The left sleeves of Kennedy's shirt and jacket are also missing. (ibid.) Is this the result of sloppy police work—or was there a cover-up?

## WAS IT A CONSPIRACY?

**THEORY #1: Los Angeles authorities deliberately destroyed evidence and aided a cover-up.**

• The LAPD failed to pursue leads, presented flawed ballistics tests as facts, and destroyed evidence while the case was still under appeal. According to a 1976 signed statement by William A. Bailey, who had been an FBI special agent assigned to the Los Angeles office in 1968, the LAPD also lied about the number of bullet holes found in door jambs and in the ceiling of the pantry where RFK was assassinated.

• Further, the coroner, Noguchi—whose autopsy report said that RFK had been shot "at point-blank range"—told the *Los Angeles Herald Examiner* that authorities urged him to perjure himself. When he was about to enter the grand jury room to present his findings, Noguchi said, he was approached by an unnamed deputy DA who pressed him to revise his estimate of the firing distance from inches to feet. Noguchi refused.

• When Noguchi was summoned to testify at Sirhan's trial, the *defense* cut Noguchi's testimony short, saying that the coroner did not have to get into the "gory details" of what angle the shots entered the body or how close the gun was.

**THEORY #2: There was a second gunman behind Robert Kennedy.**

• According to Noguchi, the shot that killed Robert Kennedy was fired at point-blank range behind the senator. And in fact, there *was* a man with a gun right behind Kennedy: Thane Eugene Cesar, a guard employed by a private company, Ace Security.

• A CBS News employee, Donald Schulman—who could see both

Sirhan and "a uniformed security guard"—said the guard returned fire when Sirhan started shooting. Schulman told a reporter that the guard accidentally hit Kennedy. The LAPD interviewed Schulman, but insisted that he was mistaken. (*The Assassination of Robert F. Kennedy*)

• Cesar denied ever drawing his company-issued gun—a Rohm .38—and he was exonerated by the FBI and the LAPD of any part in Kennedy's death. But conspiracy theorists are not so sure.

• Philip Melanson takes a different tack: "The question is not whether Cesar fired his .38, since no bullets other than .22 calibre were found. The real question is whether he carried a .22 the night of the shooting."

• Cesar did in fact own a .22 H&R pistol, which he claimed to have sold to a retiring coworker, Jim Yoder, three months before the assassination. (The two men had worked together at Lockheed; Cesar was just moonlighting at Ace Security.) However, the receipt for its sale shows that the pistol was sold three months *after* the shooting, in September 1968. The LAPD knew this by 1971, but did not publicly disclose the discrepancy.

• In 1971, the LAPD—in response to public criticism of its RFK inquiry—contacted Yoder to see if he still had the gun. But shortly after he was contacted, Yoder reported that his house had been burgled and the gun was stolen.

• Finally, although Cesar claimed that he had worked at Ace Security for six months before the assassination, independent researcher Betsy Langman discovered that he had been hired by Ace less than two weeks before. Moreover, Cesar was first assigned to guard the Ambassador Hotel on the day of the assassination. Was he planted there by conspirators?

**THEORY #3: Through LAPD officers who held key posts in the RFK inquiry, the CIA was involved in the assassination and/or its cover-up.**

• One of his brother John's closest advisors, Robert Kennedy shared JFK's distrust of the CIA. In fact, RFK suspected the agency of his brother's death. Had he become president, RFK would have likely reopened inquiries into that death. He was also an outspoken opponent of the war in Vietnam, a reason frequently cited by conspiracy theorists as the motive behind JFK's assassination.

• There are some intriguing ties between the CIA and the LAPD. In particular, two LAPD officers who vigorously quashed testimony about the polka-dot woman had at one time worked for the Agency.

• Sergeant Hank Hernandez—Sandy Serrano's interrogator—had worked for a CIA front, the Agency of International Development's (AID) Office of Public Safety. After retiring from the LAPD, he mentioned in a resumé offering his services as a private investigator that in 1963 he had played a key role in "Unified Police Command training for the CIA in Latin America." (*The Assassination of Robert F. Kennedy*)

• According to California Chief Deputy Attorney General Charles A. O'Brien in 1968, the Office of Public Safety of the AID was an "ultrasecret CIA unit...known to insiders as the 'Department of Dirty Tricks'...one of its specialties was teaching foreign 'intelligence apparats' the techniques of assassination." (ibid.)

• Another LAPD officer with purported links to the CIA and AID's Office of Public Safety was Lieutenant Manuel Pena. Pena was a supervisor for the LAPD's Special Unit Senator, "in charge of preparing the [Sirhan] case for trial and supervising 'day-watch investigators.' " Pena coordinated and approved "many of the case's most crucial witness interviews and reports." He was thus in a crucial position to direct—or misdirect—the assassination probe.

• According to Melanson, at least six of the LAPD documents Pena approved distorted or falsified eyewitness testimony concerning the polka-dot woman, or presented dates, procedures, and contents "completely at odds with the known evidence."

• Pena's ties to the CIA were fresh. In November 1967, Pena had retired from the LAPD to accept a position as "public safety advisor" with AID's Office of Public Safety. By April of the next year, Pena was back with the LAPD. Further, FBI agent Roger LaJeunesse confided that Pena "had done CIA special assignments for a decade." (*The Assassination of Robert F. Kennedy*)

• Why would the CIA have wanted to suppress evidence or distort testimony about the polka-dot woman? According to one of the stranger theories, Sirhan may have been hypnotized to kill RFK, and the polka-dot woman was Sirhan's CIA "handler." Far-fetched as this scenario may seem, the CIA did experiment with brainwashing techniques in its top-secret MK-ULTRA program (see p. 165).

• And Sirhan himself lends some credence to this theory. Although Sirhan says he acted alone and killed Robert Kennedy, he claims a memory lapse about the shooting itself. Sirhan has repeatedly said that the last thing he remembered before the shooting was having coffee with a young woman. The next thing he claims to remember is "choking and the commotion" as he was being wrestled to the floor after the shooting. Did Sirhan have coffee with the polka-dot woman just before he slipped into a hypnotic trance?

## RECOMMENDED READING

• *The Assassination of Robert F. Kennedy: A Searching Look at the Conspiracy and Coverup, 1968-1978*, by William W. Turner and John Christian (Random House, 1978)

• *The Robert F. Kennedy Assassination: New Revelations on the Conspiracy and Cover-up, 1968-1991*, by Philip Melanson (Shapolsky Publishers, 1991)

• "Sirhan's Gun," by Betsy Langman and Alexander Cockburn (*Harper's Magazine*, Jan. 1975)

# CONSPIRACY QUEEN

*Calling herself "just a housewife interested in tennis courts and dance lessons"
before she saw Lee Harvey Oswald gunned down on national television,
Mae Brussel became one of the most driven conspiracy theorists in America.
For 17 years, until her death in 1988, she broadcast a weekly radio show in
which she presented her evidence of attacks on U.S. democracy. Here are a
few examples of the things she had to say, courtesy of The Realist.*

"Conspiracy theories remain 'theories' only when there is no court, no lawyer, no judge, no Congress with the courage to expose the evidence. In every case where the evidence is pursued, the 'theory' becomes a clear-cut case of criminal conspiracy."

"The murders of John Kennedy, Martin Luther King, Robert Kennedy, the accident at Chappaquiddick and the shooting of Governor George Wallace were plots to maintain control over the electoral system. Only one candidate gained from all this violence, and that was Richard Nixon."

"CIA espionage networks were supposed to spy out secrets of other nations. Instead they have secretly engaged in clandestine political actions, stirred revolts, overthrown governments and attempted to bring about political change....Many heads of other governments were blown off to keep their economies and institutions under the control of the United States. And when newly elected President John Kennedy indicated he was not taking orders from some invisible government then it was time for him to be assassinated."

"The object of assassinations in other countries is for a shift of power. The object of American assassinations has been to keep the power in the same hands.... Every time we are ready to change domestic and foreign policies through the electoral process, the candidate who would effect [those] changes gets smashed."

"The most important ingredient in successfully concealing American conspiracies [is] to make the cover story sound so good and repeat it so often that nobody question[s] it."

# THE PLOT TO SEIZE THE WHITE HOUSE

*Fascism in America? Some powerful Wall Street leaders were so outraged by President Franklin Roosevelt that they wanted to replace him with a dictator.*

Teddy Roosevelt once called him "the finest fighting man in America." Yet if you saw Major General Smedley Darlington Butler out of uniform, you'd probably never guess that he was one of only four Americans ever awarded the Congressional Medal of Honor twice. He was a hawk-nosed little man who never weighed more than 130 pounds in his fighting prime and was a bit stoop-shouldered from years of carrying a heavy backpack.

Smedley Butler's troops loved him. He fought in the trenches beside them, and was as fearless with his opinions as he was with his body. He'd speak his mind to anyone. When, as commandant of the Marines, he caused an international furor by calling Mussolini "a mad dog"—long before WWII began—Butler resigned from his beloved Marine Corps rather than apologize.

The incident made him a national hero, however, and he was soon giving 300 speeches a year to veterans' groups. Shortly afterward, he was in the news again. On November 20, 1934, Butler told the House Un-American Activities Committee (HUAC) that he had proof of "a plot of Wall Street interests planning to overthrow President Roosevelt and establish a Fascist dictatorship backed by a private army of 500,000 ex-soldiers and others." (*The New York Times*)

## HARD TIMES
*Was it believable that industrialists would plot to take over the government? In the 1930s it was.*

• With more than a third of the work force out of work, and millions more ruined when bank failures wiped out their life savings, America was down on its luck. President Roosevelt did what he could to get the economy moving...and big business hated him for it. For example, FDR took the dollar off the gold standard to put more money in circulation—letting debtors pay bankers back in inflated paper dollars. In response, the business press heaped abuse on FDR, calling him "a traitor to his class" and "an impulsive, uninformed opportunist, lacking policy or stability, wasteful, reckless, unreliable in act and contract."

• In fact, many American industrialists looked longingly at the growing fascist movements in Europe, and some invested heavily in rebuilding and rearming Germany. They openly admired Mussolini and Hitler for outlawing unions and strikes and sometimes emulated the dictators' methods. "In 1936," writes Charles Higham in his book *Trading with the Enemy*, "Irénée du Pont used General Motors money to finance the notorious Black Legion....The members wore hoods and black robes, with skull and crossbones. They firebombed union meetings, murdered union organizers...and dedicated their lives to destroying Jews and communists."

• Wealthy media interests also supported fascism. The Hearst papers praised Hitler (see p. 66), and the July 1934 edition of *Fortune* magazine said, "Fascism is achieving in a few years or decades such a conquest of the spirit of man as Christianity achieved only in ten centuries....The good journalist must recognize in Fascism certain ancient virtues of the race, whether or not they happen to be momentarily fashionable in his own country. Among these are Discipline, Duty, Courage, Glory, Sacrifice."

## GENERAL BUTLER'S STORY

• Shortly after retiring from the Marines in 1933, Butler told the HUAC panel, he had been visited by two officials of the American Legion, William Doyle and Gerald C. MacGuire, a Wall Street bond salesman. They told him they wanted him to run for national commander of the American Legion. Butler was interested because he thought that the organization's leaders did little for the common soldier.

• At a second meeting, MacGuire told Butler that a group of nine very wealthy businessmen would finance his campaign for the office—if he were willing to read a prepared speech to the Legion convention. The speech was a call for the U.S. to return to the gold standard, a move that would help bankers. Because the speech had nothing to do with soldiers' concerns, Butler grew suspicious and stalled.

• MacGuire wasn't discouraged. Just before Butler was scheduled to address a veterans' group in New Jersey, MacGuire showed up at the general's hotel room, grandly threw eighteen $1,000 bills down on the bed, and implied that his backers would do anything to make Butler their spokesman. Smedley was even more suspicious, but he played along. He asked to meet some of those backers.

• Shortly, Butler was visited by Robert Sterling Clark, heir to the huge Singer sewing machine fortune. Clark said he had a fortune of $30 million and was willing to spend half of it to keep the other half. Now Butler knew for sure that this group cared nothing about veterans. They wanted only to manipulate the American Legion through him to pressure Roosevelt and promote a Wall Street agenda. Butler told Clark that he wanted no part of the plan.

### The Plot Thickens

• For several months, MacGuire stopped pestering Butler. Then, on August 22, 1934—three days after Adolf Hitler assumed complete control of the German state—MacGuire contacted Butler again. MacGuire said he'd been touring Europe and studying "the role of veterans groups in the formation of the Nazi Party in Germany, the Fascisti in Italy, and the Croix de Feu movement in France." (Curt Gentry, *J. Edgar Hoover: The Man and the Secrets*)

• MacGuire told Butler that "it was time to get the soldiers together" in America and that his backers planned to build a 500,000-man army of veterans to take over the government. Butler testified that MacGuire and his backers wanted him to head that army. As *The New York Times* reported that testimony, "MacGuire represented that 'We have $3,000,000 to start with on the line and can get $300,000,000 if we need it,' " and implied that the J.P. Morgan Bank was also a backer.

• According to Butler, the purpose of the "veterans' army" would be a show of force to pressure Roosevelt into adding another member to his cabinet, a Secretary of General Affairs. That secretary would then dictate government policy to Roosevelt, reducing him largely to a figurehead. If Roosevelt did not go along, he would be removed.

• MacGuire told Butler that if he turned them down, the plotters were prepared to offer the dictatorship to Chief of Staff Douglas MacArthur, and if MacArthur refused, they would approach James Van Zandt, the national commander of the Veterans of Foreign Wars.

• Although Butler was appalled by what he heard, for once he kept his opinions to himself, hoping to find out who was behind the plot. He pressed MacGuire to name more of the backers. MacGuire declined, but made a number of predictions, including the formation of a "superorganization" of industrial leaders and patriots backed by du Pont money.

## BUTLER'S CRITICS RESPOND

• When Butler's charges first leaked out of an executive session of HUAC, the press reported them respectfully. *Newsweek* noted, "Butler has the evidence."

• But then Butler's alleged conspirators responded. Thomas LaMont, a partner in J. P. Morgan & Company, called Butler's story "perfect moonshine, too unutterably ridiculous to comment upon." Douglas MacArthur issued a statement calling it "the best laugh story of the year." For his part, MacGuire said, "I know nothing about it. The matter is made out of whole cloth. I deny the story completely."

• Robert Clark, out of the country when the charges broke, said he was "bewildered" and threatened to sue Butler unless "the whole affair [wasn't] relegated to the funny papers by Sunday." Clark's lawyer further cabled, "Reports of the Butler testimony [are] outrageous....my opinion is that a most serious libel has been committed."

## SUSPICIOUS FACTS

• Despite threats by Clark and his lawyer to sue Butler for libel, the general never recanted and they never sued.

• MacGuire *was* a dedicated fascist. Although he told HUAC that he had taken a trip to Europe solely to buy bonds, investigators noted that he had come back with detailed reports on fascist organizations in Italy, Germany, and France.

• The committee also found that on the day Butler claimed that the bond salesman had offered him $18,000 in $1,000 bills, MacGuire's bank records showed that he had at least $16,000 in his possession, most of it in $1,000 bills.

## Corroborating Witnesses

• Before going public with the story, Butler had asked *Philadelphia Record* reporter Paul French to investigate the conspiracy. French gained MacGuire's confidence, and MacGuire repeated to him much of what he'd told Butler: that he supported having a fascist government in the U.S.; that he wanted Butler to lead the uprising against FDR; and that the du Ponts were willing to use their controlling interest in the Remington Arms Company, a major weapons manufacturer, to arm the planned paramilitary force.

• After the story broke, James Van Zandt claimed that "agents of Wall Street" had also asked him—as MacGuire told Butler they would—to "lead a Fascist dictatorship in the United States under the guise of a veterans organization." Like the group that approached Butler, Van Zandt's "agents" wanted to force the return of the gold standard.

## MacGuire's Predictions

• Just as MacGuire had predicted to Butler in 1934, a right-wing "superorganization" hostile to FDR appeared shortly: the American Liberty League. Backed by the same people who were allegedly behind the planned coup—executives from J. P. Morgan & Company, Rockefeller interests, E. F. Hutton, and General Motors—the group denounced the New Deal and accused Roosevelt of "fomenting class hatred" by attacking big business.

• The American Liberty League had strong ties to MacGuire. His boss, Grayson M. P. Murphy, president of one of Wall Street's leading brokerage houses, was the League's treasurer. And Robert Clark, whom Butler claimed had met with him to discuss the conspiracy, was one of the financial backers of the group.

• The League was also affiliated with two other openly Fascist and anti-labor groups that were even further to the right: the Sentinels of the Republic, an anti-Semitic group that referred to FDR's New Deal recovery program as "Jewish Communism"; and the Southern Committee to Uphold the Constitution, described in press accounts at the time as "a hybrid organization financed by Northern money, but playing on the Ku Klux Klan prejudices of the South."

## WAS THERE A CONSPIRACY?

*Were American fascists looking for a way to take over the White House? Was there a serious plot?*

• HUAC never subpoenaed any of the people Butler implicated, other than reporter Paul French and Gerald MacGuire; its 1935 report timidly omitted a number of details, including any mention of the du Ponts and the Morgan Bank.

• Despite its caution, however, the committee said it found evidence "verifying completely the testimony of General Butler." "There is no question," it added, "that these attempts were discussed, were planned, and might have been placed in execution when and if the financial backers deemed it expedient."

• One part of the conspiracy theory still makes no sense, however: Butler's dislike of Mussolini—and fascism in general—was well known. Why would fascist conspirators try to enlist him in a plot? Perhaps MacGuire and his cronies hoped that Butler was naive politically and could be manipulated to do their bidding, or that they would eventually find his price. We don't know.

• Whatever the truth of the matter, Butler's testimony and French's newspaper exposé helped kill the American Liberty League. Notes author Curt Gentry, "By 1936, when Roosevelt ran for a second term, the league was so thoroughly discredited the Republican Party begged them not to endorse their candidate."

## RECOMMENDED READING

*The Plot to Seize the White House*, by Jules Archer (Hawthorn Books, 1973)

# JACK RUBY

*Was Jack Ruby just another "lone nut" killer, or
one of the key players in the Kennedy assassination?*

J ack Ruby was a 52-year-old nightclub owner well-known to the
Dallas underworld and the police. On Sunday, November 24—
two days after Kennedy was killed—Ruby became known to the
whole world. As the Warren Report tells it:

> At approximately 11:20 a.m. Oswald emerged from the basement jail
> office flanked by detectives on either side...a man suddenly darted out
> from an area on the right of the cameras where newsmen had been as-
> sembled. The man was carrying a Colt .38 revolver in his right hand
> and, while millions watched on television, he moved quickly to within
> a few feet of Oswald and fired one shot into Oswald's abdomen. Oswald
> groaned with pain as he fell to the floor and quickly lost conscious-
> ness...he was pronounced dead at 1:07 p.m.

> The man who killed Oswald was Jack Ruby. He was instantly arrested
> and, minutes later, confined in a cell on the fifth floor of the Dallas po-
> lice jail. Under interrogation, he denied that the killing of Oswald was
> in any way connected with a conspiracy involving the assassination of
> President Kennedy. He maintained that he had killed Oswald in a tem-
> porary fit of depression and rage over the President's death.

On March 14, 1964, Ruby was found guilty of killing Oswald and
was sentenced to death. Following an appeal, however, Ruby's conviction was overturned in October 1966—which meant he could
have gone free on bail within months. But it never happened. Two
months later, on December 9, Ruby was diagnosed as having inop-
erable cancer. On January 3, 1967, he died.

## WAS IT A CONSPIRACY?
*Was Jack Ruby just a distraught admirer of John F. Kennedy, acting on
his own—or did the Mafia order him to silence Lee Harvey Oswald?*

## SUSPICIOUS FACTS
### Anguished American?

• In an interview with the FBI, Ruby said he'd shot Oswald because he "had cried a great deal," and his anguish about the president's death finally "reached the point of insanity." The national media duly reported Ruby's grief and love of the Kennedy family as fact. Yet on Saturday, the day after Kennedy was slain, Ruby was seen at the Dallas police station joking with reporters and passing out cards to his strip joint.

• Later that same day, he visited a newspaper production room to display a "twistboard" exercising device that he was trying to sell. "Considerable merriment developed when one of the women employees of the *Times-Herald* demonstrated the board, and Ruby himself put on a demonstration." (Warren Report)

• At a polygraph hearing in 1964, Ruby himself dismissed the story he had told the FBI: "If I loved the President so much, why wasn't I at the parade [motorcade]?...It's strange that perhaps I didn't vote for Kennedy, or didn't vote at all, that I should build up such a great affection for him."

### Ruby and the Mob

• Jack Ruby's connections to the Mafia and Teamster President Jimmy Hoffa—which went back thirty years—were well-known to the Dallas police and the FBI. Yet, strangely, the news media largely ignored those ties.

• After being declared an "incorrigible youth" and put into a foster home, Ruby (known then as Jack Rubenstein) gravitated to crime. Boxer Barney Ross, a close friend of Ruby, told the FBI that he "might have run innocuous errands for Capone."

• Ruby may have been a Mob hit man. A December 9, 1939, story in the *Chicago Tribune* describes Jack Rubenstein as the prime suspect in the killing of Leon Cooke, the honest president of a local Teamster's Union, No. 20467. Because police records on the case disappeared, it's unclear how the case was resolved, but Local 20467 was soon taken over by the Mafia.

• According to David Scheim in his book, *Contract on America*, Rubenstein moved from Chicago to Dallas in 1947, as part of a

Mafia takeover of Dallas crime. There he changed his name to Ruby and bought the first of several bars. Scheim says that Ruby was a Mob "lieutenant" who made sure that Chicago bosses got their cut from Dallas gambling, prostitution, and narcotics. In time, Ruby became the Mob's "pay-off man for the Dallas Police" and eventually used those contacts to get into the police station to kill Oswald.

• According to FBI and U.S. Army Intelligence reports quoted in *Contract on America*, Ruby "was active in arranging illegal flights of weapons from Miami to the Castro organization in Cuba" in the 1950s. When Castro double-crossed the Mob and threw it out of Cuba, Ruby then began supplying weapons to anti-Castro Cubans being trained by the CIA, according to several sources.

### A Mafia-Ruby-CIA Hypothesis

• According to *Double Cross*, an account of the life of Mafia boss Sam Giancana, Ruby did more than kill Oswald. The book alleges that a CIA-Mafia plot resulted in Kennedy's death and asserts that Giancana "put Ruby in charge of overseeing the Outfit's [Mafia's] role in the assassination, collaborating in Dallas with the [CIA] government agents."

• *Double Cross* also claims that Oswald—whose uncle worked for New Orleans mobster Carlos Marcello—was in on the plot and was killed so he wouldn't talk. So, because Ruby was "the person representing the Outfit in Dallas, the task had quite naturally fallen to Ruby to silence Oswald when he was unexpectedly captured alive."

• At least one part of *Double Cross*'s theory has been corroborated. In the mid-1970s, mobster John "Handsome Johnny" Roselli, who had close ties to Ruby, "began to describe Ruby as 'one of our boys' and speak of Ruby's having been ordered to eliminate Oswald to silence him." Roselli repeated that claim to columnist Jack Anderson, Senate investigators, and others before his dismembered body was found in an oil drum in Miami's Biscayne Bay. (*Contract on America*)

### FBI Ties

• Author Jim Marrs corroborates Ruby's Mafia-CIA ties and implicates one more U.S. agency in his book *Crossfire*: "In early 1959, at a time when Jack Ruby may have been involved in smuggling activities with Cubans, he contacted the FBI and said he wanted to provide the Bureau with information....The relationship between Ruby and the Bureau was mentioned in a letter from Hoover to the Warren Commission dated June 9, 1964." The letter remained classified until 1975.

• In the letter, Hoover claimed that Ruby "furnished no information whatsoever and further contacts with him were discontinued." However, Bureau records show that FBI agents met eight times with Ruby between April and October of 1959—which makes Hoover's assertion extremely suspect. (*Crossfire*)

### The Songbird

• When Earl Warren, Gerald Ford, and lawyers from the Warren Commission interviewed Ruby in Dallas on June 7, 1964, he begged them eight times to take him back to Washington, because he feared for his life if he told the truth in Dallas. The commissioners refused.

• When it became obvious that the commissioners were leaving without really probing for what he knew, Ruby persisted, "You can get more out of me, let's not break up too soon." Finally, despairing, he said, "Well, you won't ever see me again. I tell you that.... A whole new form of government is going to take over the country, and I know I won't live to see you another time." (Warren Report)

• Not long before his death, Ruby told psychiatrist Werner Teuter that Kennedy's assassination was "an act of overthrowing the government," that he knew "who had Kennedy killed," that he had been part of that plot, and that he "was framed to kill Oswald."

### Ruby's Death

• On October 5, 1966, the Texas Court of Criminal Appeals overturned Ruby's conviction and ordered a new trial. It seemed likely that Ruby would be released in a matter of months; authorities anticipated that he would receive a short prison sentence, and that his time served would count against it. (*Crossfire*)

• "On December 9, 1966...Ruby was moved from the Dallas County Jail to Parkland Hospital after complaining of persistent coughing and nausea. Doctors initially diagnosed his problem as 'pneumonia.' The next day, however, the diagnosis was changed to cancer and shortly after, it was announced that Ruby's lung cancer was too far advanced to be treated by surgery or radiation." At 9 a.m. on January 3, 1967, "he suffered a spasm and, despite emergency procedures, he was pronounced dead at 10:30 a.m." (ibid.)

• Ruby believed that he had been injected with a carcinogen. One of Ruby's Dallas County jailers, Deputy Sheriff Al Maddox, told researchers in 1982 that "a phony doctor came in from Chicago" who, though supposed to care for all the inmates, "spent half his time up there talking with Ruby." One day, said Maddox, Ruby told him that that doctor, while pretending to treat him for a cold, had injected him with cancer cells. When Maddox said, "You don't believe that shit," Ruby replied, "I damn sure do!" (ibid.)

• Could Ruby's claim be credible? Perhaps. Such carcinogens were known at the time. A 1952 CIA memo, for example, reported on the cancer-causing effects of beryllium: "This is certainly the most toxic inorganic element and it produces a peculiar fibrotic tumor at the site of local application. The amount necessary to produce these tumors is a few micrograms." (ibid.)

## FOOTNOTE

### Did Ruby Know Oswald?

A number of witnesses claimed they saw Jack Ruby and Lee Harvey Oswald together *before* the assassination of JFK. But the Warren Report says: "All assertions that Oswald was seen in the company of Ruby or anyone else...have been investigated. None of them merits any credence."

• Karen Carlin, a stripper at Ruby's Carousel Club, talked with the Secret Service on the evening of Oswald's death. She told them that Oswald and Ruby had been involved together in a plot to assassinate President Kennedy. Terrified, she asked that any information that she gave "be kept confidential to prevent retaliation." Months later she was found shot to death in a Houston hotel. The Warren Report says: "Mrs. Carlin was...not certain that the man was Oswald nor was she sure where she had seen him."

• The Associated Press reported that William Crowe, an entertainer who specialized in memory tricks, said he was "positive" he had seen and interacted with Oswald at the Carousel Club. Crowe later told the *Dallas Morning News* that after the AP story appeared, the FBI advised him to go into hiding for a while. The Warren Report quoted Crowe as telling the Commission: "I never stated definitely, positively, and they said that I did, and all in all, what they had in the paper was hardly even close to what I told them." The report added: "When asked how certain he was that the man he saw was Oswald, Crowe testified: 'The face seemed familiar as some faces do, and I had associated it with a patron that I had seen in the club a week before. That was about it.' "

• While seated in the Carousel Club, Dallas attorney Carroll Jarnagin "overheard Jack Ruby—whom he knew well—talking with another man. Jarnagin heard the man tell Ruby, 'Don't use my real name. I'm going by the name O. H. Lee.' " According to Jarnagan, they discussed killing Governor John Connally and Robert Kennedy. Jarnagin gave the Texas Department of Public Safety this information—before JFK's assassination—but nothing came of the warning. (*Crossfire*)

## RECOMMENDED READING
• *Crossfire: The Plot to Kill Kennedy*, by Jim Marrs (Carroll & Graf, 1989)
• *Contract on America: The Mafia Murders of JFK*, by David Scheim (Zebra, 1991)
• *Double Cross*, by Sam & Chuck Giancana (Warner Books, 1992)

## TALES OF THE CIA
Quiz: What motto is inscribed on the wall of the CIA headquarters in Langley, Virginia?
A) "Keep the Faith"  B) "And Ye Shall Know the Truth and the Truth Shall Make You Free"  C) "A Secret Kept Is a Secret Saved"

Answer: B

# NIXON VS. THE REDS

*No matter who he was really running against, Dick Nixon's main opponent, early in his political career, was the Communist conspiracy. Here are a few of the things you might have heard the "old" Nixon say.*

## 1951

"Communists have infiltrated the very highest councils of this [Truman] administration, [yet]...our top administration officials have refused time and time again to recognize the existence of the fifth column in this country and to take effective action to clean subversives out of the administrative branch of our government."

## 1952

"You folks know I did the work of investigating the Communists in the United States. Ever since [then]...the Communists and left-wingers have been fighting me with every smear they have had."

"After I received the nomination for the vice-presidency, I was warned that if I continued to attack the Communists and crooks in this administration, they would smear me, and, believe me, you can expect that they will continue to do so."

"You can be sure that smears will continue to come, and the purpose of the smears is to make me, if possible, relent in my attacks on the Communists ...in the present administration."

"I'm going to expose the Communists...and those who defend them until they throw them all out of Washington."

## 1958

"Everywhere out there, the press, the radio, the magazines, etc., have been heavily infiltrated by the Commies."

## 1960

"I think it is shocking for a candidate for the Presidency [John F. Kennedy] to say that he is willing to hand over a part of the Free World to the Communist World....Let me say this to you: if you elect me President I assure you that I will not hand over one square foot of the Free World to the Communists."

## 1958 Footnote

"It is despicable to make a racket of anti-Communism."

# NAZIS IN THE CIA

*War makes strange allies, but peace can make even stranger ones.*

It was five years after the end of World War II, but one of Hitler's chief intelligence officers was still on the job. From a walled-in compound in Bavaria, General Reinhard Gehlen oversaw a vast network of intelligence agents spying on Russia. His top aides were Nazi zealots who had committed some of the most notorious crimes of the war. Why hadn't the Allies found him?

They had...and they'd hired him. Now he was an agent for the CIA.

## THE NAZI VIEW

• Gehlen, the head of Nazi military intelligence in Eastern Europe and the Soviet Union, began planning his career move long before the war ended. As he noted in his memoirs, "Early in 1944 I told my more intimate colleagues that I considered the war lost and we must begin thinking of the future...and plan for the approaching catastrophe." (*Covert Action*, Fall 1990)

• He had amassed an extraordinary amount of information about the USSR. In addition to files on roads, bridges, airfields, and factories, he had personnel files on the Soviet high command and had amassed a network of fascist collaborators in Eastern Europe and the Soviet Union.

• "He derived much of his information from his role in one of the most terrible atrocities of the war: the torture, interrogation and murder by starvation of some four million Soviet prisoners. Prisoners who refused to cooperate were often tortured or summarily executed. Many were executed even *after* they gave information, while others were simply left to starve to death." (*Blowback: America's Recruitment of Nazis and Its Effect on the Cold War*)

• As a result, Gehlen and members of his organization maneuvered to make sure that they were captured by advancing American troops rather than Russians, who would have probably executed them on the spot.

## GEHLEN'S MOVE

• Two months before Germany surrendered in 1945, the Gehlen organization made its move. "Gehlen and a small group of his most senior officers carefully microfilmed the vast holding on the USSR ...in the military section of the German army's general staff. They packed the film in watertight steel drums and secretly buried it in remote mountain meadows scattered throughout the Austrian Alps." (ibid.)

• Gehlen had to be very careful. "For one thing, the U.S. command mistrusted any type of deals offered by desperate Germans. For another, the Yalta agreements [with the Soviet Union] required the United States to turn over to the Russians captured Axis officers who had been involved in 'eastern area activities' in exchange for Soviet help in returning the thousands of American POWs who had been picked up by the Red Army." (ibid.)

## THE OFFICIAL STORY

•When Gehlen and his men surrendered, they were apparently very lucky. They might have been interrogated by someone who went by the book and felt compelled to turn them over to the Russians. But instead they were quizzed by Captain John Bokor, a pragmatist who regarded the Soviets as a potential enemy. Gehlen later wrote that Bokor "had no illusions about the way political events were turning....We became close friends and have remained so."

• During the weeks that followed, Gehlen gradually laid his cards on the table. "Not only did the former Wehrmacht general know where the precious archives were buried, but he had also maintained the embryo of an underground espionage organization that could put the records to work against the USSR. Captain Bokor was interested." (ibid.)

• According to Gehlen's memoirs, Bokor decided to proceed on his own, regardless of official policy. He kept the details of Gehlen's offer secret from the other Americans at the interrogation center and worked quietly to remove the names of Gehlen's senior command from the official lists of POWs in U.S. hands.

• Gehlen's precious cache of records was located and shipped to the interrogation center under such secrecy that not even the Army Intelligence's chain of command was informed. "Bokor feared," Gehlen related many years later, "that if he had reported our existence too early...we might have become exposed to hostile forces [within the U.S. chain of command] and then we would have been beyond salvation. I now know...that Captain Bokor was acting on his own during the earliest days." (ibid.)

• By the end of the summer, however, Bokor had won the support of General Edwin Sibert (the highest ranking U.S. Army Intelligence officer in Europe at the time) and Walter Bedell Smith, the chief of staff of the Supreme Allied Command.

• General William "Wild Bill" Donovan and Allen Dulles of America's wartime clandestine operations agency, the Office of Strategic Services (OSS), were also tipped off about Gehlen's offer. The OSS was soon jockeying with military intelligence for authority over Gehlen's microfilmed records—and control of the German spy master.

• By August, Gehlen and three assistants were surreptitiously flown to Washington, D.C. and interviewed by both the OSS and military intelligence. Within a year, the Gehlen Organization (which became known as the "Gehlen Org") was installed in West Germany to act as America's eyes and ears on Eastern Europe. In time, the Gehlen Org became West Germany's version of the CIA and America's staunch ally in the Cold War.

### WAS IT A CONSPIRACY? #1
*Did American intelligence agents intentionally break the law and flout U.S. foreign policy in hiring Gehlen?*

### SUSPICIOUS FACTS
• Gehlen's resurrection was a clear violation of the Yalta accords. Through their own network of informants and double agents, the Soviets learned that the U.S. had "secured" Gehlen, yet refused to turn him over. The Soviets "made vigorous protests against this secret agreement at least as early as the Potsdam Conference." Although this U.S. violation increased Cold War tensions, the American government ignored the Russian protests. (*Blowback*)

• It was also against U.S. law and public policy to employ Nazis, and it would have been political dynamite in America. Thus, U.S. officials denied everything. To those few insiders in government who knew the truth, the conspirators justified their actions by saying that Gehlen had promised not to hire any former SS, SD, or Gestapo agents. There were few apologies. When Allen Dulles became head of the CIA, he said of Gehlen, "He's on our side, and that's all that matters."

## WAS IT A CONSPIRACY? #2
*Was Gehlen's lucky meeting with Captain Bokor just a cover story for a plan that had been worked out while the war was still on?*

## SUSPICIOUS FACTS
### The Dulles Connection
• Immediately after World War II, "[U.S.] intelligence files on the Soviet Union were virtually empty....Even the most elementary facts were unavailable." (*Blowback*)

• However, the OSS had some extraordinary contacts within Germany. The OSS station chief in Bern, Switzerland, Allen Dulles, "had German contacts going back to his State Department posting in Berlin in the 1920s." In 1929, Dulles's Wall Street law firm, Sullivan and Cromwell, opened a Berlin office and helped build the German chemical giant I.G. Farben and rearm Germany.

• Dulles's ties to the Nazis were also personal. Hitler's "financial wizard" and president of the Reichsbank, Hjalmar Schacht, was a longtime friend. Schacht, in turn, knew almost all the German High Command. Thus, Dulles, through his post in neutral Switzerland, was in a good position to send messages to or get intelligence from officials within Nazi Germany.

### The Bokor Connection
• Gehlen's story that Bokor "acted on his own" to keep the spy master's surrender a secret is unbelievable. It's improbable that an American officer would risk his career to protect a Nazi general, and even less probable that Gehlen—who had carefully planned his move—would simply wander into an American base and surrender himself to the first soldier he met.

• On the other hand, as an intelligence chief, Gehlen undoubtedly knew that business and personal contacts frequently cross the boundaries of warring countries. He would have known which members of the German High Command had contacts in the West, whom he could trust, and who would want the information he had.

The Secret Agenda

• Dulles knew Gehlen was coming. According to Peter Dale Scott, "In April 1945, one month before the war ended, Dulles asked [an aide] to begin talks with Gehlen, who was not taken into U.S. custody until May 20." Gehlen may well have contacted Dulles sometime in 1944. (*Covert Action*, Winter 1986)

• Given the political perils of rehabbing a Nazi spy master well known and detested by the Soviets—still U.S. allies at the time—it's almost certain that President Truman knew, too. Truman's approval of Project Paperclip (see p. 37), which brought German scientists to America, further supports this theory. But it's just a theory: nearly fifty years later, the documents that could prove Truman's approval of the plan are still classified.

## WAS IT A CONSPIRACY? #3

*After the war, did the U.S. government condone hiring Nazi war criminals—and indirectly help thousands more escape justice?*

## SUSPICIOUS FACTS

• Gehlen promised not to hire former SS, SD, or Gestapo members; he hired them anyway, and the CIA didn't stop him.

• Two of Gehlen's early recruits were Emil Augsburg and Dr. Franz Six, who had been part of mobile killing squads, which killed Jews, intellectuals, and Soviet partisans wherever they found them. (Adolf Eichmann called Six a *Streber*—an "eager beaver.") Other early recruits included Willi Krichbaum, senior Gestapo leader for southeastern Europe, and the Gestapo chiefs of Paris and Kiel, Germany.

• With the encouragement of the OSS and the CIA, the Gehlen Org set up "rat lines" to get Nazi war criminals out of Europe so they wouldn't be prosecuted. By setting up transit camps and issuing phony passports, the Gehlen Org helped more than 5,000 Nazis leave Europe and relocate around the world, especially in South and Central America. There, mass murderers like Klaus Barbie (the "Butcher of Lyons") helped governments set up death squads in Chile, Argentina, El Salvador, and elsewhere.

• According to Peter Dale Scott, the OSS and the CIA foresaw this fascist network as an ally in its war against international

Communism. For example, Scott alleges, OSS officer (and later CIA chief of intelligence) James Jesus Angleton supplied new identities to Nazis held in Allied prison camps and helped them to escape. Scott also notes that Donovan and Dulles must have seen that "with a global network of its men already in place, the Gehlen Org would be an even more impressive asset in their case for a postwar CIA." (*Covert Action*, Winter 1986)

## WAS IT A CONSPIRACY? #4

*Did Gehlen and American intelligence organizations join forces to help create the Cold War?*

## SUSPICIOUS FACTS

• To protect his new position, Gehlen needed to make himself invaluable to his new employers. He realized that the blacker he painted Russian intentions, the more indispensable he would become. Consequently, Gehlen consistently misrepresented Soviet intentions and dramatically overestimated Soviet strength. For example:

√ He told the U.S. that Soviet assault troops were combat-ready and massed to attack West Germany as early as 1946. He reported that their 208 assault divisions represented a ten-to-one numerical superiority over Western forces.

√ "By late 1947 Gehlen...reported...that quiet changes already under way in Soviet billeting and leave-policies for the troops suggested a major mobilization could be in the wind. The Soviets' behavior should be interpreted as a prelude to military aggression, he argued." (*Blowback*)

√ Gehlen predicted a quick and decisive move by the Soviets. According to his intelligence information, they were ready to launch a *blitzkrieg*—a lightning-fast surprise attack—into Western Europe at any time.

• Actually, Gehlen's assertions couldn't have been further from the truth:

√ In mid-1946, U.S. military intelligence correctly reported that the Red Army was underequipped, overextended, and war weary. The Soviets even lacked motorized support vehicles to move soldiers and equipment. At least half of their transport vehicles were *horse-drawn*.

√ Furthermore, Army intelligence concluded, those forces were almost entirely tied down with administrative police and reconstruction tasks in the Russian-occupied zone. Soviet military aggression against Western Europe was highly unlikely for at least a decade, if only for logistical reasons, the army determined. (*Blowback*)

√ As for the 10-to-1 Russian superiority, Gehlen's estimate failed to acknowledge that each Soviet division averaged only a third of the manpower of a Western division, and that only a third of the Soviet divisions were "full-strength and combat ready." In reality, there was rough military parity in postwar Europe, both sides having about 800,000 troops. (*International Security*)

• When American intelligence organizations tried to reconcile these discrepancies, they decided to trust Gehlen's figures. In fact 70% of the U.S. government's information on Soviet forces and weapons came from the Gehlen Org, and it was invariably dire. According to one retired CIA official quoted in the book *Blowback*, "Gehlen's reports and analyses were sometimes simply retyped onto CIA stationary and presented to President Truman without further comment."

• Truman's response to Gehlen's concocted crisis was exactly what the military, the intelligence community, and Gehlen desired: he stopped cuts in the military budget, accelerated construction of atomic weapons, and dumped millions of dollars into a variety of covert operations and intelligence programs, including the newly born CIA. (ibid.)

• Gelen's disinformation paid big dividends for his organization as well. The United States dumped at least $200 million into it during the ten years following the war.

• The CIA's former chief analyst on Soviet military capabilities, Victor Marchetti, summed up the situation decades later: "The agency [CIA] loved Gehlen because he fed us what we wanted to hear. We used his stuff constantly, and we fed it to everybody else: the Pentagon; the White House; the newspapers. They loved it."

• Marchetti adds: "Gehlen had to make his money by creating a threat that we were afraid of, so we would give him more money to tell us about it. In my opinion, the Gehlen Organization provided nothing worthwhile for understanding or estimating Soviet military or political capabilities in Eastern Europe or anywhere else."

• In the end, Gehlen's biased intelligence helped create a Cold War that lasted 45 years and cost U.S. taxpayers more than $8 *trillion.*

## RECOMMENDED READING

• *Blowback: America's Recruitment of Nazis and Its Effect on the Cold War,* by Christopher Simpson (Weidenfeld & Nicolson, 1988). An excellent book, well-researched and very readable.

• *Gehlen, Spy of the Century,* by E. H. Cookridge (Random House, 1971)

• "How Allen Dulles and the SS Preserved Each Other," by Peter Dale Scott (*Covert Action,* Winter 1986, No. 25, pp. 4-14).

## MEDIA CONSPIRACIES

On September 5, 1989, president George Bush gave a televised speech to announce his "War on Drugs" and declare drugs "public enemy #1." To show just how bad things had gotten, Bush held up a plastic bag of crack cocaine that he said had been bought from a drug dealer in Lafayette Park—right across the street from the White House. But, according to *Propaganda Review:*

> Lafayette Park, across Pennsylvania Avenue from the White House, has never attracted drug dealers of any kind—the young crack dealer had been lured to Lafayette Park, with great difficulty, by the DEA (Drug Enforcement Agency).
>
> When Bush was questioned about these details a few days later by the press, he got angry and asked whether the press was siding with the dealer. He said, "I don't understand—I mean, has somebody got some advocates here for this drug guy?"
>
> He then changed the subject and nobody even attempted to question him about the Constitutional violations involved in such an arrest or about the underlying deception of staging a bust just for the purpose of his speech.

Keith Jackson, the dealer, "was found not guilty on the Lafayette Park charge." Because he had resisted undercover agents' attempts to get him to sell drugs across the street from the White House—as any streetwise dealer would—the bust was considered entrapment and was thrown out of court. Bush did not comment.

# SUSPICIOUS DEATH #5: VICKI MORGAN

*Was Vicki Morgan murdered by her mentally disturbed housemate—
or by her powerful enemies in the Republican establishment?*

T he deceased: Vicki Morgan, model and longtime mistress of Alfred Bloomingdale, one of the wealthiest men in America. (He was founder of the Diner's Club, heir to the Bloomingdale department store fortune, and a member of Ronald Reagan's Kitchen Cabinet.)

How she died: On July 7, 1983, Morgan was found dead in her apartment, beaten to death with a baseball bat. The man who shared her Studio City condo, Marvin Pancoast, confessed.

## BACKGROUND

• Morgan was Bloomingdale's mistress for twelve years—from 1970 to 1982, when Bloomingdale contracted terminal throat cancer. Once Alfred was hospitalized, his wife, Betsy, long furious about the affair, cut off Morgan's income—which was reportedly between $10,000 and $18,000 a month.

• In response, Morgan decided to go public about the affair. She first tried to place her memoirs, *Alfred's Mistress*, with the William Morris Agency. When that attempt fizzled—allegedly because of White House pressure—she filed a $10 million palimony suit against Bloomingdale in which she revealed all of Bloomingdale's indiscretions, from his taste for kinky sex—she once described him as "a drooling sadist" with a fondness for bondage and beatings—to his loose talk about "secret and delicate matters such as campaign contributions for Mr. Reagan."

• The case was thrown out, but the trial was an enormous embarrassment to Betsy Bloomingdale—Nancy Reagan's close friend—as well as to Bloomingdale's highly placed Republican cronies.

## SUSPICIOUS FACTS

### Marvin Pancoast

• Pancoast had a history of mental illness. (In fact, Morgan had met him four years earlier when they were both patients in a mental institution.) He had previously confessed to crimes he hadn't committed. At one point he even confessed to the Tate-LaBianca murders committed by the Manson family.

• The room in which Morgan was killed was spattered with blood—but, according to John Austin, author of *Hollywood's Unsolved Mysteries*, when Pancoast turned himself in, he did not have a spot of blood on him anywhere. No bloodstained clothes of his were ever found.

### Kissing and Telling

• Morgan may have been more than just Bloomingdale's mistress—Bloomingdale may have used her to gather dirt on top-level Republican officials. According to Austin, Bloomingdale had his Hollywood house wired with "state-of-the-art video cameras in every room and hidden behind false walls. Even the three johns were 'wired' behind two-way mirrors....Vicki and Pancoast would often 'share' a high ranking member of the [Reagan] Administration....Anyone who was important in the pre-Administration and the Administration of Ronald Reagan and who wanted *divertissement* called on Alfred, regardless of what his or her fetish might be." And Bloomingdale allegedly got it all on tape.

• If the tapes existed, what happened to them? Five days after Morgan's death, attorney Robert Steinberg held a press conference in Los Angeles announcing that he had received three videotapes showing "Bloomingdale and Miss Morgan engaging in group and sadomasochistic sex with top government officials." The sex tapes, Steinberg asserted, could "bring down the Reagan government." But when a court ordered Steinberg to turn them over to police, he suddenly declared that they had been stolen from a bag in his office during the press conference. The media denounced the whole thing as a hoax.

• Morgan's apartment wasn't sealed by the L.A. Police Department until more than 24 hours after the murder. According to author Anne Louise Bardach, "This is really a story of police negligence.

People could just walk in and walk out. And they did. If there were any 'sex tapes' in the condo, then they could easily have disappeared during those 24 hours."

● Morgan may have sensed that the end was near. The night before she was killed, according to her friend Gordon Basichis, "Vicki confided in me that she was afraid of being murdered. I have a feeling that someone with knowledge of the Bloomingdale 'tapes' had approached her, possibly through Pancoast, with a proposal for blackmail."

## POSSIBLE CONCLUSIONS

● **Pancoast killed her.** After all, he confessed and was sentenced in the case.

● **Someone in power had Morgan killed.** She could have been killed to silence her. If the videotapes did exist, they would have been severely damaging to the Reagan administration. Bloomingdale was a close personal friend of the president and an appointee to the Foreign Intelligence Advisory Board

## RECOMMENDED READING

● *Encyclopedia of American Scandal*, by George C. Kohn (Facts On File, 1989)

● *Hollywood's Unsolved Mysteries*, by John Austin (Shapolsky Publishers, Inc., 1990)

## TALES OF THE CIA

The ultimate in insider trading was described in Warren Hinkle and William Turner's book *Deadly Secrets*: "When the White House gave the green light for the [Bay of Pigs invasion of Cuba in 1961], a number of CIA insiders began buying the stocks of Francisco and other sugar companies, the earnings of which had been depressed by the loss of Cuban plantations. Stockbrokers became curious about the sudden influx of orders as friends were cut in on the tip that cheap sugar shares might prove a sweet gamble."

# JFK ROGUES' GALLERY #2

*Here are more of the interesting characters you'll
meet while investigating JFK's murder:*

**ALLEN DULLES.** Wall Street lawyer with close ties to the Nazi elite in the 1920s and 1930s (see p. 195); founder and later chief of the CIA; fired by JFK in 1961, when the Bay of Pigs invasion failed.

**JFK connection:** Although JFK and Dulles were antagonists, and the CIA was a plausible suspect in the assassination, LBJ appointed Dulles to the Warren Commission.

**GENERAL CHARLES CABELL.** CIA deputy director, who was fired by JFK after the Bay of Pigs fiasco.

**JFK connection:** His brother Earl was the mayor of Dallas in 1963. According to New Orleans District Attorney Jim Garrison, Earl Cabell may have rerouted Kennedy's motorcade to the slow turn by the Texas Book Depository: "The last minute change in the parade route was highly suspicious...the parade route change, along with other leads to the CIA, had been covered up by the Warren Commission." (*On the Trail of the Assassins*)

**CARLOS MARCELLO.** As the Mafia don of New Orleans, Marcello oversaw criminal activities in the southeastern U.S.—including drug smuggling and gun running. Marcello's mafiosi were thus often involved in supplying weapons to paramilitary groups such as CIA-backed Cuban exiles training in the Southeast.

**JFK connection:** Marcello figures prominently in many theories suggesting that the Mafia killed JFK. For example, John Davis, author of *Mafia Kingfish*, theorizes that Marcello, frustrated by Justice Department persecution and incensed that Attorney General Robert Kennedy had him deported, had JFK assassinated to stop RFK.

**GUY BANISTER.** Ex-FBI agent in New Orleans who was training anti-Communist Cuban exiles for the CIA in 1963.

**JFK connection:** Banister supposedly employed Oswald during the summer before Kennedy was killed, even though Oswald was supposedly pro-Castro (see p. 42).

**CLAY SHAW.** New Orleans socialite; international businessman.

**JFK connection:** According to New Orleans District Attorney Jim Garrison, Shaw conspired to kill the president with Banister and others. Shaw denied everything, and a jury acquitted him in 1969 after less than an hour's deliberation. However, Richard Helms, director of CIA covert operations in 1963, later admitted that Shaw had in fact been a CIA operative.

**DAVID FERRIE.** Vehement anti-Communist who allegedly trained and supplied Cuban exiles preparing for a second CIA-backed invasion of Cuba. Ferrie also had strong ties to Carlos Marcello and other Mafia figures.

**JFK connection:** Ferrie was a pilot who worked with Banister and Oswald the summer before President Kennedy was killed. According to *Double Cross*, he also flew Marcello back into the U.S. after Marcello had been deported by Robert Kennedy. Jim Garrison named him a chief suspect in the plot to kill Kennedy; shortly after, on February 22, 1967, he died under mysterious circumstances.

**LT. COL. PIERRE FINCK.** Army doctor on the staff of the Bethesda Medical Center in Maryland.

**JFK connection:** Assisted autopsies of JFK and RFK, according to Garrison. When asked why he didn't investigate JFK's neck wound, Finck replied that he had been outranked by several officers in the crowded autopsy room and "when you are a lieutenant colonel in the Army you just follow orders." (*On the Trail of the Assassins*)

**DR. LOUIS JOYLON "JOLLY" WEST.** Pioneer of LSD research for the CIA (see p. 165). According to the book *Acid Dreams*, West once destroyed an elephant by giving it 300,000 micrograms of acid.

**JFK connection:** While Jack Ruby was in prison, Dr. West examined him and diagnosed Oswald's killer as having "visual and auditory hallucinations" and "delusions" that America was being taken over by a fascist plot. On the basis of West's diagnosis Ruby was given "happy pills." (*Acid Dreams*)

# WHO KILLED MALCOLM X?

*Malcolm X was one of the most charismatic and militant black leaders of the 1960s. When this self-proclaimed former "hoodlum, dope-peddler and pimp" became an international spokesman, he urged African nations to denounce U.S. government racism. Did it get him killed?*

On February 21, 1965, Malcolm X rose to address a largely black crowd in the Audubon Ballroom in New York City. But before he could begin speaking, a scuffle broke out in the audience.

In *Seven Days,* Alan Berger described what happened next: "All heads turned to see what was happening...Malcolm's bodyguards moved down from the stage toward the disturbance. Malcolm himself stepped out from behind the podium and toward the front of the stage.

"There was a muffled explosion at the rear of the hall and smoke... a woman screamed. A man in one of the front rows held up a sawed-off shotgun and fired into Malcolm's chest. As Malcolm keeled over, two or three men were seen standing in the front row, 'like a firing squad,' pumping bullets into him. After he had fallen, the gunmen emptied their revolvers into the inert body."

According to a 1967 article in *The Realist,* "All eyewitness reports of the assassination indicated a total of five gunmen had been involved, but only one, Thomas Hagan, was caught after he was slowed by a thrown chair and shot in the leg." Hagan was a member of a militant religious sect—the Black Muslims—from which Malcolm had recently broken off. The following week, two more suspects (both Black Muslim "enforcers") were arrested. All three were convicted and sentenced to life.

## BACKGROUND

• Malcolm X's pilgrimage from street tough to international figure began in prison when he discovered the writings of Elijah Mohammed. This Black Muslim philosophy of racial separation and black self-reliance appealed to Malcolm, and when he was released from jail in 1952, he joined the group. He quickly became their most effective evangelist...and their most prominent spokesman. He was often quoted in the national press.

• In 1963, while the country was still grieving the death of President Kennedy, he remarked that the murder was just a case of "the chickens coming home to roost." His remark so incensed the public that the Black Muslims suspended him.

• Unrepentant, he quit the church in March, 1964, and started his own group, taking so many Black Muslims with him that Elijah Mohammed's followers vowed revenge. Malcolm repeatedly told aides that he had been "marked for death."

• From the beginning of the investigation, the police and the FBI assumed that the killing had been ordered by the Black Muslims. The media echoed that official story. The *New York Herald Tribune*'s report was typical: "Now the hatred and violence that he preached has overwhelmed him, and he has fallen at the hand of Negroes."

## WAS IT A CONSPIRACY?

*Many prominent blacks saw a different reason why Malcolm X had been killed. Some suspected the U.S. government. Said CORE National Director James Farmer in* The New York Times, *"The killing of Malcolm X was a political act, with international implications and not necessarily connected with black nationalism."*

## A THORN IN THE SIDE OF GOVERNMENT

• In 1964, Malcolm visited Mecca and Africa. He was greeted as the roving ambassador of an American black nation; he met with presidents, prime ministers, and kings. In Ghana, for example, he addressed a joint session of the Ghanian parliament—the first American to do so. Wherever he went, he encouraged African governments to speak out against American racism and reported that wherever he went in Africa, he was followed by CIA agents.

• In July 1964, he traveled to Cairo to address the Summit Conference of African prime minsters. There he introduced a program to "bring the American racial problem before the U.N. under the Human Rights provision of its charter, as South Africa had been." (*The Realist*)

• A few weeks later, the State Department and Justice Department acknowledged that they considered Malcolm a threat. A spokesman told the *New York Times*: "If [Malcolm X] succeeds in convincing just one African government to bring up the charge at the United Nations, the United States government would be faced with a touchy problem."

• After returning to the U.S., Malcolm X continued to push for his U.N. program. In the fall of 1964, he spent most of his time at the U.N., lobbying African delegates to support his efforts. In November, 1964, the US intervened in the Congo Civil War. Malcolm X warned African leaders that if they didn't speak out, "the same thing can happen to you."

• They took his advice. During a U.N. General Assembly debate on the Congo, African delegates condemned the U.S. as being indifferent to the fate of blacks everywhere, citing as evidence the U.S. government's attitude toward the civil rights struggle in Mississippi. The State Department reportedly blamed Malcolm X for their embarrassment.

• Friends and family were concerned that Malcolm X was taking a great risk by interfering in American foreign policy. He was under constant surveillance. His half sister, Ella Collins, said she had heard from reliable sources that there were even CIA agents in the group Malcolm X had founded, the Organization of Afro-American Unity. "Malcolm knew the dangers, but he said he had to go ahead." (*Seven Days*)

• Just before he was killed, Malcolm X told his biographer, Alex Haley, that he no longer believed that the biggest threat to his life was the Black Muslim organization. "I know what they can do, and what they can't, and they can't do some of the stuff recently going on." (ibid.)

## SUSPICIOUS FACTS
### In Cairo

• The U.S. State Department didn't want Malcolm X to attend the summit in Cairo. The U.S. embassy in Cairo tried, and failed, to get the Egyptian government to bar his appearance. (*The New York Times*)

• The day before Malcolm X was scheduled to speak at the summit, he ate dinner at the Hilton Hotel in Cairo. Shortly after the meal, he collapsed with severe stomach pains. He was rushed to a hospital.

• "His stomach was pumped out, cleaned thoroughly, and that saved him," said an associate. "Malcolm said afterwards he would have died if he had not got immediate treatment." Reportedly, a "toxic substance" was found and natural food poisoning was ruled out. Malcolm suspected the CIA. (*The Realist*)

In France

• Two weeks before he was killed, Malcolm X was scheduled to address a conference in France, as he had on other occasions. But when his plane landed, he was told he could not disembark—the French Government had branded him "an undesirable person." He was ordered to leave the country immediately.

• Three months earlier Malcolm X had visited France without incident, so he was baffled by the expulsion order: "I was surprised when I arrived in Paris and was prohibited from landing. I thought that if there were any country in Europe that was liberal in its approach to the problem it was France."

• After the assassination, a prominent North African diplomat approached an American journalist with information about the incident. "This official, who insists on anonymity, said that the French Department of Alien Documentation and Counter Espionage had been quietly informed that the CIA planned to murder Malcolm, and France feared he might be liquidated on its soil." (*Seven Days*)

Firebombing

• Ten hours after Malcolm X's return from France, four fire bombs were hurled into his home in Queens, New York. It looked like a professional hit job, with bombs positioned to block all possible escapes. Fortunately the fourth bomb glanced off a window pane and exploded harmlessly on the front lawn, allowing Malcolm, his wife, and their four children to narrowly escape. The house was destroyed.

• To Malcolm X, the timing of the attack could not be chalked up to coincidence: "It was no accident that I was barred from France, and ten hours after I arrived home my home was bombed," he declared at a February 17, 1965, press conference.

• Malcolm X announced, "We are demanding an immediate investigation by the FBI of the bombing. We feel a conspiracy has been entered into at the local level, with some local police, firemen and press. Neither I, nor my wife and child have insurance, and we stand in no way to gain from the bombing....My attorney has instructed me and my wife to submit to a lie detector test and will ask that the same test be given to police and firemen at the scene." But Malcolm X's hopes of pursuing this investigation were cut short eight days later.

## THE ASSASSINATION

### Police Protection

• Malcolm X had held meetings in the Audubon Ballroom many times before. Usually, there was a large contingent of uniformed police to prevent violence from followers of Elijah Mohammed. But on the day he was murdered, there were only two uniformed police officers—posted at the exit. (*Seven Days*)

• After the murder, New York Deputy Police Commissioner Walter Arm claimed that protection had been offered Malcolm X, but that he had refused it. But, according to Alex Haley, Malcolm had made repeated requests for increased protection, but the police ignored him. (*Seven Days*)

### Gene Roberts

• The police certainly knew about the threats against Malcolm X. His chief bodyguard, Gene Roberts—who was with him when he was assassinated—was an undercover New York City policeman.

• Roberts actually did his best to save Malcolm X. He attacked one of the armed assailants with a chair and chased him into a crowd. When the assailant was captured by the crowd, Roberts returned to give Malcolm mouth-to-mouth resuscitation.

• According to *Newsday*, later in the evening, Roberts was called by his supervisors and questioned extensively. Why had he, for example, given Malcolm mouth-to-mouth resuscitation and tried to stop the gunman? "Isn't that what I'm supposed to do?" Roberts responded. "I'm a cop. It's my job to save people's lives. What was I supposed to do...let him bleed to death?"

• Years after the assassination Roberts voiced his doubts about the integrity of the police and raised questions about a larger conspiracy. Certain events at that meeting seemed particularly suspicious to Roberts:

√ After the shooting, "people were trying to get medical help from Columbia-Presbyterian Hospital," which was across the street from the hall. "It damn near took them a half an hour."

√ No other policemen came to Gene's assistance. "The cops were outside. None of them came inside."

## The Patsies

• Although eyewitness accounts suggest there were as many as five gunmen, only three were captured, and only one of those was actually apprehended in the ballroom.

• Thomas Hagan was shot in the leg as he fled the ballroom and was quickly trapped by the crowd and arrested by police. But it was only after an "intensive investigation" that Norman Butler and Thomas Johnson were arrested weeks later. Both were "enforcers" for the Black Muslims who were awaiting trial for the shooting of a Muslim defector.

• When Hagan stood trial he confessed to the murder, but he told the court that the other two suspects were innocent: "I just want the truth to be known—that Butler and Johnson didn't have anything to do with this crime. Because I was there. I know what happened and I know the people who were there." (*Seven Days*)

• On March 1, 1966, *The New York Times* reported that Hagan "said that he had three accomplices, but he declined to name them. He said he had been approached early in the month of the murder and offered money for the job, but he declined to say by whom....One thing he did know, he said, was that no one involved in the murder was a Black Muslim."

• Regardless, on April 16, 1966, Hagan, Johnson, and Butler were each sentenced to life imprisonment for the murder of Malcolm X.

## The One That Got Away

• There may have been another suspect caught at the scene who mysteriously disappeared. The first edition of *The New York Times* the next day reported that one of the two police officers at the exit "said he 'grabbed a suspect' whom people were chasing. 'As I brought him to the front of the ballroom, the crowd began beating me and the suspect,' Patrolman Hoy said. He said he put this man—not otherwise identified later for newsmen—into a police car to be taken to the Wadsworth Avenue station." (*The Realist*)

• That second suspect was never heard from again, and the press did not pursue the issue. In later editions of the *Times*, the story had been changed and the earlier subhead, "Police Hold Two For Question," had been changed to "One Is Held In Killing." (ibid.)

• What makes the case of this "mystery suspect" even more intriguing is that his appearance—"a thin-lipped, olive-skinned Latin-looking man"—matches the description of a man whom Malcolm X had noticed trailing him through London and on the plane to New York one week before his death. (ibid.)

## BURYING THE TRUTH

### The Films

• According to a February 25, 1965, article in *The New York Times:* "the police were in possession of motion pictures that had been taken at the Audubon Ballroom...where the killing took place." These films would have been invaluable evidence—but there was no further mention of them by press or police. (*The Realist*)

### The Mysterious Death of Leon Ameer

• Leon Ameer was the New England representative of Malcolm X's group, the Organization of Afro-American Unity—and many believed him to be Malcolm X's hand-picked successor. On March 13, 1965, he announced, "I have facts in my possession as to who *really* killed Malcolm X. The killers aren't from Chicago [Muslim headquarters]. They're from Washington." (*The Realist*)

• Ameer promised to hold a press conference to reveal evidence proving the "power structure's" involvement in the killing, including documents and a tape recording Malcolm X had given him.

• The next morning, Ameer's body was discovered by a maid in Boston's Sherry Biltmore Hotel. The police announced that he had died of an epileptic fit, but Ameer's wife contended that her husband had had a complete medical checkup just one month before—"and there was no hint of epilepsy." (ibid.)

## RECOMMENDED READING

• "The Murder of Malcolm X," by Eric Norden (*The Realist*, Feb. 1967)

• "Who Killed Malcolm X?," by Alan Berger (*Seven Days*, March 24 and April 7, 1978)

# NICARAGUA REPORTS

*Did the Reagan White House really believe the contras were
"freedom fighters," as it reported so often in the 1980s?
Or was it just manipulating the American public?*

In 1979, the left-wing Sandinista rebels overthrew Anastasio Somoza, a U.S.-backed dictator whose family had ruled Nicaragua
for more than forty years.

Although neither the American public nor the Congress was
particularly disturbed by Somoza's fall, the Reagan administration
saw it as a serious Communist threat to the Americas. Overthrowing the Sandinista government became a Reagan priority, and to
accomplish it, the White House authorized the funding and training of a counter-revolutionary army, the "contras."

The Reagan administration seemed willing to do almost anything to undermine the Sandinistas—from mining Managua's harbors to lying repeatedly to the American public. In fact, the White
House directed the CIA to launch an illegal propaganda campaign—to misinform and manipulate the American people.

Here is a partial account of their conspiracy against the truth,
taken from Martin Lee's and Norman Solomon's excellent book,
*Unreliable Sources.*

## PSYCHOLOGICAL WARFARE

Much of the [government's] propaganda against Nicaragua was coordinated by an Orwellian agency known as the Office of Public
Diplomacy (OPD). Ostensibly part of the State Department, OPD
actually took its marching orders from the National Security Council and indirectly from the CIA. A senior U.S. official described
OPD as "a vast psychological warfare operation of the kind the military conducts to influence a population in enemy territory"—only
in this case the target was the American people.

In order to elude legal prohibitions against CIA involvement in
domestic operations, CIA Director William Casey transferred one
of his propaganda specialists, Walter Raymond, to the National

Security Council in 1982. Raymond's job was to help organize a massive public diplomacy effort that would generate grassroots support for Reagan's controversial—and hitherto unpopular—foreign policy ventures. Toward this end, OPD recruited five "psy-ops" specialists from the 4th Psychological Operations Group in Fort Bragg, North Carolina. Skilled in what OPD chief Otto Reich called "persuasive communications," these psychological warfare experts prepared "studies, papers, speeches, and memoranda to support [OPD] activities."

A July 1986 memo described the crux of OPD's efforts: "In the specific case of Nica[ragua], concentrate on gluing black hats on the Sandinistas and white hats on [the contras]." The idea was to slowly turn the Nicaraguan government "into a real enemy and threat in the minds of the American people, thereby eroding their resistance to U.S. support for the contras and, perhaps, to a future U.S. military intervention in the region," a U.S. official told the *Miami Herald*.

## OPD STRIKES

OPD inundated the media with glossy booklets, reports and other material, while behind the scenes it planted stories, coached journalists, and lobbied members of Congress. Media critic Alexander Cockburn summarized the modus operandi of Reagan's public diplomacy offensive against Nicaragua: "Erect a mountain of lies, and as members of the press examine each new falsehood, they find themselves on a foundation of older lies still taken for granted as natural features of the landscape."

Financed with taxpayers' money, OPD functioned as "an officially sanctioned leaks bureau" that sought to deceive the American people. A March 13, 1985, "Eyes Only" memo to White House Communications Director Patrick Buchanan mentioned "five illustrative examples" of OPD's ongoing "White Propaganda Operation." That week OPD helped compose a *Wall Street Journal* column about "the Nicaraguan arms build-up"; assisted in "a positive piece" on the contras by Fred Francis on "NBC Nightly News"; wrote op-ed columns in the names of contra leaders to appear in leading dailies; arranged a media tour for a contra leader; and prepared to leak a State Department cable to embarrass the

Sandinistas. "Do not be surprised," OPD told Buchanan, "if this cable somehow hits the evening news."

## GOOD TIMING

One of OPD's specialties was creating a crisis to sway public opinion at a crucial moment. In November 1984, OPD officials leaked false information about an impending shipment of Soviet MIG fighters to Nicaragua. Bolstered by over 30 OPD background briefings, the MIGs story dominated the headlines for a few days until journalists began to realize that no MIGs were headed for Nicaragua. By this time, OPD had already succeeded in drawing attention away from Nicaragua's elections, which otherwise might have legitimized a government that the Reagan administration was trying to overthrow. As former contra leader Edgar Chamorro said of the phantom MIGs: "The timing was controlled. Events can be neutralized when people are confused or distracted. That's why timing is so important."

## SWAYING CONGRESS

OPD operations kicked into high gear whenever a congressional vote on contra aid drew near. On December 10, 1987, the day before Congress was scheduled to decide on additional funds for the contras, OPD officials unveiled a Sandinista defector, Major Roger Miranda Bengoechea—who told a hand-picked group of four U.S. reporters that the Nicaraguan government planned to expand its military force to a half million soldiers, and that Soviet MIGs would be delivered by the early 1990s.

Among those present during the Miranda briefing was AP correspondent George Gedda, who ignored State Department documents that contradicted claims of a massive Nicaraguan military buildup. Gedda and fellow practitioners of Foggy Bottom journalism broke the story without mentioning a relevant fact: The U.S. government was paying Miranda $800,000 to make his ominous disclosures. As it turned out, no major expansion of Nicaragua's regular army was being planned; the evidence actually pointed toward a troop reduction, according to *Newsday*, which picked apart Miranda's charges days after Congress passed $8.1 million in new contra aid.

## LIES THAT ECHO

In addition to concocting scare stories and parading dubious defectors before the press, OPD planted articles in leading U.S. newspapers. An op-ed in *The Wall Street Journal* by Professor John Guilmartin ("Nicaragua Is Armed for Trouble") pretended to offer independent confirmation of White House assertions. "The Soviet doctrinal model, which the Sandinistas are clearly following, is inherently offensive in nature," said Guilmartin, who was described as an OPD "consultant" in a secret State Department memo dated March 13, 1985. In keeping with OPD's "low profile," the memo cautioned, "Officially, this office had no role in [the article's] preparation."

Guilmartin's opinion piece was rebutted a few weeks later in the *Journal*'s news pages when [two reporters] obtained a once-classified 1984 intelligence report which indicated that "Soviet arms shipments to Nicaragua turned sharply upward only after the Reagan administration launched the contra war." The report asserted that Nicaragua's build-up "is primarily defense oriented, and much of the recent effort has been devoted to improving counter-insurgency capabilities." This article prompted an angry letter from OPD chief Otto Reich in which he touted Guilmartin's op-ed and attacked the *Journal*'s disclosure as "an echo of Sandinista propaganda"—a remarkable charge given that Reich himself was "echoing" propaganda his office had covertly generated.

## EXPORTING REVOLUTION

For years, the Reagan administration alleged that Nicaragua was seeking to export its revolution by supplying arms to leftist guerrillas in El Salvador. Stories about this supposed "arms flow" continued to appear in the press even after the disclosures of David Mac-Michael, a former CIA analyst who resigned in protest over what he described as efforts to fake evidence of Nicaraguan military involvement in El Salvador. In June 1984, MacMichael told *The New York Times* that the CIA had "systematically" doctored evidence "to justify efforts to overthrow the Nicaraguan government." He reiterated these charges in testimony before the World Court, which ruled that the U.S. had violated international law by mining Nicaraguan harbors and directing the contra war. That same year a declassified State Department memo noted, "Intelligence officials claim that they can 'hear a toilet flush in Managua.' Yet they have not produced even a captured van or one downed plane."

OPD efforts to glue white hats on the contras stuck, as many top journalists adopted White House terminology, calling the CIA's mercenary army "freedom fighters" and the "Nicaraguan Resistance." For example: NBC News correspondent Robin Lloyd described Reagan's meeting with contra military chief Enrique Bermudez—a twenty-five-year veteran of dictator Anastasio Somoza's brutal National Guard—as evidence of the president's "commitment to democracy."

## THE OPD AT WORK

In addition to promoting disinformation, OPD sought to pressure journalists when they filed stories deemed objectionable by the Reagan administration. "I talked to reporters, editors, producers, anyone who would listen to our side," said OPD chief Otto Reich. "I had lots of meetings with editorial boards of newspapers." After National Public Radio aired a critical report about the contras, Reich paid a visit to NPR, which he called the "little Havana on the Potomac." According to NPR employees, Reich said his efforts had convinced editors at other media to change the tenor of their reporting, which resulted in journalists' being removed from the Central America beat. He also boasted that he had a team of people who monitored all NPR programs, as well as other broadcast networks. An NPR staffer described Reich's remarks as a "calculated attempt to intimidate." Reich's courtesy call succeeded in getting NPR reporters to second-guess themselves.

## THE END OF OPD

A 1987 probe of OPD by the General Accounting Office found that the Reagan administration had engaged in "prohibited, covert propaganda activities." Representative Jack Brooks called it an "illegal operation" designed "to manipulate public opinion and congressional action." The U.S. media quietly let the matter drop without further investigation.

OPD was disbanded at the end of 1987 as a result of the Iran-Contra scandal. By this time, official lies about Nicaragua had become ingrained media truths.

# AGENT ORANGE

*Did American chemical manufacturers knowingly poison U.S. soldiers with Agent Orange during the Vietnam War—and did the U.S. government cover it up? You be the judge.*

In 1962, American forces began spraying herbicides on the Vietnamese countryside in order to defoliate the jungle, thus exposing Viet Cong supply lines and destroying their cover. The most commonly used herbicide was called Agent Orange, which got its name from the bright orange stripes on the steel drums that contained it.

Agent Orange contained a synthetic growth hormone that caused plants literally to grow themselves to death—a banana, for example, would grow two feet long...then explode. "After spraying," writes Russell Mokhiber in his book *Corporate Crimes and Violence,* "the jungles went silent. There were no more sounds of insects, birds or other animals. Fish floated in the rivers. The soldiers labeled Agent Orange-sprayed forests, 'the land of the dead.'"

Spraying increased as the war heated up in 1967 and 1968, and so did reports of Vietnamese women miscarrying and bearing deformed children. At first the U.S. government dismissed the stories as Communist propaganda, but stateside studies on lab animals soon corroborated the chemical's effect.

In 1969, the U.S. began phasing out Agent Orange, but by that time, 11 million gallons had been sprayed on Vietnam, and at least 60,000 American troops had been exposed to it.

## AFTEREFFECTS

• Less than a decade after the war, thousands of American veterans reported strikingly similar symptoms: rashes, numb fingers and toes, impotence, debilitating fatigue, liver disorders, cancer, and children born deformed. Convinced that these problems were related to exposure to Agent Orange, many vets sought compensation from the Veterans Administration. The VA turned them down, arguing that there was no scientific proof that Agent Orange caused lasting health problems.

• When the vets fought the decision, they found two legal obstacles: 1) by law, the VA is the only major federal agency whose decisions cannot be reviewed in court, and 2) because of a 1950 Supreme Court ruling, military personnel can't sue the government for injuries suffered while on duty.

## CHEMICAL SUIT

• As a last resort, in 1978, the veterans sued seven companies, including Dow Chemical, Monsanto, and Uniroyal, that had manufactured Agent Orange and other herbicides.

• The veterans charged that the herbicides had been adulterated with a dioxin, one of the most lethal chemicals known ("170,000 times more deadly than cyanide," according to *U.S. News & World Report*). The veterans, *Science News* reported, also asserted that "the chemical companies never warned the military of the contaminant nor its potential for human harm—even though [they] knew or should have known."

• The suit was settled out of court in May 1984, when the chemical companies agreed to pay representatives of 16,000 veterans $180 million—the largest mass-damage award ever negotiated, but still only $11,125 per veteran represented in the suit.

• As part of the settlement, the companies admitted no liability and, according to the *Washington Post*, deprived the plaintiffs of what would have been "a forum to probe corporate officials on what they secretly knew or didn't know about the dangers of their chemicals."

• Many vets were bitter about the settlement. Former Marine Corps infantryman David P. Martin told the *Washington Post*, "We wanted our day in court...I want the truth to be told and the truth to come out." The *Post* also quoted *Agent Orange Dispatch*, a newsletter for New Jersey veterans: "We want the world to hear how Dow Chemical poisoned Americans in Vietnam. No amount of blood money could ever be enough to repay what the bastards did to us and our children."

## WAS IT A CONSPIRACY? #1

*Did the seven chemical companies know that Agent Orange was toxic to humans, yet fail to tell the military? Evidence suggests they did.*

## SUSPICIOUS FACTS

• "Agent Orange was no ordinary defoliant," Mokhiber writes in *Corporate Crimes and Violence.* "There were other effective jungle-killer chemicals that could force the enemy to seek new hideouts, but Agent Orange was a superagent with super ingredients. Its active ingredients were [chemicals called] 2,4,5-T and 2,4-D—and with 2,4,5-T came a deadly sidekick contaminant, dioxin....Today dioxin is known as one of the most deadly manmade chemicals. Three ounces of dioxin placed in New York City's drinking water could wipe out the city's entire populace."

• In 1970, a Dow vice president told a senate subcommittee: "Since 1950 we have been keenly aware of the possibility of a highly toxic impurity being formed" in Agent Orange's ingredients.

• According to a report in *Newsweek*, in 1983 a New York court released evidence showing that Dow knew the Agent Orange it made for use in Vietnam "contained levels of dioxin that might be harmful to humans"—and that the company knew this five years before it told the government or the public. The *Newsweek* account cites "a 1965 memo by Dow's toxicology director warning that dioxin could be 'exceptionally toxic,' and another by the company's medical director saying that dioxin-related 'fatalities have been reported in the literature.' "

## WAS IT A CONSPIRACY? #2
*Did the White House try to quash any government studies that might have linked Agent Orange to ailments suffered by thousands of American service personnel (and tens of thousands of Vietnamese civilians)?*

## SUSPICIOUS FACTS

• In 1990, a House subcommittee chaired by Representative Ted Weiss issued a report accusing the Reagan White House of obstructing a Centers for Disease Control (CDC) study of Agent Orange exposure.

• The study had been ordered in 1982 by Congress. More than $40 million had been spent on it by the time it was cancelled by the White House in 1987—after, the subcommittee report charged, the administration "had secretly taken a legal position to resist demands to compensate victims" exposed to the chemical. "While the Reagan administration defended the Vietnam conflict as an honorable war," said Weiss, "it worked behind the scenes to deny benefits to the very people who sacrificed their health for their country."

• Testifying before the Weiss subcommittee, Admiral Elmo R. Zumwalt, Jr., former chief of naval operations in Vietnam, supported the charges. He said that that Dr. Vernon Houk, the CDC official in charge of the study—and a former member of the Reagan administration's Agent Orange group—had "made it his mission to manipulate and prevent the true facts from being determined."

• Zumwalt also charged that federal officials were ignoring the "more than enough verifiable, credible evidence...linking certain cancers and other illnesses with Agent Orange," and that "government and industry officials [responsible for] examining such linkage intentionally manipulated or withheld compelling information of the adverse health effects." Ironically, Zumwalt was the officer who had ordered the Mekong Delta sprayed with Agent Orange. His son, Elmo Zumwalt III, died in 1988 from a rare form of lymphoma—a result, Zumwalt believes, of his own exposure to Agent Orange.

## RECOMMENDED READING

*Corporate Crime and Violence: Big Business and the Abuse of the Public Trust,* by Russell Mokhiber (Sierra Club Books, 1989)

## TALES OF THE CIA

In its war against Fidel Castro during the 1960s, the CIA literally tried to play hardball politics. "The CIA tried to cut off the supply of baseballs to Cuba. Agents persuaded suppliers in other countries not to ship them. (U.S. baseballs were already banned by the trade embargo the U.S. had declared.)" The bizarre embargo was effective. Some balls got through, "but the supply was so limited that the government had to ask fans to throw foul balls and home runs back onto the field for continued play."

—Jonathan Kwitny, *Endless Enemies*

# WHO KILLED KENNEDY?

*Who killed JFK? There are dozens of theories floating around.
Here are eight of the most plausible ones.*

THEORY #1: Lee Harvey Oswald did it.
*A maladjusted loner and Communist sympathizer, Oswald killed
Kennedy because of the president's hostility toward Cuba.*

**Advocates:** The Warren Commission, the major media, the U.S.
government (until 1978), and William Manchester, author of *Death
of a President*.

**Strengths:** Easily understood and endlessly repeated, this explanation reassured Americans that even though the president was dead,
democracy was alive and well. Manchester still believes in the Warren Commission's findings: he points out that Oswald's target, "the
presidential limousine, was only 88 yards away from his sniper's nest.
At that distance, a marksman could scarcely miss." Manchester feels
that current conspiracy theories about Kennedy's assassination are
little more than attempts "to invest the President's death with meaning....He would have died for something." (*The New York Times*)

**Weaknesses:** Almost nobody believes it anymore. In fact, in 1978,
the House Select Committee on Assassinations found evidence of a
conspiracy in the murder of JFK, thus putting one branch of the U.S.
government on record as believing that there *was* a conspiracy.

THEORY #2: The Communists did it.
*Oswald was a Marxist zealot who became a KGB agent after he defected
to Russia. Some theories even speculate that the "Oswald" whom Jack
Ruby shot in Dallas was a Russian-born KGB agent doubling for the real
Lee Harvey Oswald born in New Orleans.*

**Advocates:** Anti-Communist publications such as the John Birch
Society's *New American* magazine.

**Strengths:** Oswald called himself a Marxist, and his flirtation with
Communism can be documented back to his Marine stint, when he
used to receive Marxist reading materials. Years later he defected to
Russia and married the niece of a Soviet colonel.

**Weaknesses:** Neither the Russians nor Castro wanted Kennedy dead. After the Cuban missile crisis of 1962, Soviet Premier Nikita Khrushchev had a grudging respect for JFK, and Kennedy had promised not to invade Cuba. Nor do theories that Castro retaliated for CIA assassination plots against him make much sense. Kennedy was trying to normalize relations with Cuba.

### THEORY #3: Cuban exiles did it.

*Anti-Castro Cuban exiles never forgave JFK for denying them air support during the Bay of Pigs invasion. When rumors circulated that Kennedy was seeking peace with Castro, the exiles killed him.*

**Advocates:** Many conspiracy theorists, from Sam and Chuck Giancana, to New Orleans D.A. Jim Garrison, to lawyer Mark Lane, to Jack Ruby—who had run guns to Cuban exiles—theorize that anti-Communist Cubans were key players in the plot to kill Kennedy.

**Strengths:** Cuban veterans of the Bay of Pigs were motivated, disciplined, well trained by the CIA—and willing to die for their cause. Former CIA officer Ray Clines said of the Cuban exiles, "You train them and put them into business, it's not that easy to turn them off." Moreover, links between prominent Cuban exiles and the Mafia are well documented: before Castro took power, Cuba was a major gambling and drug-transshipment center; many Cubans who fled were employed in those Mafia-controlled trades. (Thus it was not surprising to see, two decades later, some of those same CIA-trained Cuban exiles running drugs and guns to fund the CIA's contra war in Nicaragua.)

**Weaknesses:** Cuban exiles may have been hit-men, or "cut-outs" (hired assassins used to do the dirty work so the CIA couldn't be directly implicated), but they didn't have the resources to orchestrate an extensive cover-up. Many theorists hypothesize that the CIA planned the murder and Cuban exiles executed it.

### THEORY #4: The FBI did it.

*Or, at the very least, it aided and abetted a cover-up.*

**Advocates:** Many conspiracy theorists, including Mark Lane, author of *Rush to Judgment* and *Plausible Denial*, accuse the FBI of a cover-up. Warren Commission members Hale Boggs, Richard Russell—and even Earl Warren himself—felt that the FBI had prejudged the case and withheld information.

**Strengths:** J. Edgar Hoover detested the Kennedys, and the feeling was mutual. Rightly suspecting that they wanted to fire him, Hoover kept incriminating files on the Kennedys' extramarital affairs, which he would have leaked to the press if they had tried to sack him, according to Curt Gentry, author of the definitive *J. Edgar Hoover: The Man and the Secrets*. Hoover was also a close friend of Kennedy rivals LBJ and Richard Nixon. But, personalities aside: the FBI allegedly ignored a telex several days before the assassination, warning of a plot to kill JFK; it may have faked Oswald's palm print on the rifle allegedly used to kill Kennedy; shortly after the assassination, former FBI agent James Hosty was ordered to destroy a note Oswald had written to the FBI's Dallas office months earlier; and, according to Mark Lane, Hoover suppressed information that Jack Ruby had been an FBI informant.

**Weaknesses:** The FBI clearly failed to protect the president and withheld information that contradicted the government's official explanation that a "lone nut" killed JFK. But few theorists suggest that the FBI initiated the plot to kill Kennedy; it could easily have destroyed his presidency without murdering him. A better guess is that Hoover, badly embarrassed by the Bureau's failure to detect the conspiracy, limited the investigation and encouraged the "lone nut" theory to protect the FBI's reputation.

### THEORY #5: Lyndon Johnson did it.
*Then, as president, he engineered a cover-up.*

**Advocates:** Lee Harvey Oswald's killer, Jack Ruby, specifically accused Johnson of planning the assassination and trying to silence him. (Ruby asserted that J. E. Haley's right-wing diatribe, *A Texan Looks at Lyndon: A Study in Illegitimate Power*, would prove his claims.)

**Strengths:** Johnson's reputation as a ruthless politician has been well documented by such historians as Robert Caro. Johnson hated the Kennedys; behind his back they called him "Uncle Cornpone." Johnson had access to virtually unlimited funds for a plot: Brown and Root, the Texas construction firm that became one of the biggest contractors in Vietnam, "lavishly poured money into his campaigns" from the start, according to Caro. Sam and Chuck Giancana's book, *Double Cross*, alleges that the Mafia also gave often and well to LBJ's campaigns. LBJ also had strong ties to the defense industry, which Kennedy was alienating. Washington pundits called Johnson "the senator from the Pentagon."

Suspicious facts:

√ Johnson created the Warren Commission and hand-picked its members to forestall other more independent investigations.

√ Senator Ralph Yarborough (D-Texas) was shocked to learn that "all vital assassination information was sent to President Johnson before it went to the Warren Commission."

√ LBJ ordered the limousine in which JFK was killed to be competely stripped and refurbished, thus destroying forensic evidence.

√ Johnson's Executive Order #11652 sealed assassination evidence until the year 2039.

Weaknesses: Plausible, but no facts have yet emerged that directly link Johnson to an assassination plot. Ruby's testimony was too incoherent to be worth much. Moreover, according to Jim Marrs in his book *Crossfire*, Johnson himself confided to his close friend Marvin Watson that he thought "the CIA had something to do with this plot."

## THEORY #6: The Mafia did it.

*According to the book* Double Cross, *Mob boss Sam Giancana had done a number of favors for JFK's father, Joe Kennedy, a former bootlegger; and, through vote rigging in Chicago, helped JFK win a very tight presidential race. In return, JFK supposedly agreed to stop Bobby Kennedy's prosecution of organized crime and get rid of Fidel Castro (who had confiscated Mafia casinos and disrupted a major drug route from Europe to America.)*

• Once in office, however, Kennedy welshed on the deal. After the Bay of Pigs invasion failed, JFK quietly sought to improve relations with Castro and, far from reining in his brother's attacks on the Mob, made him Attorney General.

• Robert Kennedy is the catalyst in many of the theories alleging Mafia involvement. One of the most widely held is that the Mob was really after RFK, but they realized that if they killed him, his brother the president would hunt them down. So they decided to kill JFK to neutralize RFK. Or, as New Orleans Mafia don Carlos Marcello reportedly said, "If you want to kill a dog, you don't cut off the tail. You cut off the head."

**Advocates:** David Scheim, author of *Contract on America*; John Davis, author of *Mafia Kingfish*; Sam and Chuck Giancana (godson and brother of Mob boss Sam Giancana), authors of *Double Cross*.

**Strengths:** The Mafia has few scruples about killing people and lots of experience doing it. Jack Ruby had Mafia ties going back as far as the 1930s. There was bad blood between Bobby Kennedy and the Mafia because of his attempts to bust Jimmy Hoffa, president of the Teamsters Union, whose pension fund was a Mafia cash cow. Nor was the FBI a serious impediment to the Mob. Through cowardice or complicity, J. Edgar Hoover claimed that organized crime didn't exist and so did nothing to stop it.

**Weaknesses:** The theory is plausible, but JFK's broken promises are only hearsay. The Mob couldn't have pulled off the whole cover-up alone, but it had plenty of allies in government—especially the CIA—who were willing to set up JFK and manage the cover-up.

### THEORY #7: The military-industrial complex did it.

*It killed Kennedy because he was planning to disengage the U.S. from the Vietnam War, thus denying prestige and power to military professionals, as well as enormous profits to defense contractors.*

**Advocates:** Oliver Stone, director of the movie *JFK*; Colonel L. Fletcher Prouty, USAF (ret.), former Chief of Special Operations for the Joint Chiefs of Staff, who advised Stone on his film. (John Newman, author of the book *JFK and Vietnam*, does not focus on the assassination, but he does document Kennedy's intentions to pull out of Vietnam.)

**Strengths:** This theory sees the killing of Kennedy as a political act that altered the direction of U.S. policy. It is less concerned with who did it than why. There are facts to support it: Kennedy's National Security memo #263 called for the removal of 1,000 troops from Vietnam by Christmas of 1963, whereas Lyndon Johnson's memo #273, signed the day Kennedy was buried, reversed JFK's withdrawal policy and led to the escalation of the war.

**Weaknesses:** The term "military-industrial complex" is so broad that it includes just about everyone and indicts no one. But asking why JFK was killed and who benefited from his death is a good place to start.

**THEORY #8: The CIA did it.**
President Kennedy had fired Allen Dulles, the director of the CIA, and humiliated the agency after the Bay of Pigs fiasco in 1961. Moreover, JFK had vowed to "splinter the CIA into a thousand pieces and scatter it in the wind." By starting to pull out of the Vietnam War, a war the CIA helped to start, Kennedy also alienated powerful corporations that were using the CIA as their own international police force.

**Advocates:** Many people, including attorney Mark Lane, author of *Rush to Judgment* and *Plausible Denial* (in which he claims that CIA veteran E. Howard Hunt was the paymaster for the JFK assassination).

**Strengths:** The CIA is an organization with virtually unlimited funds, experience in clandestine operations, and ties to every level of government, the underworld, and the media. Many key players, from Lee Harvey Oswald to Warren Commission member Allen Dulles, had arguably strong ties to the Agency. Robert Kennedy apparently also suspected the CIA. According to Kennedy aide Walter Sheriden, RFK called CIA Director John McCone within hours of the assassination and asked, "John, did you kill my brother?" (*J. Edgar Hoover: The Man and the Secrets*)

**Weaknesses:** The CIA denies it.

## MEDIA CONSPIRACIES

In 1966, working with Haitian exiles, anti-Castro Cubans came up with a scheme to get rid of Haitian dictator 'Papa Doc' Duvalier and use Haiti as a base for actions against Castro. Their ally and financial backer in the struggle: *CBS News*.

"Needing funding, the plotters met with officials of CBS and offered to sell exclusive coverage of the coup, 'including the hanging of President Duvalier!' In…violation of neutrality laws, the network paid …thousands of dollars, but to no avail—the plotters were arrested by the Coast Guard as they set sail from the shores of Florida."

—Jim Hougan, *Spooks*

# DEREGULATION QUIZ

*When Ronald Reagan took office, he said that "getting government off the backs of the people"—deregulating American businesses and reducing federal regulations—was his first priority. But who really benefited from deregulation? Here's a quiz to see if you know.*

**1.** To make sure that deregulation helped "mom & pop businesses tied up in government red tape," whom did Reagan appoint to head the Task Force on Regulatory Relief?
a. a small-town grocer
b. a Texas oil millionaire
c. the former head of the CIA

**2.** To gather the best ideas for improving federal agencies, the task force:
a. met with civic leaders
b. set up an 800 number so the public could offer suggestions
c. met secretly

**3.** How much did corporations spend annually to lobby Congress and sell deregulation to the American people?
a. $100,000
b. $100 million
c. $1 billion

**4.** As head of the Office of Occupational Safety and Health, Reagan appointed:
a. a doctor who specialized in industrial accidents
b. a malpractice lawyer
c. a contractor who had received 48 safety violations from OSHA

**5.** To head the Environmental Protection Agency, Reagan appointed a Colorado legislator who had:
a. obstructed state hazardous-waste regulation
b. fought strip-mining controls
c. resisted toxics regulation
d. all of the above

**6.** Price controls hurt the "little guy," Reagan claimed. A month after the president decontrolled oil prices:
a. oil prices dropped by 60%
b. oil executives contributed lavishly to redecorate the White House
c. Exxon announced that it was bankrupt

**7.** After the government deregulated buses, trains and airlines:
a. 3,763 communities lost interstate bus service
b. 1200 towns lost rail service
c. 150 airlines went bankrupt
d. all of the above

**8.** In 1983, Reagan blamed regulation for "holding back free enterprise." At the time, how many Americans agreed that workplace and consumer-protection regulations were "too strict"?
a. 90%
b. 65%
c. 30%
d. 5%

**9.** After AT&T was allowed to slough off many of its cumbersome federal regulations, what happened?
a. The cost of local phone calls went up 32%.
b. AT&T moved much of its equipment manufacturing to Third World countries
c. 78,000 unionized telephone workers lost their jobs

**10.** When President Reagan signed the bill that deregulated S&Ls, he chuckled:
a. "It'll be years before they figure this one out."
b. "I think FDR just rolled over in his grave."
c. "All in all, I think we've hit the jackpot."
d. "This one penstroke creates great opportunities not only for all Americans, but also their children."

Answers: (1) b & c [George Bush] (2) b (3) c (4) c (5) d (6) b (7) d (8) d (9) all of them (10) c—sure, we used it in the S&L quiz too, but it deserves to be repeated.

## RANDOM THOUGHTS

"A Nixon-Agnew administration will abolish the credibility gap and re-establish the truth, the whole truth, as its policy."
—*Spiro T. Agnew, Republican candidate for vice president*

"Anyone who opposes us we'll destroy. As a matter of fact, anyone who doesn't support us, we'll destroy."
—*Nixon aide (and White House plumber) Egil Krogh*

# OCTOBER SURPRISE

*Did Reagan's 1980 campaign team cut a secret deal with Iran to keep the American hostages captive—and keep Jimmy Carter from being reelected?*

In early 1979, Islamic fundamentalists led by Ayatollah Ruhollah Khomeini took power in Iran, ending the rule of the Shah, whose corrupt and brutal regime had finally collapsed under its own weight. They immediately began a propaganda war against the United States—"the Great Satan"—which had been the Shah's staunchest ally.

Later in the year, the Shah contracted cancer, and President Jimmy Carter allowed him into the U.S. for medical treatment. It was a terrible mistake. Unable to exact revenge on the Shah, militant Iranian students struck at his benefactor instead, seizing the U.S. Embassy in Teheran on November 4, 1979, and taking 52 Americans hostage.

The hostages instantly became the focus of the American media, and freeing them became an obsession of the Carter White House. In April 1980, the U.S. attempted a military rescue mission in the desert, but it failed miserably (see p. 81).

## BACKING OFF

• As the months went by and the Khomeini regime consolidated its power, it no longer needed the hostages for propaganda purposes. Moreover, in September, Iraq invaded Iran, launching a bloody war that would last eight years. Iran desperately needed the billions of dollars of Iranian assets and arms shipments that Carter had frozen when the hostages were seized. (Those shipments included $300 million in military hardware that the Shah had paid for but never received.) With the war going badly and many of its planes grounded because of a parts shortage, Iran finally seemed ready to cut a deal with the Great Satan. Suddenly, there were rumors that Iran was willing to negotiate the hostages return.

• Carter needed no prodding to talk; he was clearly concerned about the imprisoned Americans. Plus, it was an election year, and his adversaries (Republicans *and* Democrats) were shellacking him in the polls by talking tough about Iranian terrorists.

• So, despite his consistent stand against bargaining with terrorists, Carter authorized secret contacts with Iranian representatives in an effort to negotiate the hostages' release.

• Early contacts proved encouraging. Through West German intermediaries, the Carter administration and the Iranians talked on into the fall. By early October, negotiations were going so well that it looked like the hostages would be released before the election.

## CLAMMING UP

• Then, suddenly, in mid-October, the Iranians broke off negotiations and rejected all deals with the Carter government. Baffled, U.S. officials continued to press for a resolution, but the Iranians issued bizarre, untenable demands and then simply stalled until, in the last few days before the American election, it became clear that there would be no happy ending for the Carter presidency. Jimmy Carter, who had closed to a virtual dead heat with Reagan in the opinion polls, lost badly.

• The Carter White House continued working to free the hostages, however. Serious negotiations resumed in December, and, in the waning days of Carter's term, Iran agreed to terms that cost it billions. (Iran agreed, for example, to pay off loans to the Shah.)

• Carter hoped to welcome the hostages home, as president. But instead, the hostages were freed just past noon, Washington time, on January 20, 1981—minutes after Reagan took the oath of office. The timing of their release was dramatic and ironic, but most observers chalked it up to the Ayatollah Khomeini's vindictiveness towards Jimmy Carter, and a wish to humiliate him one last time.

• In the wake of the Iran-Contra scandal, however, rumors began circulating that the timing of the hostages' release was due neither to coincidence nor the Ayatollah's malice. Rather, the rumors said, a secret, illegal maneuver between high officials in the Reagan-Bush campaign and the Iranians had kept the hostages in captivity until Reagan's inauguration, thus denying Carter reelection and any share of the glory when the hostages did return.

## WHAT HAPPENED

• According to *October Surprise: America's Hostages in Iran and the Election of Ronald Reagan*, by Gary Sick, Reagan's campaign manager and later CIA director, William Casey, and other campaign officials met several times in Madrid and Paris in the summer and fall of 1980 with Iranian-born arms dealers, representatives of the Iranian government, and Israeli intelligence agents. During these meetings, Casey and his colleagues persuaded Iran to abandon talks with the Carter administration and strike a deal with the Reagan team instead.

• Sick, who was a National Security Council analyst on Iran during both the Carter and Reagan administrations, says the deal included these terms:

√ The hostages would not be released until after the American election—possibly not until after Reagan's inauguration—but they would be well treated until their release.

√ The Republicans, not yet in power, promised to encourage Israel to begin shipping arms and spare parts to Iran, thus circumventing official U.S. policy. (Israeli hard-liners had already decided their future lay with Reagan, not Carter.)

√ If the hostages were freed after Reagan assumed the presidency, his administration would unfreeze Iranian assets, release equipment that Iran had paid for, and resume arms sales and shipments to Iran.

• This deal was concluded in Paris in mid-October 1980; within days, negotiations between the Iranians and Carter's representatives collapsed. The Reagan team's meetings with the Iranians were in direct violation of U.S. law, which prohibits private American citizens from conducting diplomatic negotiations with foreign powers. What's more, Gary Sick notes, "to the extent that these people may have attempted to thwart the legitimate policies of the U.S. government or to manipulate the electoral processes, they were engaged in nothing less than a political coup." And, he adds, these acts, if indeed they were committed, "were not only strictly illegal but bordered on treason."

## SUSPICIOUS FACTS

• The Reagan-Bush campaign was obsessed with the possibility that Carter would win the hostages' release before the election and thus ensure his victory. Allegedly, George Bush himself coined the phrase "October Surprise" to describe such a move by Carter.

• The Reagan-Bush campaign had an extensive network of intelligence operatives monitoring Carter's attempts to free the hostages. The network, which included CIA officials and military officers assigned to the White House staff, kept the Republicans current on the Carter administration's secret negotiations with Iran and impending rescue plans.

• Gary Sick claims that former President Richard Nixon met in London with the head of a British helicopter service to discuss the possibility of a Republican-sponsored rescue mission. A Nixon spokesperson, asked about this incident, said, "We will neither confirm nor deny this story. We have nothing to say."

### Making Contact

• The first illegal meetings between Republicans and Iranians reportedly began around July 27 in Madrid. William Casey's records showed that from July 26 to July 30, he was indeed out of the country—at the Anglo-American Conference on the History of the Second World War, in London. Sick reports—and investigations by the PBS TV series "Frontline" confirm—that Casey was unaccountably absent from the conference for enough time to have flown to Madrid, conducted the meetings, and returned to London for his conference appearances.

• Shortly after the Republicans allegedly cut their deal, a European arms dealer who had been developing a sale with Iran was told by his contact that their deal was off, since Iran could now get all the arms it needed from another source. (*October Surprise*)

• According to self-described "Israeli operative" Ari Ben-Menache, CIA officials encouraged Israelis to cooperate with Republican initiatives to free the hostages. In the four months following the alleged first Madrid meetings between Casey and the Iranians—and in violation of the U.S. embargo—Israel sent Iran four shipments totalling approximately $150 million worth of ammunition and other military equipment. (ibid.)

**Scattered Shots**

• In September 1980, a full decade before most other accounts, Iranian Foreign Minister Sadegh Ghotbzadeh was quoted by Agence France Presse as saying that candidate Ronald Reagan was "trying to block a solution" to the hostage dilemma. (ibid.)

• In late October, Benjamin Fernandez, Reagan's campaign advisor on minority issues, said it would be "better for the Republic as a whole" if the hostages were not released until after the election. (A Reagan spokesperson later denied that this was the candidate's position.)

• In June 1991, Ronald Reagan, asked about this episode, denied any personal contacts between himself and the Iranian government, but admitted "efforts on [his] part...directed at getting [the hostages] home." He did not elaborate.

• George Bush has specifically denied that he attended Paris meetings with Iranian representatives, but has not specifically commented on whether some members of the 1980 GOP campaign team went to such meetings.

• Republican campaign official (and Bush aide) Donald Gregg, later appointed ambassador to South Korea, was also said to have been at the Paris meetings. As proof that he was not there, Gregg offered a photograph showing him on a sunny Delaware beach. But a meteorologist has testified that the cloud formations in the photo were inconsistent with Delaware weather data on the weekend in question.

• On November 24, 1980, Teheran radio quoted a prominent mullah, Hojjat ol-Eslam Sadegh Khalkhali, as saying the hostages would not be released before Reagan was inaugurated. (*October Surprise*)

**Major Offensives**

• In December 1991, *The New York Times* reported that, shortly after taking power, the Reagan administration "secretly and abruptly changed U.S. policy and allowed Israel to sell several billion dollars' worth of American-made arms, spare parts and ammunition to the Iranian Government." The shipments continued, the report said, "even as the Reagan Administration aggressively promoted a public campaign, known as Operation Staunch, to stop worldwide transfer of military goods to Iran." (*The New York Times*)

• Cyrus Hashemi was an Iranian-born arms dealer who, with his brother Jamshid, allegedly introduced Casey to the representatives of the Iranian government and helped orchestrate their meetings. In July 1986, he died under mysterious circumstances in London after a two-day illness. He supposedly succumbed to acute myeloblastic leukemia, but his death came two days after he played a "vigorous" round of tennis, and less than a week after he had had a thorough medical examination that revealed no leukemia. The autopsy revealed "injection sites at both elbows with surrounding bruising." Hashemi had been under criminal investigation by the Carter-era FBI; the investigation was suspended abruptly after Reagan took office. He later cooperated with the Justice Department in a sting operation that resulted in the arrest of several international arms dealers, and major charges against him were dropped.

## WAS IT A CONSPIRACY?

### THEORY #1: Yes

• According to Gary Sick, "[T]he Reagan-Bush campaign mounted a professionally organized intelligence operation to subvert the American democratic process," convincing Iran to keep the American hostages captive in return for billions of dollars in arms.

• This was not the last the American public would hear of "arms-for-hostages" deals. In 1986, the Iran-Contra scandal broke open, uncovering another elaborate scheme in which arms sold to Iran helped fund an illegal war in Nicaragua. This suggests that the Iran-Contra affair—far from being an "aberration" dreamed up by Oliver North—was actually a continuation of illicit arms deals with Iran that began before Ronald Reagan was even in the White House.

### THEORY #2: No

• There was no conspiracy, said former CIA agent Frank Snepp in a February 1992 article in the *Village Voice*. "It appears that none of Sick's key informants named in his book had any original knowledge of the Surprise plot," Snepp notes. "Only by swapping rumors and tacking with the latest ones were they able to create an impression that they knew of the event firsthand. The picture that ultimately emerges...is a self-perpetuating fraud."

• A November 18, 1991, piece in *The New Republic* also questions Sick's sources: "The key sources on whose word the story rests are documented frauds and imposters....Almost every primary source cited by Sick has been indicted or was the subject of a federal investigation prior to claiming to be a participant in the October Surprise." (Note: On the other hand, the Hashemi brothers didn't make their claims until after charges against them were dropped.)

• One prominent source, Abolhassan Bani-Sadr, president of Iran from January 1980 through June 1981, changed his story of the Paris meeting repeatedly. He didn't know about the Casey meeting in advance, then he did. George Bush attended, then he didn't. In fact, "Bani-Sadr had nothing to do with the negotiations. He was completely out of it," according to a 1988 story in the *Los Angeles Times*.

• Self-proclaimed "CIA operative" Richard Brenneke, on whom Sick relied heavily for information, is a good example of how flimsy the theory's proof is. When he was interrogated by a Senate subcommittee in February 1987, Brenneke never mentioned the October Surprise. But by August 1988, after he had met with Barbara Honegger, another author who has written about the October Surprise, Brenneke suddenly began claiming that he had actually taken part in meetings in Paris and Madrid with Bill Casey and other conspirators in 1980. But, says Snepp, Brenneke's credit card receipts between 1980 and 1982 show that he "was never away from his favorite Portland [Oregon] shopping malls for more than a few days at a time"—despite Brenneke's claims that he flew planeloads of guns to Iran for "four to five weeks at a time."

## FOOTNOTES
• In 1992 the PBS television series "Frontline" revealed that at least one person who spread inaccurate information about the October Surprise conspiracy claimed to have been paid by U.S. government agents to mount a disinformation campaign to discredit all the theories.

## RECOMMENDED READING
• *October Surprise: America's Hostages in Iran and the Election of Ronald Reagan*, by Gary Sick (Random House, 1992).

# WATERGATE

*Watergate was more than just a conspiracy—
it was a series of conspiracies.*

CONSPIRACY #1: THE BREAK-IN.
On June 17, 1971, five men dressed in business suits and blue Playtex gloves were arrested breaking into the Democratic National Committee (DNC) headquarters at the Watergate office complex in Washington, D.C.

At first it seemed like a run-of-the-mill burglary. But the burglars were carrying photographic equipment and eavesdropping devices—hardly the stuff of a routine break-in. It turned out that four of them had ties to the CIA (Three were Cuban veterans of the Bay of Pigs invasion. The other, James McCord, was the security coordinator for President Nixon's Committee to Re-elect the President (CRP)). In addition, two of them were carrying the phone number of E. Howard Hunt, a consultant working for the White House.

The burglars were later revealed to be a part of a secret intelligence team known as "the White House Plumbers," assigned to plug information leaks in the Nixon administration. But what were they doing in Watergate? The original explanation was that they were trying to bug the office of DNC chairman Lawrence O'Brien. But some experts consider that just a cover story. We may never know the truth about their mission, but here are some theories:

THEORY #1: The plumbers were trying to find out what kind of dirt the Democrats—particularly Democratic National Committee Chairman Lawrence O'Brien—had on Nixon.

• In his book *Will*, Watergate conspirator G. Gordon Liddy wrote, "The purpose of the Watergate break-in was to find out what O'Brien had of a derogatory nature about us."

• Reportedly, Nixon was obsessed with the idea that the Democrats had dug up information about Nixon's shady land dealings with, and under-the-table cash from, Howard Hughes.

• Nixon's defensiveness about Hughes dated back to 1960, when

Nixon was running for president against JFK. In the midst of that campaign, revelations about a $205,000 "loan" made in 1956 from the Hughes Tool Company to Donald Nixon (the president's brother) caused a scandal that some historians feel cost Nixon the election. Determined not to be brought down by another Hughes scandal, Nixon supposedly ordered the break-in to find out what O'Brien knew.

**THEORY #2: They were trying to get proof that the DNC— particularly Lawrence O'Brien—was also secretly involved with Howard Hughes.**

• Although the Democrats were critical of Nixon's relationship with Hughes, their own ties to the billionaire were also extensive. According to Nixon biographer Stephen Ambrose in *Nixon: The Triumph of a Politician*, O'Brien had been secretly paid a $15,000-a-month retainer fee to represent the billionaire's interests in Washington, D.C., and, according to one account, Hughes had surreptitiously paid off more than $9 million of the debts left over from Hubert Humphrey's 1968 presidential campaign.

• Proving such links would have been a political bombshell for Nixon against the Democrats. According to Ambrose: "For years, Nixon had been accused of being Howard Hughes's hired man in Washington. How sweet it would be to turn the tables and reveal that the chairman of the Democratic National Committee had been on a secret retainer for Hughes."

**THEORY #3: They were trying to get information on the DNC's involvement with a prostitution ring.**

• On June 9—only 8 days before the Watergate break-in, the *Washington Star* ran a front-page article on a prostitution ring that had been uncovered by the FBI. According to the article, the ring was "headed by a Washington attorney and staffed by secretaries and office workers from Capitol Hill and involved at least one White House secretary." Among the evidence seized were address books naming the prostitutes and their clients.

• In his book *Secret Agenda*, Jim Hougan suggests that the prostitution ring was directly linked to the DNC. Unknown to the

Democrats, Philip Bailley, a politically connected attorney (who was later sentenced to 5 years in prison for his involvement in the ring), was using a telephone line in the DNC to arrange meetings between "high-rolling pols" and prostitutes in a nearby apartment. The phone was in the office of R. Spencer Oliver, director of the Association of Democratic State Chairmen, who was often on the road. (Oliver had no knowledge of the arrangement.) According to Hougan, a secretary in the DNC "would tell the prospective clients that soon after entering Oliver's vacant office the telephone would ring twice. They were not to answer it. Immediately afterward, the telephone would ring again, and this time they were to pick it up." The secretary would also call the prostitute and tell her that a customer was waiting in the office for the call.

• At its peak, Bailley later claimed, the prostitution ring served at least one DNC-referred client every day. Some historians believe that the break-in was ordered to discover if the DNC connection existed and to collect information on the ring in order to embarrass the Democrats. In their book *Silent Coup*, authors Len Colodny and Robert Gettlin say, "Howard Hunt and two of the burglars recently told us [that] the real target was the frequently used telephone that was in the portion of the DNC that contained the offices of R. Spencer Oliver."

• When the burglars were caught, they were carrying the key to Oliver's secretary's desk.

**Alternative theory:** The break-in was designed to put a lid on the story and limit the political damage. Though the Democrats allegedly were the most deeply involved in the prostitution ring, it also threatened to tar the Republicans. According to one account, "The involvement of some White House employees was indisputable...[including] sexually explicit photos of a female attorney who... worked in the Executive Office of the President." The White House may have ordered the Watergate burglary to find out what the Democrats knew about possible Republican involvement in the prostitution ring—and to keep it quiet.

**THEORY #4: To protect the reputation of John Dean's girlfriend.**

• In *Silent Coup*, Colodny and Gettlin develop the theory even further: they allege that Maurine Biner, John Dean's girlfriend (later his wife), was one of the women listed in Bailley's address book; she was also the roommate of Erika Rikan, the alleged madam of the prostitution ring. (Biner's *direct* alleged involvement in the ring, if any, is unclear.)

• Colodny and Gettlin suggest that "the pressure to go into the Watergate had come...specifically from John Dean." In order to protect his girlfriend's name, they allege, Dean ordered the break-in, was a key figure in the cover-up, and left Nixon to take the fall when the scandal exploded. (Note: After *Silent Coup* was published, John Dean sued the authors for libel.)

## CONSPIRACY #2: THE CAPTURE

The burglars were caught after a security guard at the Watergate office complex discovered that one of the doors had been taped so that it wouldn't lock. At first he did nothing; he just untaped the door. But when he came back later and saw that the door had been retaped, he called the police. A plainclothes unit was less than two blocks away; it arrived on the scene within minutes. Together with the security guard, it searched the building and discovered the burglars in the offices of the DNC.

But was the capture an unlucky break for the burglars...or did someone set it up so they were sure to get caught?

### Suspicious Facts

• James McCord was in charge of the burglary. Before taking the job as head of security for Nixon's reelection campaign, McCord had spent more than 20 years working for the CIA. By the time he allegedly retired, he was a high-level security chief. Before joining the CIA, he'd worked as a special agent for the FBI. Yet despite this extensive experience in intelligence work, McCord made several uncharacteristically inept mistakes during the break-in. As a direct result, the burglary team was caught in the act, arrested, and ultimately traced back to the Nixon White House.

### For example:

√ The hotel room the team rented across from the Watergate office complex to serve as a lookout point was rented in the name of McCord's security company. It could have easily been traced.

√ Another hotel room the team used during the burglary was rented in the name of a company that one of the burglars, Bernard Barker, was connected with. It, too, would have been easy to trace.

√ McCord tried to get FCC clearance for the walkie-talkie frequencies the team used during the break-in. Gordon Liddy likened this to "registering a gun you're going to use in a holdup."

√ McCord's attempts to tape the doors so that they didn't attract attention doomed the mission. According to one account, "had the tape been placed horizontally (i.e., visible from the outside) the building guard would have assumed that it had been done by maintenance men, who would have no incentive to conceal their handiwork. The hidden tape placement was a dead giveaway" that a burglary was in progress.

√ McCord had the burglars turn off their walkie-talkies just when they needed them most: when the police were searching the building. As the search team drew close, McCord assured the other burglars that it was just the security guard making his rounds. But he told them to turn off their walkie-talkies "so that no one would hear the static." This prevented the burglars from communicating with their lookouts in the hotel across the street, who could have warned them and helped them get away.

*How could McCord have bungled the operation so badly?*

**THEORY #1: It was an accident.**

The Watergate break-in was a small-time job for someone with McCord's experience and had been hastily planned. Moreover, the job seemed so easy that McCord wouldn't have expected to get caught. He may have just been sloppy.

**THEORY #2: He did it deliberately.**

McCord—who might have still been working for the CIA even after his "retirement"—may have been an Agency plant on the White House staff who had been ordered to sabotage the mission.

Why? "The answer should not be surmised from the effect that the sabotage had on the Nixon presidency," suggests Hougan in *Secret Agenda*. "McCord could not have predicted that the arrests would cause a scandal of such dimensions that the Nixon administration would collapse. Indeed, all that could have been foreseen at the time was that the sabotage would lead to the temporary embarrassment of the administration, and, just as certainly, that it would put an end to any further assaults on the DNC. Clearly, [that] was the…goal that McCord pursued."

Hougan provides evidence that calls between prostitutes and the DNC were bugged (he says by the CIA), and he speculates that McCord, on orders from superiors at the CIA, acted to keep the Republicans from learning any more details about the prostitution ring. "Neither [McCord], nor the Agency, wanted the…operation exposed," writes Hougan.

## CONSPIRACY #3: THE COVER-UP

The White House denied any knowledge of or involvement in the break-in from the very beginning. The morning after the arrests, White House Press Secretary Ron Zeigler described the incident as "a third rate burglary." In the months to come, the White House would denounce press reports of the break-in as "shabby journalism," "unfounded and unsubstantiated allegations," and "using innuendo, third-person hearsay, unsubstantiated charges, anonymous sources, and huge scare headlines."

### The White House

• Nearly every White House official with the power to obstruct the Watergate investigation got involved in the cover-up. And whether or not President Nixon personally ordered the break-in, he certainly tried to hide White House involvement in it from the very beginning.

• As the scandal unfolded, it turned out that Nixon had ordered the CIA to pressure the FBI to limit its investigation of the scandal; authorized more than $200,000 in hush payments to the Watergate burglars; fired the Watergate special prosecutor; refused to turn over his secret White House tapes; and erased—or had someone else erase—sensitive conversations from the tapes when he was forced to turn them over.

### The Smoking Gun

• Strangely, despite his efforts to destroy evidence and hide the truth, Nixon left a "smoking gun"—the tape of a conversation he had with White House Chief of Staff H. R. Haldeman on June 23,

1972, less than a week after the break-in. In it, Nixon instructed Haldeman how to handle the cover-up—an indication that he had known about the break-in and perhaps directed it from the very beginning.

• The contents of this taped conversation were made public on August 5, 1974; two days later the president resigned. At 10:00 a.m. on August 7, 1974, Nixon boarded Air Force One for his last presidential flight to San Clemente. At 12:00 noon, in the skies over Kansas City halfway through the flight, Nixon's term of office expired and Vice President Gerald Ford was sworn in as president.

It was Nixon's involvement in the cover-up—not the Watergate break-in itself—that destroyed his presidency. So why didn't he just come clean in the very beginning? One theory is that he thought he could get away with it. Except for the outcome, Watergate had been like any other crisis in his political career. And this time he had all the powers of the presidency to help him hide the truth.

## CONSPIRACY #4: DEEP THROAT

Although *Washington Post* reporters Bob Woodward and Carl Bernstein took much of the credit for exposing Watergate, they couldn't have done it without the help of "Deep Throat," a source in the executive branch who had access to information at CRP as well as the White House—a man who occupied an "extremely sensitive" position in the government. Deep Throat was a crucial source for the reporters; whenever the trail leading to the president grew cold, he provided them with information to warm it up.

Why would a top government official rat on his boss? Until recently it was assumed that Deep Throat was a whistle-blower in the classic sense—an honest man who wanted to expose the corruption in the Nixon administration. But new facts have come to light that suggest that Deep Throat's motives may have been far less noble; he may actually have been working with the military to topple the president.

### The Motive

• Top brass in the military had a reason to get rid of Nixon: he had been excluding them from major foreign-policy decisions, even issues as important as troop activities in the Vietnam War and the thawing of relations with Communist China.

• According to Colodny and Gettlin in *Silent Coup*, the Joint Chiefs of Staff were so cut off from foreign policy that they were forced to steal "uncounted documents—just thousands, thousands of documents" in order to keep informed on White House activities. Their mole in the White House allegedly was Navy Yeoman Charles Radford, aide-de-camp to General Alexander Haig. Radford pilfered papers concerning "contingency plans, political agreements, security conferences going on between the U.S. government and foreign governments," and other documents from Haig and Haig's boss, Henry Kissinger.

• According to this theory, the Joint Chiefs became so enraged with their almost total exclusion from foreign policy that they decided to derail President Nixon. Working through Deep Throat, they leaked information that ultimately forced Nixon from power.

### Suspicious Facts

• Some theorists believe that General Alexander Haig, a career military officer, was Deep Throat. Appointed White House chief of staff after H. R. Haldeman resigned under fire, Haig was one of only a handful of people close enough to President Nixon to have had access to the kind of information Deep Throat passed on to Woodward and Bernstein.

• Was this consistent with Haig's character? According to Attorney General John Mitchell, "Haig was no great supporter of Nixon's; he was in business for himself." And as a military man, Haig was one of the few people on the White House staff who didn't owe his career to the president.

• Though Woodward denies it, there is evidence to suggest that Woodward had a closer relationship to the military—and to General Haig—than he has admitted. An ROTC cadet while a student at Yale, Woodward joined the Navy after his graduation. He was eventually promoted to the post of duty officer for Admiral Thomas Moorer, a member of the Joint Chiefs of Staff who would eventually become its chairman.

• When he was duty officer, Woodward supervised the encoding, decoding, routing, and prioritizing of top secret information among the White House, the CIA, and other government agencies. It was also his duty to brief government and military officials on this information. One person Woodward allegedly briefed regularly was General Haig. (Note: Hougan says that, "told he was alleged to have regularly briefed Alexander Haig when Haig was Kissinger's deputy on the National Security Council, Woodward says no. 'Not to my knowledge anyway—though he may have been part of some large group [that I briefed]. But if he was,' Woodward adds, 'I wasn't aware of it.' " However, Admiral Moorer and former Secretary of Defense Melvin Laird, among others, confirm that Woodward did brief Haig.)

• Although he refuses to identify who Deep Throat was, Woodward describes him as an "old friend" who held an "extremely sensitive" job in the Nixon administration. Few—if any—White House officials fit this description as well as Haig.

• Even if he wasn't Deep Throat, Haig made a strange move as White House Chief of Staff: he argued *against* destroying the "smoking gun" tape of June 23, 1972. The tape was the one piece of evidence linking Nixon directly to the cover-up. If Nixon had destroyed it, he might have been able to save his presidency.

### Alternative Theories
Not everyone agrees with Colodny and Gettlin. J. Anthony Lukas, in his definitive book, *Nightmare: The Underside of the Nixon Years*, suggests Deep Throat may have been W. Mark Felt, Jr., deputy associate director of the FBI. Jim Hougan says, "Deep Throat is probably a spook—someone in the intelligence community—with sources in high places." One possibility he names is Admiral Bobby Ray Inman, "a quintessential spook [who] satisfies some of the most obvious criteria for any Deep Throat candidate: e.g., he was in Washington throughout the period that Woodward was secretly meeting with his source, and at some point or other, he himself became a source of Woodward's."

## CONSPIRACY #5: THE PARDON
On September 8, President Ford granted Nixon a "full, free and absolute pardon…for all offenses against the United States which he…has committed or may have committed or taken part in during the period from January 20, 1969, through August 9, 1974"— Nixon's entire term of office.

According to Stephen Ambrose, Ford privately listed a number of reasons for issuing the pardon:

√ To avoid the degrading spectacle of a former president in the prisoner's dock in a criminal court

√ The difficulty, not to say impossibility, of meeting Supreme Court standards for an unbiased jury

√ The length of time it would take to prosecute Nixon

√ The likelihood that if Nixon were convicted, whoever was president at the time would pardon him

### *Was there a deal?*

Did Ford promise to pardon Nixon as part of a deal, in exchange for being selected to replace resigning Vice President Spiro Agnew?

### THEORY #1: Yes.

Many theorists reason that once Agnew resigned, Nixon used the vice presidency—and ultimately the presidency itself—as a bargaining chip. After all, his entire political career—not to mention his freedom—was at stake.

### THEORY #2: No.

Stephen Ambrose believes that Nixon did *not* cut a deal: "It was the Vice President, not the President, who occupied a position of strength....Ford had widespread support from the public and the Congress. Nixon did not. Nixon could not say, 'Look, either you promise to pardon, or I'll never resign.' The Presidency was not his either to give or to keep....It seems likely that Nixon knew that it was inevitable that Ford was going to have to pardon him, and he did not need to...extract such a promise....No deal was struck."

## RECOMMENDED READING

• *Silent Coup: The Removal of a President,* by Len Colodny and Robert Gettlin (St. Martin's Press, 1991)

• *Nixon,* by Stephen Ambrose (Simon and Schuster, 1987-1991) *An excellent three-volume work.*

• *Nightmare: The Underside of the Nixon Years,* by J. Anthony Lukas (Viking, 1976)

• *Secret Agenda: Watergate, Deep Throat, and the CIA,* by Jim Hougan (Random House, 1984)

# WHO SAID IT?

*See if you can guess which of the conspirators listed below made
the following statements. Answers are at the bottom of the page.*

**1.** "There's something addicting about a secret."

**2.** "We did not—repeat, did not—trade weapons or anything else for hostages, nor will we."

**3.** "This life I'm leading is going to change....If I could walk around and see things without mobs of people, be free, it would be worth a million dollars, if only for a week."

**4.** "The press is the enemy."

**5.** "Our government has kept us in a perpetual state of fear....Always there has been some terrible evil about to gobble us up if we did not blindly rally to it....Yet in retrospect, these disasters...seem never to have been quite real."

**6.** "I want you to know lying does not come easy to me."

**7.** "Urine tests are the loyalty oaths of the 1990s."

**8.** "The Communists within our borders have been more responsible for the success of Communism abroad than Soviet Russia."

**9.** "Everything on paper will be used against me."

**10.** "The great masses of people will more easily fall victims to a great lie than to a small one."

---

**A.** Adolph Hitler

**B.** Harry Truman

**C.** Douglas MacArthur

**D.** Elvis

**E.** Oliver North

**F.** Joseph McCarthy

**G.** Abbie Hoffman

**H.** Richard Nixon

**I.** Henry Kissinger

**J.** Ronald Reagan

**K.** J. Edgar Hoover

# RECOMMENDED READING

*We've recommended references at the end of some of our chapters, but here is a more extensive list of resources we think you should know about.*

## PERIODICALS

• *Covert Action Information Bulletin*, P.O. Box 50272, Washington, DC 20004.

• *The Defense Monitor*, The Center for Defense Information, 1500 Massachusetts Avenue NW, Washington, DC 20005.

• *Extra!* (a bi-monthly "journal of media analysis") published by Fairness and Accuracy in Media (FAIR), 130 W. 25 Street, NY, NY 10001.

• *Left Business Observer*, 250 W 85th Street, New York, NY 10024.

• *Lies of Our Times*, 145 W 4th Street, New York, NY 10012.

• *Mother Jones*, 1663 Mission St., 2nd Floor, San Francisco, CA 94103.

• *The Nation*.P.O. Box 10763, Des Moines, IA 50340-0763.

• *The Realist*, Box 1230, Venice, CA 90294.

• *Z Magazine*, 116 St. Botolph St., Boston, MA 02115.

## BOOKS

Most of these titles are current; the rest are worth looking for at a library or used book shop.

• Austin, John, *Hollywood's Unsolved Mysteries*, and *More of Hollywood's Unsolved Mysteries* (Shapolsky, 1991)

• Bates, Stephen, *If No News, Send Rumors* (St. Martin's Press, 1989)

• Canfield, Michael and Alan Weberman, *Coup d'Etat in America* (1985)

• Davis, John H., *Mafia Kingfish: Carlos Marcello and the Assassination of John F. Kennedy* (New American Library, 1989)

- Davis, Kenneth C., *Don't Know Much About History* (Avon, 1991)

- Donner, Frank J., *The Age of Surveillance: The Aims and Methods of America's Political Intelligence System* (Vintage Books, 1981)

- Garrison, Jim, *On the Trail of the Assassins: My Investigation and Prosecution of the Murder of President Kennedy* (Sheridan Square, 1988)

- Gentry, Curt, *J. Edgar Hoover: The Man and the Secrets* (W. W. Norton & Co., 1991)

- Giancana, Sam and Chuck, *Double Cross* (Warner Books, 1992).

- Herman, Edward S., and Noam Chomsky, *Manufacturing Consent: The Political Economy of the Mass Media* (Pantheon, 1988)

- Higham, Charles, *Trading with the Enemy: An Exposé of the Nazi-American Money Plot 1933-1949* (Delacorte Press, 1983)

- Hinkle, Warren, and Bill Turner, *Deadly Secrets: The CIA-Mafia War Against Castro and the Assassination of JFK* (Thunders Mouth, 1992)

- Hougan, Jim, *Spooks* (Bantam, 1979)

- Kohn, George C., *Encyclopedia of American Scandal,* (Facts on File, 1989)

- Kwitny, Jonathan, *Endless Enemies: The Making of an Unfriendly World* (Congdon & Weed, 1984)

- Lane, Mark, *Plausible Denial: Was the CIA Involved in the Assassination of JFK?* (Thunders Mouth, 1992)

- Lee, Martin, and Bruce Shlain, *Acid Dreams: The CIA, LSD and the Sixties Rebellion* (Grove Press, 1985)

- Lee, Martin, and Norman Solomon, *Unreliable Sources: A Guide to Detecting Bias in News Media* (Lyle Stuart, 1991)

- Marrs, Jim, *Crossfire: The Plot that Killed Kennedy* (Carroll & Graf Publishers, 1989)

- Marshall, Jonathan, Peter Dale Scott, and Jane Hunter, *The Iran-Contra Connection: Secret Teams and Covert Operations in the Reagan Era* (South End Press, 1987)

- Matthiessen, Peter, *In the Spirit of Crazy Horse* (Viking Press, 1991)

- McCoy, Alfred, *The Politics of Heroin: CIA Complicity in the Global Drug Trade* (Chicago Review Press, 1991)

- Mokhiber, Russell, *Corporate Crime and Violence: Big Business and the Abuse of the Public Trust* (Sierra Club Books, 1989)

- Moyers, Bill, *The Secret Government* (7 Locks Press, 1990)

- Pizzo, Stephen, Mary Fricker, and Paul Muolo, *Inside Job: The Looting of America's Savings and Loans* (HarperCollins, 1991)

- Scheim, David, *Contract On America: The Mafia Murder of a President* (Shapolsky, 1988)

- Seldes, George, *Facts and Fascism*. Seldes, one of the great muckrakers of the century, did his best work from the 1930s to 1950. Check your library. Other titles include: *Iron, Blood and Profits*; *Sawdust Caesar*; and *Freedom of the Press*.

- Simpson, Christopher, *Blowback: The First Full Account of America's Recruitment of Nazis, and Its Disastrous Effect on Our Domestic and Foreign Policy* (Wiedenfeld & Nicolson, 1988)

- Stone, I. F., *The Hidden History of the Korean War, 1950-51* (Little, Brown, 1988)

- Summers, Anthony, *Conspiracy* (McGraw-Hill, 1980), and *Goddess* (McMillan, 1985)

- Vankin, Jonathan, *Conspiracies, Cover-ups and Crimes* (Paragon Press, 1991)

- Zinn, Howard, *The Twentieth Century: A People's History*, (Harper & Row, 1984)

## OTHER RESOURCES

- Eclipse Enterprises Trading Cards, P.O. Box 1099, Forestville, CA 95436. Their catalog includes the *Savings and Loan Scandal*, *Iran-Contra Scandal*, *Drug Wars*, *Coup d'Etat: The Assassination of JFK*, and more. Ask for their list.

- "Flashpoints," a radio program produced by KPFA (Berkeley) and syndicated through the Pacifica radio network (WBAI, New York; KPFK, Los Angeles, etc.), is doing some of the best investigative reporting in America. Catch it. Coproduced by Dennis Bernstein and Julie Light.

"Secrecy is the freedom zealots dream of: no watchman to check the door, no accountant to check the books, no judge to check the law. The secret government has no constitution. The rules it follows are the rules it makes up."

—Bill Moyers,
*The Secret Government: The Constitution in Crisis*

# BECOME A CARD-CARRYING MEMBER!

## *Join the National Insecurity Council!*

### Attention, Conspiracy Buffs!

Now you can infiltrate the National Insecurity Council.
Send a self-addressed, stamped envelope to our mail drop (below).
Your free NIC membership card will be delivered by a
uniformed agent of the U.S. government.

### WE HAVE WAYS TO MAKE YOU TALK!

Clue us in on *your* favorite conspiracy theories:
Tell us about your favorite conspiracy books and
sources of information. If we use something you've sent,
we'll send you a free copy of *It's a Conspiracy, Volume II*.

### WRITE TO:
The National Insecurity Council
1400 Shattuck Avenue, Suite 25
Berkeley, CA 94709